Jane Austen's
Transatlantic Sister

Jane Austen's
Transatlantic Sister

The Life and Letters
of Fanny Palmer Austen

SHEILA JOHNSON KINDRED

McGill-Queen's University Press

Montreal & Kingston • London • Chicago

ISBN 978-0-7735-5131-2 (cloth)
ISBN 978-0-7735-5708-6 (paper)
ISBN 978-0-7735-5208-1 (ePDF)
ISBN 978-0-7735-5209-8 (ePUB)

Legal deposit third quarter 2017
Bibliothèque nationale du Québec
First paperback edition 2018

Printed in Canada on acid-free paper

We acknowledge the support of the Canada Council for the Arts, which last year invested $153 million to bring the arts to Canadians throughout the country.

Nous remercions le Conseil des arts du Canada de son soutien. L'an dernier, le Conseil a investi 153 millions de dollars pour mettre de l'art dans la vie des Canadiennes et des Canadiens de tout le pays.

Library and Archives Canada Cataloguing in Publication

Kindred, Sheila Johnson, 1943–, author
        Jane Austen's transatlantic sister : the life and letters of Fanny Palmer
Austen / Sheila Johnson Kindred.

Includes bibliographical references and index.
Issued in print and electronic formats.
ISBN 978-0-7735-5131-2 (hardcover).–ISBN 978-0-7735-5708-6 (paperback).
–ISBN 978-0-7735-5208-1 (ePDF).–ISBN 978-0-7735-5209-8 (ePUB)

    1. Austen, Fanny, 1790–1814. 2. Austen, Fanny, 1790–1814–
Correspondence. 3. Great Britain. Royal Navy–Military life–History–
18th century. 4. Great Britain. Royal Navy–History–18th century.
5. Great Britain–History, Naval–18th century. 6. Officers' spouses–
Great Britain–Correspondence. 7. Officers' spouses–Great Britain–
Biography. 8. Officers' spouses–Great Britain–Social conditions–18th
century. 9. Austen, Jane, 1775–1817–Family. 10. Austen, Charles.
I. Title.

V737.K56 2017   940.2'7341092   C2017-903712-9
                                               C2017-903713-7

This book is for Hugh

Contents

Illustrations

Preface

JUST OVER TWO HUNDRED YEARS AGO a young naval wife spent an anxious summer during 1810 in Halifax, Nova Scotia. It was the later years of the Napoleonic Wars. Her husband had been suddenly called away on a mission to transport troops to a war zone off the coast of Portugal. During the months that followed she waited for his return with growing trepidation until she finally welcomed back to port her "beloved Charles." The genteel young woman was the beautiful, Bermuda-born Fanny Palmer Austen; her husband was Captain Charles John Austen, a naval officer, then serving on the North American Station of the British navy, and the youngest brother of the novelist Jane Austen.

This vignette, derived from Fanny Austen's own letters, has turned out to be an inspiration for me. Since 2005 I had been writing extensively about Charles Austen's career in North American waters, about the excitement of his first command and his pursuit of naval prize, but I had not paid much attention to his falling in love and marrying Fanny Palmer. More recently I became intrigued by the evidence that Fanny Austen had spent parts of two years in the place which I call home – Halifax. I wanted to find out about her personality and character, as well as about the kind of life she led in Halifax and elsewhere. There was much to explore, beginning with her formative years in St George's, Bermuda, through her naval travels with Charles in

North America to her later years in England when she came to know the other members of the Austen family. This book presents what I have learned about Fanny Palmer Austen in all the ordinary and extraordinary aspects of her short life and exciting times.

My investigations began with Fanny's letters, which have proved to be a treasure trove of personal narrative and contemporary detail. As a result of extensive original research, I have been able to present the letters in the social and cultural context of Fanny's life. The picture of a lively, resourceful, and articulate young woman has emerged. I discovered a wife intimately involved with her husband's naval career and a new and significant member of the Austen family.

The narrative of Fanny's life that I have been able to uncover is particularly instructive of what it was like to be a young woman living at sea with her husband and small children in early nineteenth-century wartime. Naval historian N.A.M. Rodger has observed that "unfortunately there has been virtually no research undertaken into what one might call the female half of the naval community as a whole ... They represent an enormous void of ignorance, and our knowledge of the social history of the Navy will never be complete until someone fills it" (*Command of the Ocean*, 2004). Despite Rodger's plea, little has since been published about wives who had immediate experience of their husbands' professional careers and naval society. Fanny Austen's letters, along with the story that surrounds them, provide a unique insight into female life in the theatres of naval warfare on both sides of the Atlantic during this tumultuous time.

Through her marriage to Charles, Fanny became closely connected with other members of his family. In particular, Fanny developed a relationship with Jane that excited my attention. Their sisterly association gave me grounds to investigate whether Fanny's experiences may have influenced Jane Austen in the writing of her fiction. Because Fanny was both with Charles on the North American Station of the British navy (1807–11) and then with him and their children aboard HMS *Namur* stationed off Sheerness, Kent (1812–14), she had a truly transatlantic experience within his naval world that she could impart to Jane. Hence the title of this book, *Jane Austen's Transatlantic Sister.*

Other artefacts in addition to Fanny's letters became important sources for my research. The discovery of Fanny's small, red morocco leather pocket diary for 1814 was an exciting find. Entries identifying her domestic needs, noting the existence of books to be bound, laundry sent out, coaches hired, and treats of cake and tea acquired, personalize the profile of a young mother trying to run her household with care and economy. Additionally, a fine oil painting executed by British artist Robert Field in Halifax in 1810 gives a strong impression of Fanny. Her red-gold hair and clear blue eyes are striking; her gaze is direct and her mood reflective. The painting invites conjecture about her character and her emotions.

As I liked the idea of allowing Fanny to recount her own story, the full texts of her letters are placed within the main body of the book. I have added two important but hitherto unpublished letters about her, written in 1808, by her sister Esther and her husband Charles (Appendix 2). I have traced Fanny's ancestral roots through her connections to the Irish and English Palmers and the aristocratic British Strangways family (Appendix 3). The endnotes also add significant details to the context of Fanny's letters. They identify important individuals and locations, and provide brief explanations of naval and other unfamiliar references, in addition to citing sources of information. The notes and the extensive bibliography are intended to enrich an appreciation of Fanny Austen's life, yet the style of writing will allow a general reader to enjoy the book without consulting these materials.

I was fortunate to obtain numerous illustrations, some rarely seen, that connect Fanny to the places and people she knew. These contemporary nineteenth-century images illuminate her life in Bermuda, Nova Scotia, and England. Of special interest are several items from private collections: the wonderful portraits by Robert Field of Fanny and Charles, a sketch by Cassandra and a handsome watercolour of Halifax town and harbour by Charles's nephew, Herbert Grey Austen, a naval officer of the next generation.

As I write this in the 200th anniversary year of Jane Austen's death, there is a noticeable resurgence of interest in her novels, in fact in all things Austen. My study of the life and letters of Fanny Austen adds to our knowledge of the Austen family and of Jane's fiction. Fanny's time in England coincided with the years of Jane Austen's most productive period, which were highlighted by the publication of *Sense and Sensibility* (1811), *Pride and Prejudice* (1813), *Mansfield Park* (1814), and her initial work on *Emma*. Fanny was party to the secret that Jane was the author of these very well received novels, and she was present to witness the great pleasure their publication brought to their author. In a special way Fanny's association with Jane may have contributed to Jane Austen's creative process. To celebrate them together is fitting and timely.

Sheila Johnson Kindred
Halifax, Nova Scotia
31 March 2017

Acknowledgments

I WISH TO EXTEND HEARTFELT THANKS to the many people whose support and assistance has made my writing of this book possible. I am hugely indebted to Deirdre Le Faye, who has helped and encouraged me throughout this project. She not only shared significant primary material about Fanny Austen when I began but has also been exceptionally generous in answering questions and clarifying many points of detail along the way. Her *Family Record* and *Chronology* have been invaluable resources of information. Without them, the telling of Fanny's story would have been incomplete.

Sarah Emsley and Barbara Garner have given me unstinting support and advice for which I thank them profusely. Barbara assiduously reviewed and commented on several drafts as I crafted the manuscript. Sarah advised on the revision of an early draft and was party to many helpful and enjoyable conversations about Jane Austen's family and her fiction. I am also very grateful to Isabel Huggan for her counsel and willingness to discuss the challenges of writing nonfiction. Clive Caplan, Matthew Huntley, and Maggie Lane kindly read early drafts and made useful suggestions. I would also like to thank the two anonymous reviewers for McGill-Queen's University Press. They made insightful comments that I greatly appreciate and led me to improve both the clarity and content of the book.

My sincere appreciation goes to three late Austen scholars, Clive Caplan, David Gilson, and Brian Southam, who willingly shared their expertise.

Several historians have been liberal with their knowledge about naval detail, in particular, Dan Conlin, Julian Gwyn, and Roger Marsters.

I am deeply appreciative to Francis Austen, Ruth Shepley, Patrick Stokes, and Derek and Brian Willan for their interest in my efforts to portray Fanny Austen's life and letters, and for their willingness to make available important information about her and her family.

I am also thankful for the assistance of Darren Bevin, Sheryl Craig, Shelagh Crooks, Grant Curtis, Ronald Dunning, Philip Girard, Margie Lloyd, Brenton Haliburton, Philip Hartling, Clea Kindred, Kerry Kindred-Barnes, Rebecca Lilley, Tinker McKay, Cathy Morley, Dianne O'Neill, Elise Outerbridge, Shannon Parker, Michèle Raymond, Rosemary Seale, Rohan Shastri, Karen Smith, Isabel Snowdon, Maureen Stiller, Chris Viveash, Jill Webster, Peter Wingfield-Digby, Susanne Wise, and members of the Jane Austen Societies in North America, in particular the Nova Scotia Region and in the Jane Austen Society in England, especially the Kent branch.

I value the help provided by the archives, libraries, and museums that have assisted me in so many ways. I am grateful for access to their holdings and the guidance of their staffs. In England, I have explored the resources of the Bodleian Library, British Library, Caird Library, National Maritime Museum, Kemsing Library, Southend Forum Library, and the National Archives. In Canada, I have made use of the services of Dalhousie University Library, Library Archives Canada, Nova Scotia Archives, and Saint Mary's University Library; and in the United States, the Morgan Library and Museum.

For supplying images and giving permission for their use as illustrations, my thanks are extended to David Brandreth, Chawton House Library, Godmersham Park Heritage Centre, Jane Austen's House Museum, National Maritime Museum, National Portrait Gallery, Southend Forum Library; Art Gallery of Nova Scotia, Maritime Museum of the Atlantic, Special Collections of Dalhousie University Libraries, St Paul's Church Archives, Halifax; Bermuda National Trust, Masterworks Museum of Bermuda Art; National Gallery of Art, Washington; and several private collections.

At McGill-Queen's University Press, I wish to thank my acquisitions editor Mark Abley, whose wisdom, advice, and support have been exemplary, his assistant, Joanne Pisano, managing editor Ryan Van Huijstee, and executive director, Philip Cercone. Thanks also to my efficient and effective copy editor, Judith Turnbull.

My greatest debt of appreciation is to my husband, Hugh. Together we have followed in Fanny Austen's footsteps to many sites in Bermuda, Nova Scotia, and England. Hugh has provided the skills of a research assistant with an accompanying sense of humour and perspective that has been truly encouraging. He has also read many drafts of chapters and made cogent comments and suggestions. My debt of gratitude to Hugh is huge.

Jane Austen's
Transatlantic Sister

Here is the intimacy of heart and mind
speaking to heart and mind
across distance and across time.

P.D. JAMES, FOREWORD TO OLGA KENYON, ED.,
800 Years of Women's Letters

Introduction

"A VERY PLEASING LITTLE WOMAN, she is gentle and amiable in her manners, and appears to make [Charles] very happy"[1] (Fig. 1). Such were the words of Cassandra Austen when she and her sister Jane first met Fanny Palmer, their brother Charles's Bermuda-born wife. Yet, this charming profile of Fanny Austen masks the spirited and resilient woman who, as the wife of Captain Austen, endured with fortitude the rigours of naval life. Fanny wrote about her life experiences in a number of letters. The twelve extant ones, some of which are of considerable length, as they include instalments written over several weeks, are transcribed and contextualized in this biography.[2] They help us to discover the strength of her character and to appreciate the difficulty of the conditions in which she struggled to create a home for her family on ship and on shore. Her affectionate association with Charles's sisters, foreshadowed by Cassandra's first impression of Fanny, provided her with supportive female company and also afforded Jane a female perspective on naval life and society. Though Fanny's life would be short (1789–1814), it is intriguing to consider her lasting impact as a source of information and inspiration for the female naval characters in Jane Austen's novel *Persuasion*.

Fanny's life spanned turbulent years of Britain's war with Napoleonic France. Born in Bermuda in 1789, she met Charles Austen there in 1805 and married him in 1807 (Fig. 2). Their years together coincided with the last major incidents of the war at sea and the events leading up to the culminating

Fig. 1   Fanny Palmer Austen, painted in Halifax by British artist Robert Field, 1810.

battle on land at Waterloo in 1815. The British navy established its dominance by sea in European waters at the battle of Trafalgar on 21 October 1805 and defeated the French fleet in West Indian waters at the battle of San Domingo on 6 February 1806. The next year the Danish fleet surrendered after the British attacked Copenhagen on 7 September. Subsequent naval expeditions organized from Halifax, Nova Scotia, took control of the French islands of Martinique (24 February 1809) and Guadeloupe (6 February 1810).

Fig. 2 Captain Charles John Austen RN, Fanny's husband, a companion portrait to hers, also painted by Field.

The pattern of Fanny's life was conditioned by Charles's career in the British navy. As a young junior officer Charles was posted to the Royal Navy's North American Station in 1805, where he experienced his first solo command in the sloop of war, HMS *Indian*. As part of the squadron, Charles spent long periods at sea cruising for trade protection, escorting convoys, and transporting troops, all in the face of danger and possible disaster. Fanny was aware of the risks he faced and the attendant anxieties for herself and her young family. She knew that at sea Charles was vulnerable to attack from armed and marauding French vessels, in addition to the possibility that his wooden ship would fall victim to the fierce autumn and winter storms of the North Atlantic. She experienced the anguish of uncertainty during their periods of enforced separation.

While Charles was in North America, Fanny sometimes travelled with him between Bermuda, the southern base of the station, and Halifax, Nova Scotia, its northern base, but his extensive duties of cruising at sea meant that Fanny lived primarily in Bermuda. Later, Fanny found that being a naval wife would disrupt the familiar aspects of shore-based life in her island home. From mid-1811 Charles's career took him into English waters and Fanny became a transatlantic traveller. She braved a potentially hazardous crossing of the North Atlantic and on arrival undertook the courageous initiative of making a home for the two of them and their family of young daughters aboard a working vessel, the guard and receiving ship HMS *Namur* (74 guns).

This unlikely situation presented Fanny with many unusual domestic problems that tested her determination and ingenuity. Household management was distinctly more difficult aboard ship. Help for Fanny from reliable servants and the support of other genteel women were hard to come by. Nurturing and educating her young children, which Fanny took very seriously, presented a unique set of complications for her. Yet throughout their married life, Fanny was a loyal and sensitive supporter of Charles, both when his career in the sea service advanced and when it stalled, and she was happiest when they could be continuously together even under the testing conditions of living at sea.

Through her letters, Fanny becomes the narrator of her own life story. The letters provide an intimate, engaging, and frank self-portrait, revealing her emotions, attitudes, and aspirations. They chart the course of a young woman as she reflects on her situation and adapts to the varying demands on her feelings and capabilities. Her letters also reveal the sophistication of Fanny's dealing with her duties and anxieties in her daily family life both when Charles is with her, and when his naval duties dictate they must be separated. They reveal her maturation as a wife and mother. Altogether, Fanny's life as a naval wife during war time was excitingly diverse and challenging compared to the lives of other refined young ladies of the period. Access to the full text of Fanny's letters transports us directly into her social milieu and familiarizes us with the trials she faced, especially those of the naval world that she inhabited with Charles.

Fanny was confined by the social and cultural conventions of genteel Georgian society. She was susceptible to expectations about the appropriate behaviour of young women of her class; she was influenced by the ideology of domesticity to which they were expected to conform. Her letters show that she recognized the importance of a particular code of conduct but that at the same time she was developing her own sense of identity and autonomy, including certain behaviour and attitudes that nowadays would be considered as reflecting feminist values.

Kinship ties helped ground Fanny. Her letters record the interactions within the various "families" to which she belonged: her own nuclear household with Charles and her children; her blood relatives, including her parents and siblings, Esther, Harriet, and Robert John; Esther's husband, James Christie Esten; and members of the Austen family, especially Cassandra and Jane, among whom Fanny was addressed as sister, rather than sister-in-law, as was the custom of the time. Additionally, friendships with Charles's professional colleagues, particularly those forged while on the close-knit North American Station, entailed membership in an extended naval family that provided support, solidarity, and companionship for both Fanny and Charles.

Among these kinship relations, Fanny had a particularly fascinating connection to Jane Austen, first as a family member but, in addition, as a source for literary invention. Jane was very devoted to Charles. This emotional tie predisposed her to take a strong interest in his young wife and children. Jane had viewed this marriage from afar during its first four years, when Fanny and Charles were still in North America, but on their return to England she spent time in Fanny's company at Chawton and Godmersham and corresponded with her when they were apart. She appreciated the trials Fanny and Charles faced as a family living primarily at sea, and she sometimes shared in the care of their young children. In consequence, she had close access to the pleasures and pains of the unusual domestic life that this young couple experienced. Knowing their story provided her with a better understanding of the complexities of human actions and interactions, a theme that fascinated Jane Austen as a writer and that she addressed so brilliantly in her novels. Additionally, Jane had an empathetic understanding of Fanny's life as a naval wife. What Jane learned from Fanny provided a repository of personal as well as naval detail upon which she could draw in creating her own fictional female characters associated with the navy, notably *Persuasion*'s Mrs Croft, Mrs Harville, and Anne Elliot.[3]

The narrative of Fanny's life, told in her wonderfully evocative correspondence, affords an entry into Fanny's world, the domain of an articulate, educated, and engaging nineteenth-century gentlewoman and letter writer.

CHAPTER I

From Birth to Marriage and Motherhood,

1789–1809

FRANCES (FANNY) FITZWILLIAMS PALMER was born on 3 December 1789 into a household of comfort and gentility in St George's, Bermuda.[1] Her future looked promising, for as the daughter of John Grove Palmer, the attorney general of Bermuda,[2] she could expect to enjoy a life of relative ease in a welcoming, close-knit colonial community. Yet her marriage to a British naval officer in a time of war would lead to risky foreign travel, unexpected places of abode, new family connections, and a fortuitous relationship with Jane Austen of significance for both women. From easy and uncomplicated beginnings, Fanny was to have a life rich in diverse experiences.

Fanny grew up as the youngest and fourth surviving child in her family and in the company of sisters Esther and Harriet and brother Robert John (known as John). To her parents and siblings' great sorrow, four subsequent children to Fanny – babies Mary, Georgina, William, and Thomas[3] – all died in infancy before Fanny was eight. The youngest child in a family sometimes enjoys a close relationship with the next oldest. In the Palmer family it was different. Esther, the eldest, was fourteen years older than Fanny, and these two were always very close. It was not apparent for some years, but Esther was to play an important role in both Fanny's late childhood and her adult life.

Fanny's birthplace has an intriguing history. Bermuda was first discovered by the Spanish in 1505 but it was not then settled. In 1609 it provided refuge for the shipwrecked passengers of *Sea Venture*, the flagship of the ill-fated

The Square, St Georges, Bermudas.

Fig. 3   *The Square, St George's, Bermudas* by Thomas Driver, 1823. King's Square looks
very much as it did during Fanny's early years in St George's. The tower of St Peter's
Church, where she married Charles in May 1807, can be seen towards the left.

English expedition of George Somers, which, with eight other vessels, was
attempting to bring settlers and relief supplies to the fledgling colony of
Jamestown, Virginia. A hurricane blew the flotilla off course and the *Sea
Venture* was wrecked on a reef, near Discovery Bay, Bermuda. During the
next ten months, the passengers and crew built houses and a church, thus
starting the colony of Bermuda. In 1612 about sixty colonists arrived and
established what became the town of St George's. By 1620 the House of
Assembly was established, and the handsome stone State House was built
four years later, to be used by the island's courts and the General Assembly.
In 1758 James Cook observed Bermuda from his vessel *Pembroke*, saying it
appeared like "the hulk of a ship."

At the time of Fanny's birth, St George's was the capital of Bermuda, the
seat of government, and home to the island's garrison (Fig. 3). Bermuda was
a small colony, its population numbering about nine thousand, but it had
gained large significance for Britain after the loss of the American colonies.
St George's was the only legal port of entry to Bermuda for all trading vessels,

Fig. 4 *St George's Harbour* by Thomas Driver, 1821. The artist effectively depicts the shape of the town in relation to the curve of the harbour and its busyness.

and the commercial warehouses that lined the waterfront of the harbour were busy with the steady traffic of merchant ships (Fig. 4). Bermuda's position in the North Atlantic, 650 miles east of North Carolina, made it a strategic location from which the British could watch the North American coast and thus a natural choice for the southern base of the Royal Navy's North American Station. Halifax, as noted earlier, served as the northern base.

Bermuda was an idyllic place for Fanny to grow up. Although surrounded to the north and the west by extensive, treacherous reefs, the islands of the Bermuda archipelago were beautiful to behold. Signature stands of tall, evergreen cedars lined the bays and inlets; turquoise waters bordered pink sand beaches. There were eastern blue birds, red cardinals, white-tailed tropicbirds, and white-eyed vireos. Bougainvillea, hibiscus, oleander, and sweet-smelling shrubs and fruits thrived in the mostly gentle climate. In St George's, white, grey, and yellow limestone houses clustered on either side of narrow streets and alleys with fairy-tale names, such as Featherbed, Shinbone, Needle and Thread, and Blockade. Visiting naval captain Philip Broke noted "the pleasingly picturesque appearance of the town – irregularly situated on a broken slope – so much of the space occupied by gardens."[4] In that immediate neighbourhood, the John Grove Palmer family occupied a well-appointed "commodious dwelling house [with] excellent kitchen, two large gardens and every other accommodation for a genteel family."[5] This was probably the property that records show Fanny's father had purchased in February 1800,[6] situated at the corner of Clarence Street and Governor's Alley. It was a desirable location; the house and garden were valued at £1,040 the year before he bought it.[7]

Fanny grew up in a household that had a history of servants and slaves. Slavery had been practised in Bermuda since the early seventeenth century, but unlike the West Indies, it was not a colony of sugar plantations with their notorious stories of cruel conditions and brutality. In Bermuda, slaves worked as domestics, in trades, and as seamen. As a consequence, according to Virginia Bernhard, a historian of Bermuda slavery, "white and black families in Bermuda lived in much closer proximity than in England's other colonies, and the harshness of slavery was constantly mitigated by the personal nature of the contact between slaveholder and slave."[8] In many cases domestic slaves lived under the same roof and ate the same food as the family and until adolescence young white children found playmates among their family's slave children. In some cases, "black and white childhood playmates fostered attachments that lasted for life."[9]

The black population of Bermuda, which throughout Fanny's life time roughly equalled the number of whites, consisted of both slaves and freed individuals.[10] The Palmer family is known to have liberated at least four black slaves in their possession. Sometime in the 1790s, when Fanny was a young girl, her parents freed "a woman and her three boys." According to Bermuda historian Henry Wilkinson, "Mrs. Palmer did not set her Lettice free until she had undertaken to contribute a quarter of her wages for the upbringing of her own three younger brothers."[11] Presumably Lettice remained in the Palmer employ, as she would need an income in the future for herself as well as to ensure her siblings' well-being. Most likely there were or had been other slaves in the Palmer household engaged in domestic work both inside and outside Fanny's home. But whether they served as slaves or as freed servants, Fanny grew up in close association with a number of black Bermudians as well as with her white relatives in the same household.[12]

Fanny was most likely schooled at home in reading and writing, in the essentials of plain sewing and needlework, and in the principles of household management. A young Georgian lady was also expected to have a pleasing manner and air. These qualities came easily to Fanny. She liked company, adored dancing, appreciated music, and was lovely to look at, possessing a small, graceful figure and luxuriant, curly red-gold hair. Her father's status in the legal community had secured the Palmers a place among Bermuda's first families, and in such a situation Fanny's life was comfortable and happy.

In 1802 a big change occurred in Fanny's life. Her parents and sister Harriet left Bermuda to live in England, while her favourite sister, Esther, and her husband, James Christie Esten, a Yale-educated Bermuda-born lawyer,[13] moved into the Palmer family home. Fanny did not go to England with her parents; instead she stayed in Bermuda and joined the household of James and Esther. Although this arrangement may seem odd, it was not uncommon for households to include brothers or sisters of either the wife or the husband. Remaining in Bermuda may have been Fanny's own choice. She presumably felt at home in the town where she had grown up and in the congenial company of Esther and James,[14] who had been appointed to her father's former position of attorney-general. Sixteen-year-old Harriet Palmer's situation was different. If she was to marry well, England and particularly London provided many more suitable bachelors than did tiny Bermuda. Additionally, as Harriet's health appeared delicate, a larger metropolis and a place in her parents' household must have seemed more advantageous for her.

John Grove Palmer's removal to London had all the earmarks of a long-range plan. A somewhat taciturn and opinionated man, he had recently failed to gain a seat in either the Bermuda House of Assembly or Council. In the words of Austen biographer Park Honan, he had "enforced an unconstitutional law against the Methodists"[15] that had led to divided opinion in Bermuda about religious freedom. On his father's death in 1801, John had inherited rental properties in the English counties of Essex and Hertfordshire as well as real estate in County Kerry, Ireland.[16] Now wishing to be closer to his sources of income, he secured the tenancy of 22 Keppel Street, Bloomsbury, London, a prime location in a fashionable new area of residential development favoured by the business and professional classes on lands belonging to the Duke of Bedford's estate and a few minutes walk to the British Museum. Henceforth his life and career would be in England.

Fanny's contacts with her British Palmer family were now restricted to a transatlantic correspondence. Nine years would elapse before her parents welcomed Fanny to their Keppel Street house. In the interim, Fanny's life changed dramatically, especially because of her relationship with a handsome young British naval officer. He was Charles John Austen, a man who combined good looks and charm with an "affectionate disposition [and] untiring enthusiasm."[17] What else is known of this dashing youngest brother of Jane Austen with whom Fanny would fall in love and marry?

Charles Austen was a special favourite of his sister Jane, who affectionately referred to him as "our own particular little brother."[18] Cassandra Austen recollected that "a few of the trifles [in vol. 1 of Jane's *Juvenilia*] were written expressly for [Charles's] early amusement"[19] in about 1788, when he was nine. These were Jane's stories, "Sir William Montague" and "Memoirs of Mr. Clifford," which she expressly dedicated to him. Jane and Charles were the two youngest of the Austen siblings and grew up together in close company in their father's vicarage at Steventon, Hampshire, until Charles left for the Royal Naval Academy, Portsmouth, when Jane was fifteen. She proudly followed his career from its beginning – the initial three-year period of study at the Academy, a further three years at sea as midshipman, and his subsequent promotion and service as a lieutenant.

By 1804 Charles's career had progressed further. In consequence of service of some distinction as first lieutenant on board HMS *Endymion* (44 guns), Charles was promoted in October of that year to the rank of commander and commissioned into the sloop of war HMS *Indian*, a vessel then being built in Bermuda and intended for service with the North American squadron. The title of commander was given to the captain of a sloop, which was a three-masted single-decked vessel carrying eighteen guns and the smallest warship in the British navy. Charles would be designated "Captain Austen" – though this was a courtesy title – until he was further promoted to post-captain, when he would hold both the rank and title of captain.[20] Although it was thrilling to be selected to command a vessel, it was unlucky that his promotion came when it did. About four months after he left her, the *Endymion* captured four Spanish treasure ships; these were legal prizes, as Britain was at war with Spain between 1804 and 1808.[21] The vessels included the *Brillante* from Veracruz, carrying 88 chests of money, and a vessel from Lima with 240 boxes of dollars. Had Charles still been one of her three lieutenants, he would have received the magnificent bounty of £4,000 in prize money. The modern equivalent of this sum would be between £400,000 and £600,000.[22]

Charles's posting to North America was the decision of the Board of Admiralty, a government department located in London, which controlled naval affairs and determined which officers were commissioned into what vessels and for what purposes. He was excited to be undertaking his first command and new responsibilities on the other side of the Atlantic. However, he had no idea how long his commission on the *Indian* would last; it might be years before he would see his Austen family in England again, a state of affairs that his devoted sisters Jane and Cassandra must have particularly regretted.

Once he arrived in North America, Charles and Jane corresponded regularly, but unfortunately none of their letters have survived. She was naturally curious about the state of his new vessel, what his naval duties entailed, the identity of his fellow officers, and the social milieu at both bases in Bermuda and Halifax. It is not known when Charles first mentioned his acquaintance with Fanny Palmer. It was probably quite soon after his arrival, for although Charles spent the early months of 1805 attending to the building, manning, and provisioning of the *Indian*, he was soon enjoying the entertainments of the local families of note, a circle that included Fanny Palmer and Esther and James Esten. Frequent balls were held at the State House in St George's, which would thus have been a likely and pleasing place for a first meeting with Fanny. She was fifteen and so was just entering society. Charles was twenty-six.

Charles's new vessel, the *Indian*, was still on the stocks at Tyne Yard, Devonshire Parish, when he arrived in Bermuda in January 1805, but by 14 March she was launched, towed to St George's harbour, and anchored at Edward Goodrich's wharf, near the central King's Square. Charles was very pleased with the look and the capabilities of his three-masted sloop of 399 tons, a vessel he would later refer to approvingly as "dear little Indian."[23] She was built chiefly of local Bermuda cedar, which is well known for its resistance to rot. She was a well-equipped vessel, fitted with 16 × 24 pounder

Fig. 5   Bermuda-built HMS *Atalante* (18 guns), sister ship to HMS *Indian*, which was Charles's first command, 1805–10.

carronades (short-barrelled guns) that fired sixty-eight-pound shot over a short distance and two 6-pounder chase guns (cannons) that could be mounted at either the bow or stern of the vessel as required. When fully manned, the *Indian* would have a crew of 121 men. As she was one of the British navy's first completed Bermuda Class sloops of war, she naturally became an object of interest and curiosity among the local inhabitants (Fig. 5). Fanny often had shopping to do near the town square and could easily stop, if she wished, and observe the latest stages of work on the new vessel. Should Charles be about, she would likely have an enthusiastic guide to explain the tasks of the carpenters, painters, and sail riggers and the importance of loading ballast correctly.

As the *Indian* neared completion, Charles published a notice in the *Bermuda Gazette*, 13 April 1805 (Fig. 6). Its wording reflected his enthusiasm for his vessel and his commitment to be actively involved in the hostilities. The advertisement began with the words "SPANISH WAR Now or Never," a phrase that assured the recruits that this would be a fighting ship. The reference to Spain was particularly apt. In reprisal for Spanish attacks on British ships, an order dated 12 January 1805 directed that "all ships and vessels belonging to Spain [are] to be seized or destroyed."[24] Charles's notice described the *Indian* as the "finest most beautiful sloop of war ever built, such

THE

Bermuda Gazette,

And WEEKLY ADVERTISER.

No. 1105.   SATURDAY, APRIL 13, 1805.

SPANISH WAR
Now or Never.
W A N T E D,
SEAMEN and STOUT LANDS-
MEN
To compleat the Crew of His Majef-
ty's Sloop of War the
I. N D I A N,
Of Twenty Guns,
CHARLES JOHN AUSTEN, Efq.
Commander.

THE INDIAN is the
fineft and moft beautiful
Man of War ever built, and
her conftruction puts her faft
failing beyond a doubt. Therefore
plenty of Spanifh Doubloons and
Dollars will fall to the lot of all thofe
fpirited Young Men who come forward
without delay and repair on board the
faid Sloop now fitting alongfide of Mr.
Goodrich's Wharf, in St. George's.
N. B. There are a number of Petty
Officers births vacant, who are five fhare
Men.
Grog and Frefh Beef every day at
twelve o'clock.
GOD SAVE the KING,
A N D
Succefs to the TIGHT LITTLE ISLAND.

Fig. 6   Charles enthusiastically advertised for crew members for the newly built
HMS *Indian*, 1805.

that her construction puts her fast sailing without a doubt." He promised
the "Seamen and Stout Landsmen" who joined him "plenty of Doubloons
and Dollars"[25] and "grog and fresh beef every day."[26] By late July Charles
was at sea and at work.

Charles was beginning his North American service at a time of political
tension and insecurity internationally. The navy was vigorously engaged

on both sides of the Atlantic. In Europe, Britain was at war with France, harassing and blockading the French and Spanish fleets and trying to prevent vital supplies from reaching France and her allies. British relations with the United States were also troubled, and they would become more so, especially after 1807 when a British vessel, HMS *Leopard* (50 guns), mounted an unprovoked attack on the American frigate USS *Constitution* (44 guns) over the contentious issue of British deserters serving as seamen on American ships.

Given the state of hostilities, the North American squadron was charged with the surveillance of the Atlantic for Britain. It was required to collect intelligence, to protect British commerce, to blockade and disrupt American trade with Napoleonic Europe, to escort and convoy troops to theatres of conflict, to recover deserters from British warships, and, after 1807, to police the illegal slave trade. Many of these tasks were routine and repetitive. They were assigned to frigates and sloops that were sent on cruises to patrol a specified sea area of the station for months at a time. The full range of jurisdiction was huge, as the station extended from the St Lawrence River to Cape Canaveral, Florida, and included the waters north, south, and east of Bermuda. Resources were inevitably spread thin due to the modest number and size of the vessels assigned to the squadron.

For the remainder of 1805, the *Indian*'s assignments took Charles as far north as Halifax and as far south as the West Indies. Thus the demands of his naval duties conflicted with his desire to see Fanny and hers to see more of him. He was back in Bermuda for parts of January, March, April, May, June, August, and most of September of 1806. In the words of Bermuda historian Henry Wilkinson, the St George's of the period was known for its "intermittent vivacity, its parades, balls, amateur theatricals, raffles and ... lending library."[27] The 99th Regiment was stationed at St George's, and its officers, as well as the regular influx of naval captains, animated the social life of the town. In this congenial setting Charles and Fanny fell deeply in love. Esther and James Esten were surely delighted with their courtship, as they were very fond of Charles. James sponsored Charles for membership in the St John's Lodge of the Worshipful Company of Masons, thus securing a useful social connection for him when he was in Bermuda, Halifax, or elsewhere. The two men maintained a close lifelong friendship.

Fanny was beginning to meet some of Charles's friends in the officer corps, young men in their early twenties who were seriously engaged with their naval careers. The first of these was twenty-two-year-old Captain Edward Hawker. He was onshore in Bermuda for the first half of 1805, as his frigate, HMS *Tartar* (32 guns), had been badly damaged on a reef and was undergoing repairs by shipwright-caulkers[28] sent to Bermuda from the Halifax Naval Yard. Edward Hawker was a genial, likable fellow. By 1805 he had already had nineteen years of recorded service, for his naval father, James Hawker, had put him on the books of Prince (later King) William Henry's frigate HMS *Pegasus* at the age of four,[29] although he did not actually go to sea until he was aged ten. When the repair of the *Tartar* was completed, Captain Hawker showed his appreciation by the unusual gesture of giving "a supper and a Ball to the Shipwrights from Halifax."[30]

In the following months, Fanny would be introduced to the amiable twenty-one-year-old James, Lord Townshend, who became the commander of HMS *Halifax* (18 guns) in 1806. He was a younger son of George, 4th Viscount and 1st Marquis Townshend. Fanny would later also come to know Samuel John Pechell, an able fellow who was promoted to post-captain's rank in 1807, when he was only twenty-two. Fanny must have liked him particularly, for she later refers to him as "my very great favorite Capt. Pechell."[31] He eventually inherited a baronetcy and became an expert in naval gunnery. A fourth friend was Frederick Hickey. At the rank of commander, he was captain of HMS *Atalante* (18 guns), a sister ship to the *Indian*. He was apparently a bit of a tease, as he ribbed Fanny about her weight gain when she became pregnant in 1808. She also became acquainted with Captain Sir Robert Laurie of HMS *Milan* (44 guns), who was described by Esther Esten as "our worthy friend";[32] Captain John Shortland of HMS *Squirrel* (24 guns) and HMS *Junon* (38 guns); and Captain Robert Simpson of HMS *Driver* (18 guns) and HMS *Cleopatra* (32 guns). Other captains who worked with Charles and whom Fanny would have encountered in St Georges's included captains William Byam and Gustavus Stupart.[33]

Most of the time, Charles was engaged in the routine tasks of his squadron; however, while he and his fellow officers were at sea, they kept a sharp lookout for enemy warships and merchant vessels or neutral vessels, irrespective of nationality, clandestinely transporting goods and munitions to Napoleonic Europe or to French possessions such as Haiti, Guadeloupe, Martinique, and Spanish Puerto Rico in the West Indies. Such vessels were legitimate objects of chase and sometimes of capture when seized in accordance with the law of prize. A captured vessel was often referred to as a "prize" from the moment of seizure, although, strictly speaking, the term refers to a "captured enemy warship or merchant vessel, later condemned by a Vice Admiralty Court."[34] The taking of a prize could be a huge benefit to the captain and crew of the capturing vessel but not before a lengthy legal process of proof was satisfied. Once a capture was made, the captor installed a prize crew from his own vessel who sailed the prize to either Halifax or Bermuda, whichever was nearer, for adjudication at the Vice Admiralty Court. It was the job of the court to assess the legitimacy of the capture and the value of the vessel and its contents. Should the court rule that the captured vessel and/or its cargo were "good and lawful prize" and there was no successful appeal to the High Court of Admiralty in London, the capturing captain(s) became the legal owners of the condemned items, which were then sold at public auction. If the court ruled against the captain's claim, the captured vessel and/or its cargo were returned to the owners and the costs of the legal process were levied against the captor.

Prize monies were divided in proportional shares according to a prescribed formula. Until June 1808, the capturing captain, or captains in the case of joint captures, received a quarter of the monies raised by the auction of the prize vessel and goods, less fees and court costs. The admiral of the station received a one-eighth share. The seamen and marines divided one quarter of the prize money in equal shares, while those in the ranks in between divided the remaining three-eighths share.[35] A captain needed the services of a fair and scrupulous shore based agent for the efficient management of his prize business. Prize agents were usually local businessmen employed to act on a captain's behalf and their duties were regulated by statute.[36] Over a period of time, Charles employed as his agents the Honourable Andrew Belcher[37] in Halifax (Fig. 7), Goodrich and Shedden in Bermuda, and Austen[38] and Maunde in England. He was apparently satisfied with their services.

Charles had been involved in the pursuit of naval prizes during his earlier commissions, and he had received a share of prize money. While he was a

Fig. 7   Hon. Andrew Belcher, Charles's prize agent in Halifax, Nova Scotia, painted by Robert Field, 1808.

midshipman on HMS *Unicorn* (32 guns), he participated in the capture of the Dutch brig *Comet* (18 guns) in 1795 and the French troopship *Ville d'Orient* (36 guns) in 1797. As a twenty-year-old lieutenant on HMS *Endymion*, Charles was central to the surrender during a violent gale of the French vessel *Le Scipio* (18 guns) and 140 men. He "very intrepidly put off in a boat with only four men, and, having boarded the vessel, succeeded in retaining possession of her until the following day" when more help materialized.

During July and August 1803, the *Endymion* added three enemy men-of-war and two privateers to her prize total.[39]

Now that he was captain of his own vessel, Charles would be taking the initiative in the pursuit and seizure of prize captures. This situation had several benefits in relation to Fanny. Charles's involvement with naval prizes gave him a romantic and adventurous air that very likely appealed to her. At a practical level, as the captain of the *Indian*, he would receive a greater share of any prize monies than he had previously. In addition, if they were to have a future together, sums of prize money would be a welcome supplement to Charles's salary, which at the commander level was £246 3s. 10d. net per year.[40] This salary was sufficient to sustain a single man in uniform with his officer's quarters and rations provided aboard ship, but it was a very modest sum for setting up and maintaining a home for a wife and possibly children. For these reasons, Fanny plausibly took a strong interest in the details of Charles's prize business from the very beginning.

Initially Charles's pursuit of prize vessels and prize money in North American waters met with success. The American ship *Ocean* was captured on 1 September 1805 by the *Indian* together with HMS *Cambrian* (40 guns) and HMS *Cleopatra* (32 guns), although it was five years before Charles received his final share of prize money. He seized two more vessels: *Dygden*, a Swedish ship,[41] taken with HMS *Cleopatra* on 23 August 1805; and *Rosalie*, a Spanish schooner, taken with Robert Reilly of HMS *Busy* (18 guns) on 1 March 1806. They were sent for adjudication by the Halifax Vice Admiralty Court, where they were both ruled to be lawful prizes. As a result, the capturing captains became the owners of part of the cargo in the case of the *Dygden* and owners of both the vessel and the cargo in the case of the *Rosalie*. The latter was carrying a valuable mixed cargo, including brandy (164 cases), wine, rum, silk handkerchiefs, Persian satin ribbons, sheeting, earthenware, macaroni, tar, sugar, and pitch.[42] An advertisement in the local newspaper shows that the net proceeds from the *Rosalie* were paid out in October 1806 from Andrew Belcher's counting house on Water Street in Halifax.[43]

That same year the Bermuda Vice Admiralty Court ruled in Charles's favour regarding his solo captures of the Spanish schooners the *Nuestra Senora del Carmen* and *La Lustorina*.[44] Once again he collected prize money, £112 in the case of the *Nuestra Senora del Carmen*.[45] This sum represented nearly half his net annual salary. But after Spain became allied with Britain on 1 July 1808, Spanish vessels could no longer be targeted as prizes. Charles probably wondered how this political development might further affect his tally of prize captures.

In counterbalance to the successful captures and adjudications and pay-outs of 1806–07, other claims Charles brought before the Vice Admiralty Courts were dismissed. In one instance, what seemed to be a clear case in the captor's favour proved to be the opposite. On 12 July 1806 Charles and his good friend Edward Hawker co-captured the American brig *Sally*. Judge Alexander Croke of the Halifax Vice Admiralty Court ruled in their favour; the sale of *Sally* and her cargo at auction went ahead, yielding almost £4,000. Consequently, Charles and Edward happily anticipated a share of about £500 each. Alas, Croke's judgment was successfully appealed to the High Court of Admiralty in London and, instead of considerable prize money, the two captains became responsible for the administrative costs incurred during the prolonged court proceedings.[46] There was also disappointing news for Charles the next year when the Bermuda Vice Admiralty Court restored the *Joseph*, an American brig, and the *Eliza*, an American ship, to their owners.

Fanny was well situated to monitor some of those aspects of Charles's prize business that took place in Bermuda. She was able to become familiar with the vessels he sent in with prize crews as they rode at anchor in full view in the harbour until their adjudication and sale occurred. The *Bermuda Gazette* advertised the times for prize auctions and listed the items of cargo to be sold. Moreover, Fanny knew when the court would be hearing Charles's prize cases because her brother-in-law, James Christie Esten, was the advocate general in the Vice Admiralty Court, a post previously held by her father, John Grove Palmer. The advocate general acted as a barrister representing the Crown and thus the captor's interests when a prize case was brought before the court. In September 1808 Esten successfully argued the case for what turned out to be Charles's most profitable single prize, the French privateer *La Jeune Estelle* (4 guns), carrying a crew of twenty-five men. He had captured her on 19 June 1808 at latitude 32° north and longitude 68° west, off the coast of South Carolina while she was on route from Florida to Santo Domingo with supplies. The legal process in this case proceeded with admirable swiftness,

ALL Perſons who were actually on board His Majeſty's Sloop of War INDIAN, CHARLES JOHN AUSTEN, Eſquire, Commander, and are entitled to ſhare for the French Schooner JEUNE ESTELLE and Cargo, captured on the 19th June, 1808, and condemned in the Vice Admiralty Court of theſe Iſlands, prize to His Majeſty's ſaid Sloop, are requeſted to take

NOTICE

That a Diſtribution of the Nett Proceeds, of the ſaid Veſſel and Cargo will take place on Wedneſday the 28th. inſtant; all Perſons who do not then appear are informed that attendance will be given at the Compting Houſe of the Subſcribers, in St. George's, from 10 to 2 o'clock every Tueſday and Friday, until the 28th of December next, unleſs the whole ſhould be previouſly diſcharged.

EDWARD GOODRICH,
ARCHIBALD SHEDDEN, } Agents.
GEORGE REDMOND HULBERT,
St. George's, Sept. 24, 1808.

Fig. 8   The payout notice for prize money from the sale of the French privateer *La Jeune Estelle* (4 guns) and her cargo. She was Charles's most lucrative enemy capture, earning him about £540.

for by 24 September the *Bermuda Gazette* advertised the payout of prize money. Charles's share of the prize money was £540 14s. 1d.[47] (Fig. 8). In the currency used, "£" stands for pound sterling, "s" for shilling, and "d" for penny. There were 20 shillings in a pound and 12 pence in a shilling. A guinea was worth 1 pound and 1 shilling. The amount of Charles's prize money has been calculated on the assumption that the court's adjudication in his favour in September was in accordance with the long-standing rules for the sharing of prize money. New rules of distribution had been determined in England that June by the Admiralty in England, but it appears that they were not yet officially received and in operation in Bermuda. Had the case come under the revised rules whereby the captain's share was reduced from one-quarter share to one-quarter less a third, Charles would have received about £180 less. The efficiency of the court proceedings in this case may have been due to the agency of James Christie Esten, who would have been aware of the benefits of a swift adjudication for Charles.

La Jeune Estelle is Charles's only prize for which there is a complete record, thanks to the very detailed financial bookkeeping of prize agent George Hulbert.[48] The sale of her cargo at auction on 27 July 1808 yielded very gratifying results. The superfine flour, pork, beef, fish, herrings, bread, butter, cheese, lard, pease, hams, soap, tallow, and casks of claret brought good prices, even though Esther Esten, in a report to the absent Charles, observed that she had been "a little nervous for you last week, lest an Arrival of Provisions shou'd lower the sale of yours."[49] Esther's concerns were well founded, for had there been concurrent auctions of similar prize goods or merchant vessels arriving with comparable items at the same time, Charles's property would have fetched much less.

The Austen family in England were delighted when Charles's report to his admiral describing *La Jeune Estelle*'s capture was published on the front page of the *London Gazette*, 20–23 August 1808. About this time Jane Austen observed that her other naval brother, Frank, "wants nothing but a good Prize to be a perfect Character."[50] This comment suggests the esteem in which she now held Charles.

Since Charles corresponded with Jane, he likely wrote to her from the station about his experiences regarding naval prizes. In fact, what she learned may have inspired certain features that she assigned to Captain Frederick Wentworth when she came to write *Persuasion*. Both men began prize taking as commanders of their own sloops, Charles's "dear old Indian"[51] and Wentworth's "dear old Asp."[52] Like Charles, Frederick hoped that his colleagues would profit from prize money and he enjoyed their working together and making joint captures. Charles's accounts to his family about naval prizes may have included reports about his friends' successes, as there were several impressive examples to describe. Over time, frigate captain Edward Hawker sent thirty-three vessels before the Vice Admiralty Courts, a good number of which resulted in prize money. Captain Robert Simpson's great coup was the capture of the American vessel *Fly*, which carried $150,000 in specie – that is, in coin as opposed to paper money. As this cash was considered part of the condemned cargo, he stood to receive about $37,000 as part of his prize money. In total, Simpson amassed £30,000[53] in prize money during only two years on the station (1806–08), before his luck changed and he died of a bilious attack in Halifax in June 1808.

The fact that captains like Hawker and Simpson became as rich as they did shows what was possible with some luck and skill. In *Persuasion*, Wentworth's description of taking "the very French frigate I wanted" and his recounting "how fast [he] made money"[54] in the Mediterranean indicate the sort of activities that made his wealth in prize money seem plausible. Jane Austen's interest in the dynamics of naval prizes may have triggered her consideration of how a fortune in prize money might alter the social and marital prospects of the recipient. In *Persuasion*, she generously bestows £25,000 prize money on her hero Captain Wentworth, a largesse that allows him to seek the affections of Anne Elliot a second time.

Jane and the family naturally hoped that other prizes would pay handsomely and thereby secure a financially sound future for Fanny and Charles. This did not happen, for at best Charles's net prize money while he was on the North American station could probably not have totalled more than £890. This sum needs to be understood in relation to the fact that at least three of Charles's prize claims[55] were dismissed by the courts and the captured property returned to their owners. In such cases, Charles had to pay the costs of the legal process and other fees, which might have been considerable. The paucity of surviving financial records for both the Halifax and Bermuda Vice Admiralty Courts makes it very difficult to estimate with much certainty the net income generated from Charles's prize business during the years 1805 to 1811.

Although it was intriguing for Fanny to fantasize about riches that might be gained from prize captures, she also came to have a very direct understanding of the particular risks involved in prize taking. Any British vessel in North American waters was potential prey for cruising enemy warships or privateers. At about the time of Fanny's engagement to Charles in 1806, the *Indian* had a very close call. While cruising 480 nautical miles southeast of Bermuda, she suddenly became the target of four fast-sailing and heavily armed French frigates. For almost fifty hours the *Indian* used every possible tactic to elude her determined pursuers: the gunroom, sail cabin, and bulkhead were dismantled and parts of them flung overboard to augment the ship's sailing speed. As the wind had dropped, some crew members took to the sweeps (oars) and rowed furiously while others cleared the deck for action. According to the ship's log, "the frigates [were] coming very fast."[56] Luckily for Charles, when all the vessels became becalmed, the *Indian*, being the much smaller and much lighter one, was able to put a safe distance between herself and her pursuers.

Charles was incredibly fortunate to have escaped what would have been a disastrous encounter for the *Indian*. The vessels in pursuit were most likely four French men-of-war: the *Clorinde* (40 guns), the *Renommée* (40 guns), the *Loire* (20 guns), and the *Seine* (20 guns).[57] They would later trap his squadron colleague, Captain John Shortland of HMS *Junon*, while he was cruising east of Antigua in December 1809. After a gallant but hopeless action, the French broadsides smashed the *Junon* before her captors destroyed her by fire. Shortland was gravely injured and died in Guadeloupe five weeks later.

The acquisition of prize money was highly desirable, but considering the risks at sea, some captains did not live long enough to enjoy it. One of these was Robert Reilly, who was due to share prize money with Charles from their joint capture of the Spanish schooner *Rosalie*. But before the money was paid out, Reilly's vessel, the *Busy*, floundered in a winter gale and was lost with all hands in February 1806 while escorting a convoy to the West Indies. This tragedy was sobering for Fanny, as it underlined what she already knew about the dangers Charles regularly faced at sea.

Indeed, the following year, Charles was on a mission very like Reilly's when the *Indian* had a harrowing escape. Charles's description of the "tremendous hurricane"[58] he survived while escorting a convoy in the waters southeast of Bermuda is truly chilling. In Charles's words: "The wind became so furious as to perfectly over power the Ship, which lay down on her beam ends, with such a weight of Water on Deck as made me fear she would never right again. To save HM [His Majesty's] ship and our lives, I ordered the main mast to be cut away, which happily for us was done so promptly that we got clear of the wreck without receiving any injury, and the ship, tho' with evident difficulty, righted herself." Yet their misfortune did not end there, for "on the gale abating the Ship rolled so violently, that the Mizzen Mast (which was rotten) went over the side."[59] In November 1807 the dismasted and tattered *Indian* limped in to port in Bermuda. To see Charles's vessel in such a mangled state was surely a terrifying sight for Fanny. Even Charles's current commander-in-chief, Admiral Sir George Berkeley, considered that the *Indian* "had a very narrow escape."[60]

How graphic a narrative of the *Indian*'s lucky escape from the French frigates would Charles share with Fanny? How much would he tell her about the horrors of a hurricane at sea if she had not seen for herself the terrific damage the *Indian* had suffered? However circumspect Charles was, Fanny was bound to discover some details. She read the *Bermuda Gazette*, which enthusiastically reported both naval adventures and misadventures. Moreover, Fanny was often in the company of their naval friends such as captains Edward Hawker and Frederick Hickey, and on these occasions, conversations must have touched on the officers' recent exploits at sea. Given her many sources of information, Fanny could not avoid acquiring a realistic grasp of the many dangers Charles often faced in the navy.

Fanny married Charles on the lovely morning of 18 May 1807. The ceremony took place in the beautiful seventeenth-century parish church of St Peter's at St George's,[61] where Fanny had been baptised on 21 February 1790.[62] Now, seventeen years later, she came here as a bride, accompanied by Esther and her husband, James. To their regret, her parents and sister Harriet were thousands of miles away in London. Though Fanny was a young bride, marriage at her age was not uncommon.

Early nineteenth-century marriages of the upper and middle ranks of society were grounded on certain expectations. Each partner's role was well-defined and mutually understood. The husband was expected to ensure their financial security; his wife was charged with the management of their home and their household. She arranged for the material and emotional comforts of her husband and whatever children they might have. Some of these stipulations did not apply to Fanny and Charles, who did not yet have their own establishment. With Charles so often at sea and Fanny's close and affectionate ties to her sister Esther, it made little sense for seventeen-year-old

Fanny to be out on her own in his absence. She remained in Esther's household, which was in the original Palmer house where Fanny had grown up. There Charles joined her when he was in port. Fanny was deeply in love with her handsome husband and was highly motivated to ensure his comfort and well-being. In the years ahead she became a devoted and caring mother to their children.

A marriage was a means of uniting families. Charles was already very friendly with Esther and James Esten, and at some point a mutual correspondence began with the Keppel Street Palmers. Fanny must have introduced Charles to various other Bermuda relatives early in their relationship, including individuals she called "Aunt Heane" and "Aunt Diana," as well as "Uncle Ball," her mother's brother, Alexander Forbes Ball.

For the gentry class in Jane Austen's time, knowing the lineage of individuals marrying into a family was of considerable importance. The English Austens were no exception, for as Jane's letters show, there was lively interest in the pedigrees of the women and men she knew who were about to marry. Fanny's ancestral connections stood up to scrutiny. Her father, John Grove Palmer, was the only son of the Irish-born barrister and property owner John Palmer of Kentish Town, London. This John Palmer descended from a branch of the landed Palmer family of Bekesbourne, Kent, who had subsequently settled in County Kerry, Ireland, in the seventeenth century. Fanny's Palmer grandfather had married well. His wife, Dorothy, belonged to the Yorkshire branch of the aristocratic Strangways family, who claimed a common ancestry with the rich and influential Dorset Strangways. Fanny's mother, Dorothy Palmer, née Ball, was connected to several generations of well-established colonial Bermudian families of English origin, including the Balls, Smiths, and Hutchinsons.[63]

Joining the Austen family may have seemed a somewhat daunting prospect for Fanny, whose social circles in Bermuda had been small and familiar. Her new in-laws were impressive individuals. Fanny was acquiring a mother-in-law, the clever and witty Mrs George Austen,[64] the former Cassandra Leigh; and two sisters, the practical and artistic Cassandra and the imaginative, brilliant, and yet-to-be-published author, Jane. Charles also had four able and accomplished brothers: James, rector of the parish church in Steventon, Hampshire; Edward, in possession of two substantial estates, at Chawton and Godmersham; Henry, a private banker; and Francis (known in the family as Frank), a captain in the Royal Navy. Another brother, George, was mentally and physically disabled; he was cared for in a village neighbouring Steventon and was unable to take any part in adult Austen family life. In fact, Fanny may have known little about him. In addition, there were four brothers' wives: Mary (James), Elizabeth (Edward), Eliza (Henry), Mary (Frank), and an ever increasing quantity of nieces and nephews.

Letters from the Austen family in England welcoming Fanny have not survived, but it is known that family ties were forged at an early stage. Charles's niece, fourteen-year-old Fanny Knight, recorded his marriage to the "lovely" Fanny Palmer in her pocketbook for 1807, and by August she had finished "a gold twist necklace and bracelets for [her] new Aunt Mrs. C. Austen."[65] In September, Fanny Knight visited Southampton with her parents and "went in a hired boat to Hythe to call on Mrs. Palmer [Fanny Austen's mother] who called on us the day before."[66] Jane Austen's subsequent letters include periodic references to the well-being of Fanny and Charles.[67]

Fanny became pregnant with their first child in early 1808. On 26 July, Esther sent Charles a detailed progress report about "my dear Fan": "It is with great delight that I say she is doing very well, and wants nothing but your presence to make her quite comfortable. Her Appetite (by the assistance of bitters)[68] is pretty good. A very good one you cannot expect her to have just now. Indeed Capt. Hickey[69] told her yesterday, that she had grown quite plump in the face, which I was not a little proud to hear." Esther's letter further reflects her concern for Fanny's well-being. When she is unable to accompany Fanny on "her usual evening walks … our friend Mrs. Dickinson is always ready to supply my place upon all occasions." This companion on Fanny's nightly walks was her good friend, Martha Dickinson, née Esten, a sister of James Christie Esten. Esther reports that she "forgot in my list of articles for Fan, to mention flannel. You will remember to send her twenty or thirty yards, of fine white flannel, as there is none to be got here fit for her use."[70] According to then current practice, a newborn baby should be wrapped up in flannel with her mouth and nose scarcely showing.[71]

Close to the time of the birth, Charles captured a small enemy vessel in waters near Bermuda. A French schooner, laden with sugar, taken on

21 November 1808, was assigned a prize crew from the *Indian* and despatched to Bermuda for adjudication. She never arrived. The poignancy of this event, the "real misfortune" according to Charles in a letter to Cassandra, was the loss of the prize crew from the *Indian* – "the lives of twelve of my people two of them mids [midshipmen]."[72] Although income was always welcome, especially with their first child soon to be born, Charles's sorrow over the loss of his men took precedence over regrets about prize money he may have missed.[73]

Charles's current commander-in-chief, Vice-Admiral Sir John Borlase Warren, allowed the expectant father to remain in port for his wife's confinement so that Charles could "at this criticale moment support my Fanny." On Christmas Day, Charles joyously wrote Cassandra that "my beloved Fanny was safely deliver'd [of] a fine girl on the 22nd December and … they are both doing remarkably well. The Baby besides being the finest that ever was seen is really a good looking healthy young Lady of very large dimensions and as fat as butter. I mean to call her Cassandra Esten." Charles wishes his sister "a merry and happy Xmas in which Fan joins me as well as in bespeaking the Love of her Dear Grandmother and Aunts [Cassandra and Jane] &c for our little Cassandra"[74] He asked his sister Cassandra to be the child's sponsor, along with their friend "Captain Hawker of HMS Melampus" and Fanny's sister Esther. Just a week earlier, Esther Esten had given birth to a son, John Hamilton (to be known as Hamilton), a brother for three-year-old James Christie Palmer (known as Palmer). The closeness of the two impending births was known in England, for Jane wrote Cassandra that "Mrs. Esten was unluckily to lie in at the same time with Mrs. C.A. [Fanny]."[75] Charles closed his letter with the news that he was "interrupted by Mr. De Passau[76] who is going to Baptize the Children but as they are not quite made up he has consented to eat Cakes and drink some wine." Thus, on Christmas Day, Cassandra and Jane were sent the news of the joint baptisms of the two newborn babies, Cassandra Esten Austen and John Hamilton Esten.

Three months earlier, Charles's future on the North American Station[77] had appeared to be uncertain. In late August his prize agent, Andrew Belcher, requested the Halifax Vice Admiralty Court to order the release of the *Indian*'s prize money from the American ship *Ocean* because the *Indian* was about to be transferred from the station.[78] Belcher also advertised in the *Weekly Chronicle* (18 September 1808) that "all persons having demands against Capt. Austen of HMS Sloop of War Indian are [asked] to present them to Hon. A. Belcher." Such a request and notice were typical when a vessel was returning to England at the end of its commission. Yet the Board of Admiralty issued no new orders for the *Indian* and no change of command occurred. Thus, instead of some complete change of arrangements, Fanny faced new motherhood in the supportive and familiar surrounds of her Bermuda home.

Similar speculations about Charles's job surfaced again in 1809, for as Jane optimistically wrote in a verse letter to her brother Frank:

> You'll find us very snug next year,
> Perhaps with Charles & Fanny near,
> For now it often does delight us,
> To fancy them just over-right us.[79]

But there was no immediate family reunion in the village of Chawton, to which Jane, Cassandra, Mrs Austen, and their friend Martha Lloyd had moved in July 1809 to occupy a cottage owned by Edward Knight. Instead, Charles continued to serve in North American waters. He was not included in a major British offensive against the French colony of Martinique in February 1809. This assault was considered necessary so as to deprive French vessels of a safe port from which they could prey on British merchant shipping. Fanny may have been relieved that Charles was spared a role in this potentially dangerous offensive. He, on the other hand, missed a chance to be part of a successful naval venture that included some ships from his station, such as HMS *Cleopatra* captained by their friend Samuel Pechell.

CHAPTER 2

On the Move:
Between Bermuda and Halifax,
1809–1810

IN SEPTEMBER 1809 FANNY LEFT BERMUDA, probably for the first time. She set sail on a new phase of her married life, as she became a traveller in the wake of Charles's naval career. The *Indian* was ordered to Halifax for extensive repairs and refitting, and as she would be in port for several months, Fanny, who was four months pregnant, took the opportunity to sail with Charles the 789 nautical miles to Halifax. She was to make this journey between Bermuda and Halifax five more times in the next three years, before embarking on an even longer transatlantic journey. On this occasion Fanny travelled on the *Indian* with nine-month-old Cassy, in a party that also included her sister Esther and her two sons. The two families planned to share quarters onshore.

Halifax was a younger town than St George's but a centre of greater size, commercial activity, and military importance. It owed its existence to British determination to found a settlement and build a military presence to counterbalance French political and economic ambitions in eastern North America. The man designated to begin this task, Colonel Edward Cornwallis, arrived at Chebucto Bay[1] in the summer of 1749 with a potpourri of approximately 2,500 English settlers aboard thirteen transports. They were promised free passage, food and supplies for a year, tools, arms and ammunition, free grants of land, and the formation of a civil government. Some were retired military men, others were artisans, carpenters, and labourers, but many were unskilled volunteers from the streets of poverty-ridden London. Cornwallis had a generous budget, a plan for a gridiron pattern of streets, and a ready-made population. The name for the new settlement, "Halifax," was selected in honour of George Montagu-Dunk, 2nd Earl of Halifax and president of the Board of Trade and Plantations, the British government body responsible for the town's design, construction, and settlement.

What Cornwallis did not have was a pool of settlers sufficiently motivated and willing to do the hard jobs necessary to clear the land, to build a settlement from scratch, including fortifications, and to so fulfill the conditions expected of them. He had brought trained soldiers with him, but their presence did not dispel the fear that either the French or their allies, the local Mi'kmaq, might attack at any time. Thus, the initial years of Halifax were times of struggle and uncertainty. Then fortunes improved as waves of more industrious immigrants arrived: notably German and French-speaking Protestants in the 1750s; migrants from New England, known as Planters, in the 1760s; and Scots and Irish to follow. Better fortifications provided stronger protection, wharves and warehouses were built, and an influx of Yankee traders began to engage in profitable commerce with the nearby New England colonies and the West Indies.

In the ensuing years, Halifax grew in times of war but languished and suffered in periods of peace. During the Seven Years War with France (1756 to 1763), the town benefited from a huge amount of military spending by the British government. The garrison was considerably increased, and the Halifax Naval Yard's facilities were expanded and refined to cope with the greater demand for maintenance from the British navy's North American squadron. The Naval Yard also supplied the necessary ordinance required to engage the enemy in battle and made available the supply of provisions needed for the seamen, officers and marines on board ships. Two important campaigns originated from Halifax during the Seven Years War: the successful offensive against the French stronghold of Louisbourg in 1758 and the expedition that took Quebec in 1759, thus ending French control in mainland Canada.

During the American Revolutionary War (1775–1782), when the rebel colonies shut the British out of their ports, Halifax served as the strategic forward base close to the erupting conflict. After the war the town's population swelled enormously as thousands of refugees loyal to the Crown (to become known as Loyalists) fled north. This invasion included the wealthy, the poor, and recently freed black slaves. Some Loyalists moved on, but a number from the professional, administrative, and wealthy merchant classes resumed their careers and provided leadership in their newly adopted town.

Though peace severely depressed the economy and meant less financial support from England, Halifax did not languish for long. In 1793 England went to war against republican France. In 1794 twenty-seven-year-old Prince Edward, fourth in line to the British throne, arrived in Halifax to command His Majesty's forces in North America. During the next six years, he organized the building of a network of harbour fortifications, instituted a system of signal stations, and reconstructed Fort George, now known locally as the Citadel. He also erected stone Martello towers to protect the town's seaward defences and installed modern armaments at the forts. An officer who always valued punctuality, Prince Edward, now the Duke of Kent,[2] ordered a proper garrison clock to be erected on the town side of Citadel Hill. The clock, in operation for over 210 years, has become an icon of Halifax.

Halifax is famous for its huge, deep, and long natural harbour (Fig. 9).[3] On 17 September 1809, as the *Indian*, under Charles's command and carrying Fanny, Esther, and their children, worked her way up the channel to an anchorage near the Naval Yard, the landmarks of Halifax came into view. A density of wharfs and warehouses could be seen and, further up the sloping shore, the hilltop fortress of Fort George. Tall spires marked the locations of two of Halifax's oldest white-frame churches: St Paul's Anglican (Fig. 10), built in a Palladian style in 1750; and Mathers Church (which became St Mathews), established for early nonconformist settlers and completed in 1754. Further north was St George's, begun in 1800 and known as the Round Church, given its distinctive shape. From the water, Halifax gave the impression of "a long straggling assemblage of wooden houses,"[4] although once on shore Fanny would be shown the impressive stone Government House, the official residence of the lieutenant-governor, and some of the fine private homes in the same neighbourhood. But the town was by no means universally elegant. There were pockets of marked poverty, and in certain notorious areas, evidence of the drunkenness, brawling, and squalor that a port town and military base often spawned. By 1809 Halifax had a population of about 9,600 inhabitants together with an additional 4,000 more when army and navy personnel were included (Fig. 11).

Fig. 9   Map of Halifax Harbour by Anthony Lockwood, marked to show the key
locations associated with Fanny. 1. Halifax town site; 2. Site of the French prisoners of
war's craft market on Melville Island in the North West Arm of the harbour; 3. The gibbet
on Meagher's Beach, McNab's Island where corpses of guilty naval mutineers were hanged
in 1809; 4. Treacherous shoals in the vicinity of Sambro Island to be avoided when sailing
in or out of the harbour; 5. The Naval Yard and the admiral's apartment, in which Fanny
lived during the summer of 1810; 6. Birch Cove, where Fanny attended Mrs Andrew
Belcher's party on 16 June 1810.

Fig. 10 Joseph Partridge provides a splendid view of the Grand Parade and St Paul's Church at the centre of Halifax, c. 1819. It was an area frequented by Fanny in 1809 and during the summer of 1810. The painting is titled *The National School at Halifax* to call attention to that institution, located across the street from the church.

A port town such as Halifax was vulnerable to the forced impressments of men to serve on naval vessels and the violence accompanying it. The "press" was accomplished by sending a gang of ten or eleven seamen ashore at night, led by a naval lieutenant and accompanied by a marine armed with a bayonet. The waterfront taverns, crimping houses,[5] and brothels were prime hunting grounds for gangs looking to seize whatever number of men their government-issued warrant allowed them to take. There was a nasty episode in 1805, Charles's first year on the station, when excessive impressments by several British naval vessels caused huge local consternation.[6] It is said that Reverend Robert Stanser, rector of St Paul's Church, was mistakenly caught up in the melee. Due to the civil distress caused by these excesses, the provincial government made serious efforts to control future impressments; they issued no further warrants to the navy until 1812. Thus, the Halifax of 1809 was less troubled by the climate of fear that the practices of the press gangs so quickly generated.

Fanny and Esther may have felt this was a good time to be absent from Bermuda, for in late April ten captains of the squadron had strongly objected to the billing practices at the Vice Admiralty Court. This dissatisfaction

Fig. 11 *Halifax, August 1848*, a fine watercolour by Lieut. Herbert Grey Austen RN, Charles's nephew, who also served on the North American Station, 1845–48. The drawing shows Halifax as seen from the opposite shore of Dartmouth.

touched Fanny's and Esther's lives personally. Records showed that James Esten was charging fees amounting to £705 Bermuda currency, the equivalent to £470 British sterling, for representing eight vessels whose cases came before the Vice Admiralty Court in 1809.[7] The captains directly affected, as well as other captains who also favoured a uniform fee for the advocate's legal services, vehemently objected to Esten's billing practices, and a signed petition was despatched to the Admiralty in London by way of Admiral Warren.[8] Esten's critics included Edward Hawker of HMS *Melampus* and James, Lord Townshend, of HMS *Halifax*, who had each captured a small armed French vessel,[9] that was an indisputable instance of a naval prize. As their cases required no complicated legal work on Esten's part, Hawker and Townshend were convinced, as were other petitioners, that they were being overcharged when levied £75 as fees in Hawker's case and £50 in Townshend's. The controversy was not yet settled and must have caused Fanny considerable distress, for herself and for Esther. Hawker and Townshend were friends of Fanny and Charles,[10] and James Esten was her well-loved brother-in-law. Her naval sympathies and personal loyalties were in conflict.

While Fanny became accustomed to shore-based life in her new surrounds, Charles was responsible for arranging the *Indian*'s repairs and refitting at the Naval Yard.[11] The services of the yard were pivotal to Charles's safety, for, after four years at sea, the *Indian* showed considerable wear and tear to her wooden hull, sails, and rigging, and to her copper bottom. It was time she underwent a major overhaul. The *Indian*'s log provides a profile of the yard's progress: "Unbent the sails and sent them ashore to the Dockyard[12] (15 September); Readying her for heaving down, transporting her to the Careening Wharf (1, 2 November); Rattling down the Top Mast Rigging" (7 November). At the Careening Wharf, the *Indian* was taken out of the water and rolled on her side by means of lifting tackles in order to caulk the seams of her hull and repair the copper on her bottom. The work on the *Indian* was not finished until late November, fully two months after Fanny's arrival. While Fanny and Charles waited, there were many opportunities for entertainment on shore.

The heyday of elegant parties in Halifax had coincided with the presence of Prince Edward and the tenure at Government House of Frances Wentworth, the flirtatious and politically ambitious wife of Lt.-Gov. John Wentworth.[13] It was now nine years since the duke had returned to England, but Frances, who was known for her legendary entertainments, remained a presence in social circles until 1808. Tales of her more memorable extravaganzas were still in circulation. On one occasion, "On the King's birthday [she] had a branch of lights over the gateway with the British crown outlined around the letters 'GR.' On the supper table were representations of the new road to Pictou, the new flour mill of Hartshorne's, the new wind mill on the Common, and the fisheries."[14] Lady Wentworth liked to serve special ices flavoured with orgeat, a mixture of barley water, almonds, sugar and orange flower water. She also dressed magnificently for the occasion. At one ball, "Mrs. Wentworth stood first in fashion & magnificence. Her Gown and Petticoat of sylvan tissue trimmed with Italian Flowers & the finest blond lace, a train of four yards long, her hair and wrist ornamented with real Diamonds."[15]

The behaviour of Lady Wentworth and her set did not go without criticism. Judge Alexander Croke of the Halifax Vice Admiralty Court wrote a biting satirical poem, titled "The Inquisition," that speaks to the gaiety, foibles, and moral misadventures of the Halifax upper class. The poem, in the heroic couplet style of Alexander Pope, was clandestinely circulating in 1806–07 not long after Charles Austen had arrived on the station. In this verse, Croke captures the mood of the festivities enjoyed by Halifax's inner circle. On the occasion of planning a ball,

Cards fly by packs to folk of each degree,
Request the favour, and the RSVP ...
What Turkies, Chickens, Pigs and Pidgeons fell,
To grace the banquet, not the Muse could tell.

On the day of the ball,

The Dames arrive, in Muslins, gauzes, Satins,
In Chariots, Coaches, One Horse Chaise and Pattens ...
The gaudy Banners flutter to the Air,
The Silver Side Board groans with sumptuous fare;
The fiddles crash, the merry Tambours beat,
In Notes responsive to the dancers' feet.[16]

In the Halifax of 1809 the level of entertainment still retained energy
and vigour. While the *Indian* was undergoing repairs, Charles introduced
Fanny to the society of the military and local professional community.
The provincial secretary, Samuel Hood George, in correspondence with
his mother, describes a program of varied amusements. He writes: "[F]or
the next week we are to have nothing but gaity. Tomorrow [18 October]
we dine at the Commissioners [John Inglefield's] who is the gayest of the
gay and in the evening we go on board Sir Alexander Cochrane's[17] ship
Pompee [74 guns], to a Ball and supper, on Friday to Mrs Belcher's[18] party,
on Monday a play, ... and so we pass our time."[19] Charles was familiar
with this social set. Captain Inglefield was the resident commissioner who
organized and supervised the services at the Naval Yard, where Charles
had brought the *Indian* for repairs since 1805. He was well acquainted with
the Belchers, and he was linked by naval ties to Admiral Cochrane, who
was in Halifax for the refit of his squadron at the Naval Yard. Fanny's and
Charles's presence would be welcome, even sought after, for these social
events. Little Cassy was under the care of her nursemaid, thus freeing her
mother for visits and parties.

While Sir Alexander Cochrane's flagship was in port, her men gave a
spirited benefit performance of *Barbarossa, Emperor of the Turks* on behalf
of the cash-strapped Theatre Royal on Argyle Street near St Paul's Church.

For Fanny and Charles, ever keen to support naval cultural initiatives, this performance would have a particular attraction. The Theatre Royal was first established in 1794 during Prince Edward's residency in Halifax. Under the direction of professional actor Charles Stewart Powell, supported by his wife, Mary Ann, two daughters, Cordelia and Fidelia, and theatrically inclined members of the garrison, he had regularly mounted a wide variety of plays.[20] A strict protocol was expected by attendees: "Ladies were asked to dress their hair as low as possible so that the patrons behind them could see the stage," and carriages arriving to pick up patrons from the theatre must "have their horses' heads towards the Parade," presumably so as not to create a traffic jam in narrow Argyle Street.[21] Fanny and Charles enjoyed the theatre whenever they had a chance to attend, so any offerings at the Theatre Royal would appeal during their autumn visit.

Halifax offered other pleasures. Army and naval officers and their ladies regularly travelled to an unusual craft fair held at the military prison on a tiny island in the North West Arm of the harbour. Visitors were offered a wide range of ingenious trinkets and practical objects – knitted stockings and gloves, bone snuff boxes, dice and dominoes, shaving brushes, and much more – all handmade by French prisoners of war and largely fashioned from salvaged materials. One Frenchman made hats of birchbark, while others crafted model battleships rigged with silk sails and complete with cannons made from pennies. This is the sort of outing Fanny and Esther would have enjoyed – a short sail out of the main harbour, around the tip of the peninsula, into the North West Arm, an occasion for a little shopping in an unexpected venue, and the sheer pleasure of Charles's company. As their escort, he knew the way to the military prison and was familiar with how business was conducted at the fair.

Before they left Halifax, Fanny and Charles asked the Reverend Robert Stanser, the well-liked naval chaplain of the station, to christen little Cassy at St Paul's Church. This seems surprising, since there had already been a baptism in Bermuda on Christmas Day, 1808.[22] That occasion, however, appears to be an instance of baptizing a child just in case she might not survive early infancy. In October 1809 nine-month-old Cassy was thriving, and two of the sponsors, Esther Esten and Captain Edward Hawker, were also in Halifax. After the traditional celebratory cakes and ale, Reverend

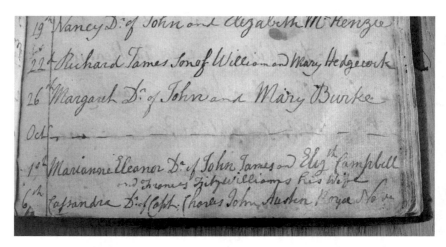

Fig. 12   Cassandra (Cassy) Austen's baptismal record in St Paul's Church, Halifax, 6 October 1809. Fanny's name in the register is the one public record of her presence in Halifax.

Stanser wrote in his baptismal register: "6 October 1809: Cassandra, D[r.23] of Capt. Charles John Austen, Royal Navy and Frances FitzWilliams his Wife"[24] (Fig. 12). Thus Jane and Cassandra Austen had a niece christened in far-off Halifax, Nova Scotia.

When the repairs to the *Indian* were complete, she was ready to return to Bermuda. On sailing into Halifax Harbour in mid-September, Fanny would have found the views from her deck pleasing and inviting – the varied townscape and wharves to port, the green woods of the biggest harbour island, McNab's, to starboard. Now Fanny would see an extraordinary sight if she looked towards McNab's as the *Indian* navigated her way down the channel. Six men from HMS *Columbine* (18 guns) had been found guilty of mutiny by a naval court martial and hanged. Since 18 September, four of their corpses were left to dangle from gibbets erected on the spit of Meagher's beach, their presence serving as warning to respect the navy's authority.[25] As the *Indian* sailed by, Charles would surely have tried to shield Fanny from this gruesome evidence of naval discipline. The provincial secretary, Samuel Hood George, voiced his disgust at this brutal display. In a letter to his father, Sir Rupert George, in London, he wrote that "it is hardly possible to go beyond George's Island without being offended by the sight of these unfortunate sufferers."[26]

The *Indian* cleared the harbour on 29 November for a voyage that would be fraught with danger. Fanny and Cassy experienced their first major storm at sea and it was terrifying. Just out of Halifax the *Indian* met "strong gales with sleet and snow." By the evening the "gale increased" and "the ship was labouring and shipping heavy seas."[27] For the next five days, the vessel lurched and rocked in the merciless gales. The *Indian* became separated from the flagship HMS *Swiftsure* (74 guns) and the three other vessels in convoy, HMS *Aeolus* (32 guns), HMS *Thistle* (10 guns), and HMS *Bream* (4 guns). On 3 December when the *Indian* signalled the *Thistle* with a blue light, which is ordinarily a sign of distress, she did not reply.[28] It was not encouraging for Charles that they were 495 nautical miles from a navigational point identified in the ship's log as Wreck Hill, Bermuda.

The erratic rolling of the vessel and the bone-chilling wind must have greatly distressed and alarmed Fanny, now almost seven months' pregnant. She needed to be brave and to try to hide her trepidation, especially as she had a terrified Cassy to calm and reassure. Finally, on 5 December the wind dropped to moderate breezes. The men surveyed the damage to the vessel and repairs began. According to the logbook, "people [were] employed repairing the rigging after the gale" and "fitting a new main sail."[29] By 10 December, the *Indian*'s deck was still awash with as much as two inches of water.[30] Imagine Fanny's relief when land was sighted and they "made all sail" for St David's Head, Bermuda, arriving in St George's on 12 December after a harrowing voyage of fifteen days, almost twice as long as the journey usually took.

Fanny settled down to await the birth of their second child. Fortunately, Charles was on shore for the arrival of Harriet Jane on 19 February 1810, a godchild for Jane Austen, Fanny's sister Harriet, and Charles's brother, Henry. Twelve days later Charles went to sea again and Fanny busied herself with her babies in Charles's absence. Even so, she must have often scanned the horizon for the signal flag, which signified the approach of a sloop of war. When that vessel was the *Indian*, Fanny welcomed Charles and delighted in his time on shore with them. When he had to leave again, her attitude and behaviour were reminiscent of another earlier naval wife, Frances (Fanny) Boscawen,[31] who assured her absent husband, Admiral Edward Boscawen, that "the most acceptable employment I can dedicate to you is the care of our dear children, and this is my study and the pleasing business of my life."[32]

On 10 May 1810 Fanny achieved the new status of flag-captain's wife when Admiral Sir John Warren appointed Charles captain of his flagship, the two-decker HMS *Swiftsure* (74 guns). She was 173 feet long and 47 feet 6 inches at the beam (middle point) and was classified as a third-rate ship, a designation made according to the number of guns she carried.[33] Charles's good fortune came as a result of the accidental death of the *Swiftsure*'s previous captain, John Conn, who had mysteriously fallen overboard and drowned on 4 May while cruising off Bermuda.[34] Charles's commission was to fill a death vacancy, and as such he knew it would be temporary, especially as Sir John Warren's term of office was coming to an end within some months. However, the appointment came with elevation to the rank of post-captain, a status that placed Charles on the list for future promotions in the Royal Navy, made according to seniority. In addition, while he was captain of HMS *Swiftsure*, his pay more than doubled, from £20 10s. to £46 7s. net per month,[35] the difference resulting from his upgrade to a third-rate vessel from the *Indian*, an unrated sloop. Charles's promotion would provide greater security for himself, Fanny, and their family, since as a post-captain and later as a higher-ranked officer he would be able to draw more "half pay"[36] whenever he was not assigned to active sea service. His new rank also meant that he might expect to get a frigate for his next commission, yet where and when that might be was uncertain and likely would depend on how long the war with France might last.

The good news of his new rank and commission was reported in the *London Gazette* on 27 June 1810: "Captain Austen of the Indian, is promoted to Post Captain and appointed to Swiftsure." Family and friends in England rejoiced over Charles's good fortune. This event was also a time of celebration for Fanny and Charles. Years later Charles remembered the day he had been made post-captain and how his "lovely and beloved wife [rejoiced] in all the good that befell me."[37]

Charles had indeed been very lucky. Admiral Warren's first choice for a replacement flag-captain was his wife's nephew and Charles's friend Captain Samuel John Pechell. However, Pechell, who was also more senior in rank to Charles, was off at sea at the time of Conn's death, and Warren, who needed to be in Halifax, could not wait for his return. Charles was the obvious choice, as he was the senior officer available in port at St George's at that

Fig. 13   Admiral Sir John Borlase Warren, Commander-in-Chief of the North American Station 1808–11, 1812–14. He promoted Charles to the coveted rank of post-captain, to the delight of both Fanny and Charles.

moment. Fanny had only days to prepare for the family's second journey to Halifax. She gathered up baby Harriet (two months) and Cassy (two years four months) and quickly packed all that she could think might be needed by the family. But frankly, she had no idea where and what Charles's future assignments on the flagship might be.

Fanny and Charles were now brought into closer contact with Admiral and Lady Warren. Sir John, in particular, was both personally and professionally an outstanding figure (Fig. 13). According to the *Naval Chronicle*, he was "one of the most accomplished officers in the service"; he possessed "the sincerity of a Seaman without the roughness of the old school ... To his friends his manner is open and impressive, [and] he commands without asperity and gains obedience and respect without the influence of terror."[38] In the mid-eighteenth century, there was a high standard for the sort of skills and personal attributes a good naval officer ought to possess. In the opinion of Admiral Vernon, it was important that he have a "good share of sense, be perfect master of his business, have some taste for honour; which last is usually the result of *a happy education, moderate reading and good company*." Such officers stood in contrast to those who were skilled seamen but, in the words of Admiral Vernon, "have the courage of brutes without any regard for the fine qualities of men."[39] Warren was a humane officer who, with his diplomatic abilities, navigational and tactical skills, as well as a master's degree from Cambridge, exemplified the model of the gentlemanly officer.

Sir John's career to date was impressive. He had inherited his father's title and fortune at the age of twenty-two. By 1809 he had served thirty-nine years in the navy, and he brought to the North American Station a reputation for successful prize taking and able, enlightened leadership. The Warrens' partnership in marriage had been long and supportive. Their first meeting had all the ingredients of a romance. Sir John sat opposite the beautiful Caroline Clavering at a dinner and was immediately smitten. He wrote her a note in French: "If you find this heart worthy of you and you deign to accept it, you will make me the happiest of men" (translation). She replied in English: "Then you shall be happy." They married in 1780.

Prior to their coming to North America, Sir John and Lady Warren had suffered repeated family tragedies. A daughter Caroline died in 1786, as did a son William in 1791. Their beloved son and heir, George, was killed at the Battle of Aboukir in 1801, and a young daughter, Diana, died unexpectedly in 1802. Their only remaining child, Frances, married her brother's best friend, George Sedley, later 4th Baron Vernon, and they were now the parents of a seven-year-old boy.[40] The Warrens' loss of so much of their own family may explain their sensitivity to the needs of the young Austen family. Fanny, in particular, would benefit from the Warrens' empathetic goodwill during her four months' stay in Halifax.

Charles's new professional relationship with Admiral Sir John Warren presented interesting possibilities. He had been very happy under his command and liked Warren personally, writing Cassandra in December 1808 that "the Admiral and his family arrived here just a Fortnight ago and are fixed for the winter. I find them as friendly as ever."[41] If he further impressed his superior in his new appointment, Warren's approbation could be useful for Charles's future career.

Fanny also had a role to play, for she and Charles were now part of Admiral and Lady Warren's immediate retinue and would be spending much more time in their company. Walter Anson, biographer of Sir John Warren, describes Lady Warren as "a woman of considerable ability, with a cheerful temper, a keen sense of humour, and a devoted wife and mother."[42] This rather generic description does little to capture the strength of Lady Warren's personality. During Sir John's appointment to the British Embassy at St Petersburg (1802–03), a mission intended to secure good diplomatic relations with Russia,[43] Lady Warren's letters to England suggest her capacity for deep feelings and strong reactions. While still in mourning for their son George, she describes how "I drive in my chariot and four grays at full gallop through the streets at 12 noon each day,"[44] and she bemoans that "a broken spirit like mine cannot combat with the young and gay world."[45] By 1810 Lady Warren had recovered her spirits. She was considered a force to be reckoned with within the social circles of the North American station, and she was somewhat notorious for her interest in her husband's squadron, as "in the opinion of the junior officers [she was inclined] to think of things for them to do."[46] Fanny must have initially wondered how she would relate to such a dynamic individual of firm views and opinions.

The *Swiftsure* made Halifax on 28 May 1810 (Fig. 14). She passed the Sambro lighthouse, built in 1759 and a necessary navigational marker for vessels on the approach to Halifax Harbour, avoided the numerous and treacherous Western Shoals, and came in sight of the familiar white granite elevation of Chebucto Head. From there she turned north up the main channel of the harbour, proceeded past McNab's Island, and arrived at her anchorage at the western side of the Narrows close by the Naval Yard. The next day a seventeen-gun salute rang out across the harbour in commemoration of the Restoration of King Charles II 150 years previously. This was most likely the first time Fanny had been present at a naval ceremony on a grand scale, and for her the sound of the guns and the sight of the men positioned aloft, evenly spaced across all the yards,[47] must have been truly

Fig. 14   *Halifax Harbour, Nova Scotia* by Vice Admiralty Judge Sir Alexander Croke, showing Admiral Warren's flagship, HMS *Swiftsure*, in the harbour. While Charles was flag-captain, Fanny sailed with him from Bermuda to Halifax in May 1810.

impressive. As she and Charles together with Cassy, Harriet, and their nurse maid, Molly, joined the Admiral's retinue to disembark, Fanny was about to fulfill a new role in a new situation.

Sir John's party proceeded to his apartments situated in the naval hospital at the northern end of the Naval Yard and known as the Admiral's Lodge (Fig. 15). Although separated from the fashionable and commercial areas of the town, the admiral's quarters at least enjoyed some advantages, as the three-wing hospital building benefited from a pleasingly rural setting, close to pasturage and small crop fields. In the past Admiral Warren had made use of the country location, although he had had bad luck in 1809 when fourteen of his sheep, twelve white and two black, marked "JBW," had disappeared from their field. According to an optimistic advertisement in the Halifax *Weekly Chronicle*, 26 October 1809, "whoever brings them back to the Admiral's Lodge will be liberally rewarded." Fanny perhaps recalled this earlier incident, since she had been in Halifax at the time and may even have been entertained at the Admiral's Lodge sometime in the fall of 1809. Now the lodge would become Fanny and Charles's temporary place of residence.

Fig. 15 *View from Fort Needham near Halifax* by G.I. Parkyns, c. 1801. The Naval Yard facilities stretch along the waterfront at the far left; Fanny lived in Admiral and Lady Warren's quarters there in the summer of 1810.

The hospital also had some architectural merit, especially from the west face where a graceful colonnade extended the length of the building. Inside, the admiral's quarters, although originally intended as the surgeon's apartment, were spacious and occupied the most southern section of the structure. From this location little Cassy and her mother were well situated to observe the spectacle of continuous marine activity in the harbour and vessels coming to and from the hospital's wharf. Yet even the most uncritical of the admiral's guests had to admit the arrangement was not ideal. The official apartment, though self-contained, was in hearing range of the patients and the working hospital because there was only a "thin board partition"[48] separating the two facilities. The acreage also accommodated what was then called a lunatic house, the morgue, and the hospital's burial ground. Although these facilities were essentially out of sight and some distance away, they were still unquestionably part of the immediate neighbourhood and did not enhance the atmosphere of the place. Furthermore, the pleasant quiet of the countryside was broken by the unmistakable sounds and smells of the Naval Yard: the clang of the yard's bell calling the men to work, the noise of machinery and labourers at work, the clacking of the turning capstan at the Sheer Wharf,[49] the clanging of anvils and caulking irons, and the smells of pitch, hot metal, wood, salt water, rope, and oily paint.

Soon after arrival Fanny witnessed a second event of patriotic significance. As the family settled into the Admiral's Lodge, the military community were preparing to celebrate King George III's seventy-second birthday on 4 June. At the lieutenant-governor's mansion, his secretary, Samuel Hood George, was fussing because "Lady Prevost's urn and ice pails did not arrive on the *Bonne Citoyenne* (20 guns) [and] there are only a few days in the year when such magnificent affairs can be used."[50] However, when the day came, the details of military pageantry were striking, with one traditional ceremonial tribute following another. On the parade ground, Lt. -Gov. George Prevost and Admiral Warren arrived to inspect the troops. Once the men were reviewed, the whole line of artillery fired the traditional rifle salute, known as a *feu de joye*. This impressive display was followed by loud gun salutes from the batteries of the town's forts and the cannons of the naval vessels in the harbour. Presumably, Fanny and Lady Warren watched the military ceremonies from a viewpoint on the parade ground. Afterwards there was a levee at Government House, where the local notables gathered with the military and naval officers and their wives to celebrate the royal birthday further. Although she had been in Halifax for only a few days, Fanny was already thrust into the forefront of its most prestigious social circle.

As part of the Warrens' retinue and as flag-captain's wife, Fanny could anticipate an entertaining whirl of balls and private parties, yet she recognized that the longer-range future was uncertain. What would the *Swiftsure*'s next assignment be and how would this affect Fanny and her young family? These were questions yet to be answered. But for the present there was the excitement of life in Halifax, about which Fanny was eager to communicate with Esther at home in Bermuda. Fanny wanted to share her observations about what she was doing and the people she was meeting as her horizons expanded and her experiences multiplied.

CHAPTER 3

In Halifax, Nova Scotia:
Summer into Autumn 1810

FANNY AUSTEN'S CORRESPONDENCE WITH HER FAMILY, and in particular with her sister Esther, was the medium that would keep her in intimate touch with those she loved. The desire to maintain a sense of community in spite of separation was central to Fanny's intentions as a letter writer. She knew that her letters were eagerly anticipated, often shared on arrival, and even reread for the pleasure and interest they provided. She took her responsibilities as a letter writer seriously.

On occasion, in order to cram in even more text, she "crossed" her letters – that is, she turned the page ninety degrees and continued in red ink instead of black, writing at right angles over the existing text. This practice was apparently used by Charles as well, as Jane Austen speaks of receiving "a nice long Black and red Letter from Charles" in November 1813.[1] Whether Fanny got this idea from Charles or not, using red ink made the letter easier to decipher, and crossing allowed the writer to say more but at the same time be economical with paper, which was expensive. A crossed letter also saved money for the recipient, who ordinarily paid for the delivery of the letter. Jane Fairfax, in Austen's novel *Emma*, was an economical correspondent who "in general … fills the whole paper and crosses half,"[2] although in her case the effect was like a "chequerboard" and deemed hard for her aunt and grandmother to decipher.

Long, frustrating waits for an anticipated letter from abroad were very common. It is therefore not surprising when Fanny laments, "[T]here is not a single letter for us"[3] in instances when the mail packet arrived from England or Bermuda without a delivery for her. Fortunately, she sometimes had an alternative means of receiving and sending letters, for navy officers regularly carried the correspondence of colleagues and friends on their vessels.

Fanny's forthright letters from Halifax detail the life of a British naval wife in a foreign port. They also provide unique access to Fanny's personality, her hopes and challenges. She is only twenty-one when her Halifax letters begin, yet she is already a wife of three years and the mother of two young children. She has a practical cast of mind. She is no fool and is willing to express her opinion about the people she meets, including a diversity of interesting characters who passed through Halifax in the summer of 1810. Fanny seems blessed with a portion of good sense. She tries to be patient when she must fit in with the schedules of her hosts. Four days after arriving in Halifax on the *Swiftsure*, Fanny wrote the first of her letters to Esther in Bermuda.

Halifax 1st June 1810 —

We arrived here my beloved Sister on the 28th May after a very comfortable passage of (I may say) 8 Days for we anchored on the evening of the 27th outside the light House — Neither Lady Warren or myself were thoroughly sick, tho' we felt uncomfortable, the first day; poor little Cass:[4] was very sick, but I think it was of great service to her, for she is looking better than I ever saw her; & is so riotous & unmanageable, that I can do nothing with her. Lady Warren has very kindly given us the room Mrs Sedle[y][5] used to have, which is on the same side, with the Drawing-Room; so that we are not at all inconvenienced, by the noises of the Hospital which you have heard Mrs. Territt[6] complain of. When I had got thus far yesterday, I was summoned to breakfast, & have not had an opportunity before this morning, of resuming my pen. (You'll see by this my dear Sister that I rise early & write before breakfast — We dined at Government House yesterday, & on our return home, found yours, my dear Brother's, & Uncle's kind letters by Mr. Meads [Mends][7] which afforded us great satisfaction, tho' the melancholy intelligence they contained, cast a gloom over us all for the rest of the evening — The Admiral & Lady Warren feel it deeply —

*[June] 12th – At length I have a leisure moment to finish this terrible scrawl,
& you will no doubt wonder what I have employed myself about for the last
ten days; why, nothing better, than receiving & returning a number of stupid
visits with Lady W [Warren]. I have executed your commissions my dear Sister
to the best of my ability, (which, <u>in shopping, you well know</u>, is not very great.)
I ventured to get you two pair of black kid shoes (tho' you did not desire it) as
they were rather cheap & very good. But there is nothing like Palmer's blue clothes
to be had here. Tell Miss Milbourne her piece of Gold lost 17s. The Shopkeepers
here, would only allow me £1.17s.9d. for it, & I have, with that, purchased her
7 Yds. of carpeting, which I shall send the bill of, & will thank you to give her.
I am endeavouring to gett a Cloak made for Mrs. Foot & hope I shall succeed.
Tell Mrs. Goodrich I received her letter, & the parcel of Dollars by Mr. Elliott,
& shall pay attention to her commission. Pray thank Mrs. Dickenson for her
kind letter & say I hope she will excuse, my not answering it by this opportunity,
as I must write to England as soon as I have finished this.*

*My dear Charles expects to sail, shortly, on a Cruize, which of course makes
me rather melancholy, but I assure you, I am as happy, as it is possible for me
to be, away from my friends. Lady Warren & the Admiral are both extremely
kind & attentive to me & are very fond of my little Cassy: her Ladyship has just
desired me to tell you, "<u>make the most of Bermuda, for it is the quietest place
in the world</u>" Lady Prevost[8] is much more gracious than she was last year, she
even vouchsafed to inquire very kindly after you & so did the Governor[9] after
my dear Brother.[10] Her Ladyship gave a splendid Bal[l] on the 7th which we
were all at; & only think of my prefering a <u>game of Commerce</u>, (to <u>Dancing</u>,)
at which I won 9 Dollars –*

After she has informed Esther of their safe arrival, Fanny draws attention
to Lady Warren's thoughtfulness. She has given Fanny and Charles the same
room that the Warrens' daughter, Mrs Sedley, occupied the year before.
Although Fanny seems happy in her new surroundings, there are clouds
on the horizon. She has learned that Charles is going "to sail, shortly on a
Cruize." This is an unlooked-for departure. She may not know the purpose
of his mission, or if she does, she cannot say. She is further troubled by
some "melancholy intelligence," probably a reference to information about
James Esten's uncertain state of health, but if this is so, Fanny hesitates to do

Fig. 16 *Government House from the S.W.* by John Elliott Woolford, 1819, showing Lt.-Gov. George Prevost's official residence, at which Fanny reported attending "a splendid Ball," seemingly "prefering a game of Commerce, (to Dancing), at which I won 9 Dollars."

more than express empathetic concern. The theme of disquiet about family well-being reappears in Fanny's August letters. Meanwhile, she busies herself with her many shopping commissions. Since Halifax stores in the area of Duke, Granville, and Hollis streets have a superior variety and quality of goods to those in Bermuda, Fanny has been given a long list of things to buy for Esther and three Bermuda friends. She diligently attempts to locate what they desire; she has an eye for bargains and a sense of value for money.

Worries can be set aside when there is a ball to attend. Fanny and Charles accompany the Warrens to an entertainment at Government House, the home of Sir George and Lady Prevost (Fig. 16). In the candle-lit glow of the ballroom, Fanny must have danced with Charles and his fellow officers. Her letter boasts about winning $9 at Commerce, a card game involving exchange and bartering. Fanny shows her social confidence in joining at cards with a group of people she may not know well and, moreover, in thoroughly enjoying the game. She can apparently afford to play Commerce; it appears she is not under financial restrictions like those that Jane Austen imposed upon herself. At an evening party Jane attended in 1808, "there were two pools at Commerce" but, as she told Cassandra, "I would not play more than one, for the Stake was three shillings, & I cannot afford to lose that, twice in an even""[11]

Fanny's letter continues:

[June] 17th – The Packet arrived on the 15th but there is not a single letter for us: I shall take the liberty of opening all yours, by every oppy. [opportunity], from our friends in England, & beg you will do the same, by any, that you may receive for me. I am quite grieved my dear Sister to think that I have not been able to find anything, for my dear Hamilton & Palmer,[12] tell them they shall be sure of some little remembrance, from dear Aunt, by the next Vessel & let me entreat you, not to let them forget me: I assure you Cassandra still retains a recollection of you all, for she frequently repeats your names: even (Aunt Heane's and Aunt Diana's: tell them this if you please) Only think of our relative Capt. Blamy[13] being here? I did not make myself known to him, but he found out by some means or other who I was & enquired very particularly about our family: He commands the Harpy Brig & has just arriv'd from England; & I assure you seems a very good sort of Man, (tho' I believe you have not a very high opinion of him)

This being Sunday the whole family (except myself) have gone to Church. The Admiral, Lady W. & Miss Hodgson to the round Church[14] & Capt. Austen has gone on board to [say] prayers but as I had a little head-ach I prefered staying at home & writing to you. You will be a little surprised to hear that I was confirmed on Friday last; but your astonishment will be very great, on hearing that Lady W. was also: we knew that there was to be a Confirmation on that day, & went to Church, out of curiosity, to see it, & to my great surprise, her Ladyship, after we got [there determined] on being confirmed herself, but did not [express an]y wish that I should, however I thought I might as well. This is quite entre nous I would not have it mentiond on any account, for fear of displeasing her Ladyship.

All the great People dined at the Rockingham[15] yesterday & the Ladies I assure you had a very pleasant party at Mrs. Belcher's (Birch Cove) which you will doubt a little when I say it consisted of Lady Prevost Lady Warren Mrs. Brinton[16] &c: but it really was very agreeable – the Gentlemen joined us in the Evening & escorted us home. Capt. Austen begs you to send him another Box of Arraroot[17] & to search for his Masonic Apron which I believe I left behind – If you can think of any thing else that you would like to have from this place, my dear Sister let me know, when you next write as you will see by your Bills that I have several of your guineas left, but I did not like to lay them out as you desired me to keep them, & purchase you some little articles in England.

I shall say nothing for my better half, as he is writing, but beg you will remember me, very affectionately to my dear Brother, Uncle[18] & all who are kind enough to think of me. Kiss my darling Palmer & Hamilton for me & accept for yourself the sincere love of Yrs. unalterably F.F. Austen

My kind rememb[rance] to Mary, Catharine &c. –

Fanny is very disappointed that the mail packet has brought no letters from her "friends." She uses this word, as was the custom of her time, to refer not only to family, both closely and distantly related, but also to personal friends and acquaintances. Usually the context of her letters provides a clue to the identity of the "friend" she mentions. In closing her letter, Fanny "sends [her] remembrance to Mary and Catharine." These two women, mentioned by their first names only, are presumably servants or slaves in Esther's home and may even have been with the Palmer family when Fanny was a girl. Fanny's subsequent letters will include queries about other servants.[19] These are people who Fanny cares about, as they are part of a wider grouping who make up her Bermuda "family."

As the flag-captain's wife and guest of Lady Warren, Fanny has been recruited to accompany her ladyship on an extensive round of making and receiving official social calls. The novelty of this obligation soon pales. Fanny even hazards to brand these niceties as "stupid." But she dares not object. She and Charles are grateful for his recent promotion, and she does not want to displease Lady Warren by showing any lack of enthusiasm on her part. It is easy to imagine the stately figure of the loquacious Lady Warren pressing forward, as the slight Fanny meekly trails a little behind.

The confirmation service probably occurred at the popular Methodist Zoar chapel, which was well-known for its evangelical outreach. Lady Warren had already proved sympathetic to Methodist projects in St George's, Bermuda, where she was patron of a Sunday School that taught literacy skills as well as religious instruction to black children and adults. On this occasion in Halifax she is apparently moved by the spirit, and Fanny diplomatically follows suit, even though she is not equally motivated nor even required by Lady Warren to participate.

Fanny attended a "very pleasant party at Mrs Belcher's (Birch Cove)" where there was much of interest to observe. She is amused by the social dynamics of a gathering that includes both Lady Warren and Lady Prevost, since each woman was particularly conscious of her status as the wife of an important administrative officer. Fanny is well placed to notice the captivating manners and air of Marianne Belcher, whose reputation as a gifted hostess and great flirt was already firmly established in Halifax. Fanny may not have known the whole inside story, but it was widely reported in fashionable circles that when Vice Admiralty Court Judge Alexander Croke wrote his poem "The Inquisition," he modelled the adulterous character Bella after the real-life Marianne Belcher. Irrespective of this damning literary reference, Marianne portrayed herself in personal correspondence as "in looks and disposition … very lively, funny & mischievous."[20] Fanny had probably met Marianne Belcher during her previous visit to Halifax the year before. She does not describe her hostess's manners and personality in her letter, probably because Esther was also already acquainted with Mrs Belcher in times past.

This expedition gave Fanny a chance to see the Belchers' handsome Georgian villa, situated on the shore of the Bedford Basin, the inner part of Halifax Harbour, and surrounded by woods and farmland. Coming here also brought Fanny into the neighbourhood of what remained of the fabled estate – known as "The Lodge" – of Prince Edward, Duke of Kent. On arrival in Halifax, he had built "a villa in the fashionable Italianate style"[21] for the pleasure of his beautiful companion, Madame Julie St Laurent. To complement the house, he created impressive landscaped gardens, wooded winding pathways, miniature Chinese temples, an ornamental heart-shaped pond and, at the basin's edge, a rotunda-shaped pavilion for summer concerts. Unfortunately, the couple's love story ended abruptly when the duke was required to abandon his mistress, marry into the proper circles, and produce an heir for the British throne. He later became the father of Queen Victoria, born in 1819. Being so close to the site of such elegance and aristocratic enjoyment must have added to the happiness Fanny experienced that day. It was an additional delight when "the gentlemen joined us in the evening and escorted us home."

While Fanny enjoyed the social life of Halifax, she was aware, once more, that the future was uncertain. Admiral Warren was waiting in Halifax for his replacement; then he and Lady Warren planned to return to England on the *Swiftsure*. If Charles was still to be captain, Fanny and the children might go with him. This possibility seems to have been on her mind for she suggests that she is saving Esther's other guineas to "purchase [for her] some little articles in England."

There was novelty in the unexpected appearance of a distant relative, Capt. George William Blamey, of the brig-sloop HMS *Harpy* (18 guns). He had previously served in the West Indies where he took soundings and made a rough sketch of the coast of Trinidad, work that was subsequently valued by the British Hydrographic Office; he had been on the North American Station before as first lieutenant on HMS *Assistance* (50 guns), a vessel well named, for it transported the Duke of Kent back to England in 1800. Fanny is curious why Blamey is so keen to identify himself as a family connection.

Fanny's first composite letter (1–17 June) was posted to Esther in mid-June. In it she has noted the progress of a myriad of shopping commissions for Bermuda friends and her activities as part of the admiral's household. She is greatly enjoying Charles's company and is watching little Cassy's development with interest and amusement. Even this early letter reveals a pattern in her narrative that is still detectable in later letters. Fanny does not simply catalogue a chronology of events. She also interjects reflections about her own behaviour and that of others. She periodically does this is by underlining words and phrases, sometimes for emphasis, sometimes for irony. When she says she prefers "a game of Commerce, (to Dancing)," she implies that she has done something Esther would not expect of her and would be amused to learn, as if she is sharing a private joke between sisters. Fanny reminds Esther that her ability "in shopping, you well know, is not very great," yet the irony in this self-deprecating remark is doubled by Fanny's subsequent list of the many purchases and commissions for friends that were completed effectively and efficiently. When describing her confirmation with Lady Warren, Fanny's use of underlining serves to convey the essential message: Esther "will be a little surprised … that I was confirmed … your astonishment will be very great … that Lady W was also … this is quite entre nous." From their outset, Fanny's letters bear the distinctive stamp of her personality.[22]

By 23 June, Charles had received his sailing orders. He was to join a squadron of five other vessels led by the senior officer on the station, Sir

Robert Laurie of HMS *Milan* (44 guns). Their mission was to cross the North Atlantic to the Rock of Lisbon and take the 1st Battalion of the 7th Fusiliers to join other British regiments fighting in the Peninsular War – a conflict between Napoleonic France and the combined forces of Britain, Portugal, and Spain over the control of the Iberian Peninsula. By mid-1810, France had encroached on Portugal, an incursion that Britain and her allies were determined to reverse. Once the soldiers were delivered, the *Swiftsure* was to return directly to Halifax.

Shortly before the expedition was about to leave, the *Weekly Chronicle* of 15 June 1810 advertised for claimants on the estate of Charles's former colleague, Captain John Shortland of HMS *Junon* (38 guns). He had died of his wounds, aged forty, when his vessel was overpowered by French frigates off Antigua earlier that year. This reminder of Shortland's grievous injury and subsequent death in captivity would be depressing for any naval wife, and particularly for Fanny, whose husband was about to head across the sea to a war zone.

On 1 July the naval community watched the small squadron of the *Milan* (44 guns), the *Martin* (18 guns), the *Swiftsure*, the *Ferret* (18 guns), the *Harpy* (18 guns), captained by Fanny's cousin George Blamey, and the transport *Ariel* tack up the harbour in company and disappear from sight. On board Charles took the bearings for Corvo, an island in the Azores, which was about 1,358 nautical miles away. Fanny settled down to await his return, knowing that she would be travelling only within the confines of Halifax during his absence and only in the more refined areas while in the company of others. Lady Sherbrooke, who came to live in Halifax the next year as wife of Lt.-Gov. Sir John Coape Sherbrooke, notes the limitations on the movements of ladies of the gentry class. While she speaks with enthusiasm of walking up Citadel Hill, saying she was "very much delighted with the view, which is extensive and beautiful," she also observes that "from the number of drunken Sailors, and other disagreeable objects that are perpetually to be seen, I am quite convinced that Sir John judged rightly in not approving of my walking in the Streets of Halifax."[23]

Fanny did not write to Esther for the next seven weeks. When she resumes the correspondence, she speaks of who has arrived and who has left. She also voices her own growing anxieties about Charles's safety, given the risks of carrying troops towards a battle zone. At this time, Fanny was unaware of the uncertainty regarding the *Swiftsure's* destination after her mission to Portugal was completed. Admiral Warren had been sent a letter, dated 20 July 1810, from Charles Yorke, First Lord of the Admiralty. In it, Yorke states that "various accidents which have happened to several of His Majesty's ships of late which have placed many in a state of requiring repairs in Dock, will in all probability prevent the Board from being able to accommodate you with the return of the Swiftsure from Lisbon.²⁴ He recommends that Sir John use HMS *Melampus* "to remove Lady Warren and the family" to England. Very fortunately for Fanny, Yorke changed his mind and the *Swiftsure* was sent back to Halifax. Had this not occurred, Fanny's immediate future would have been very unsettled. She would not know when she and her two girls might be reunited with Charles, who, in turn, could not foretell how and where he might be employed. This averted incident well demonstrates the worrisome unpredictability of Fanny's life.

Halifax August 4th 1810 –

Your letter of the 24th July my dearest Sister was, <u>to my great astonishment</u> handed me yesterday, by Mr Tudor Hinson.²⁵ Can you conceive anything so fortunate as Mrs Hodgson's arriving, just as the General²⁶ was embarking, on board the Penelope: the Admiral's Barge was actually at the Wharf, & he had come to take leave of Lady Warren, when the officer of the guard brought the report, of the Emulous's²⁷ arrival, with <u>General Hodgson's family on board</u>. The sailing of the Penelope²⁸ was of course postponed & Major Bozon²⁹ immediately dispatched to bring Mrs Hodgson & the Children on shore; which was very soon accomplished & they all dined here, slept at the Generals lodgings & embarked & sailed this Morning. – Cou'd there be any thing more complete? Mrs Hodgson has given me a charming account of you all, & speaks in the most affectionate manner, of yourself, & my dear Brother, who she informs me is <u>looking</u> much better, & <u>is so, in reallity</u> tho' you do not think so. Offer my sincere love to him, & say I received & opened his kind letter to Capt. Austen by Mr. Lagourque³⁰ & felt most truly for your anxiety respecting us: it was indeed a most tedious time before you heard of our arrival, however, I hope you were in some degree compensated, by our letter: I shou'd have written you a much longer one, but Capt. Austen's sudden departure, & the uncertainty, about his returning, [completely] upset me, as you will easily imagine: if he is not here by the middle of Sepr. I shall give him up; but I will not allow myself to think of it –

Many thanks for the straw Plaits[31] by Capt. Hickey which I am ashamed to hear was not acknowledged before, for Capt. Austen was desired to thank you for that, as well as the Matts, and Papspoon, the latter Cassy: uses constantly – I have told Molly[32] that her friends are very much displeased with her, for not writing to them by Richard, & she offers as an excuse, that she thought I was too much engaged, with my own letters, to write one for her, & did not like to make the request. She behaves uncommonly well, and has become quite a favorite of Lady Warren's –

Just after the squadron sailed, Fanny was happily distracted by the unexpected coming together of the Hodgson family, whom she had known well in Bermuda. She does not allude to the current bitter dispute in the Bermuda Legislative Assembly, which arose when, contrary to the Assembly's wishes, General Hodgson, in his capacity as governor of Bermuda, appointed William Smith as treasurer. This fracas explains why the general is now on en route to London, where he intends to argue his case with the Colonial Office.

The arrival of Mrs Hodgson was an added bonus for Fanny. The governor's wife was well connected in Bermuda, so she could bring Fanny up to date on social and political life at home and the latest news about the Estens. Mrs Hodgson was also known for the part she played on a particular occasion, when she skillfully defused a potentially awkward situation. Following a dinner at Government House, Bermuda, Colonel Orde of the 99th Regiment was about to enter the drawing room with Mrs Hodgson on his arm when Dr Territt, judge of the Vice Admiralty Court, also approached. "The question of precedence seized the mind of both gentlemen simultaneously, as they stood glaring at each other, with some ungentlemanly clamour, so that Mrs Hodgson swooned and the party broke up."[33] Mrs Hodgson, it appears, had mastered the strategic feint. Now that both Hodgsons had turned up in Halifax, Fanny was happy to dine with them at the admiral's apartment, where she and the children would remain until Charles returned.

Fanny's psychological state at the time explains why she had not been writing to Esther. It had been over a month since Charles sailed and her anxiety had increased as time passed without news of the convoy's progress. In a frank confession to Esther, Fanny expresses the depth of her worry with the pessimistic assertion: "if he is not here by the middle of Sepr. I shall give him up."

Fanny was increasingly aware of the sorts of risks sailors faced. The most common causes of deaths in the navy were shipwreck and fire, disease and accidents.[34] Any of these could occur at any time. Five years later Charles experienced the horror of fire at sea while captain of HMS *Phoenix* (36 guns). On 28 April 1815 his journal records that "an alarm was given that the ship was on fire & a great smoke was seen coming out of the afterhold. [It was caused by] a bread bag ignited by a spark from a candle ... Thank God it was found out so soon as it was as the result is shocking to think."[35] On Charles's present mission he would be most vulnerable during the approximately six hours needed to off-load the troops and their equipment at the Rock of Lisbon. His group of vessels would be about five miles offshore but easy stationary targets should hostile warships appear. With Charles so far away, it was very difficult for Fanny to keep his risks and her fears in perspective. The anguish this caused her was very great but she bravely comments, "I will not allow myself to think [of him not returning]."

[August 12] You will perceive by the different dates of this, my dear Sister, that I keep a <u>sort of journal tho' not a very regular one</u>: I think my absence from Bermuda has given me a relish for letter-writing, for I certainly, <u>dislike it, much less</u>, than I did. Capt. Jane[36] arrived here three days since & brought me some intelligence (tho' it was rather indirect) of Capt. Austen: he spoke an American Ship, which was boarded on the 12th July by one of our Lisbon fleet & the American said there were then in Company four ships & two brigs,[37] & from the Latitude & Longitude they must have been very near the Western Islands[38] which the Admiral says was doing very well in twelve days: so that I expect to see them back, in the course of the next fortnight. Capt. Jane also met with the St Albans & brought a letter from Frank Austen[39] to his Brother dated 15th July on his way home, congratulating him on his promotion, which, he learnt from Capt Bradshaw[40] who he fell in with, just 36 days before, & by whom, he has sent me some presents from China –

It is reported that Sir Richard Strachan[41] is to succeed our Admiral but it is not known officially – Poor Mr Hinson is very anxious for the arrival of the Packet as he depends on going in the Schooner which takes the Mail to Bermuda; he is very lame in one of his feet, which Capt. Hawker[42] & Lord James[43] tell him, is the gout; & he does not seem to like the idea of it at all – he lodges with them, at Grants –

As her correspondence increases, Fanny pauses to reflect on the narrative character of her letters. She sees herself as keeping "a sort of a journal tho' not a very regular one" and she thinks that her absence from Bermuda has "given [her] a relish for letter-writing." By her own admission, this activity has become more than a means of keeping in touch with family; it is establishing a record of this new phase of her life. In fact, Fanny is telling *her* story in the context of her experiences in Halifax, as witnessed in her account of the timely but unexpected coming together of the Hodgson family.

By 12 August there was much happier news to report. Fanny was hugely encouraged to learn about of the Lisbon fleet's progress as of 12 July. By then Charles had crossed the Atlantic safely. Even so, he was still nearly 400 nautical miles west of Corvo,[44] an island in the Azores 1,136 nautical miles west of Lisbon, and he still had to transfer the fusiliers to other vessels before returning to Halifax. Fanny's hopeful prediction that Charles would soon be back with her in Halifax was too optimistic.

Captain Jane also brought Fanny news about Frank Austen. He was currently sailing as an armed escort for thirteen ships of the East India Company that were returning from Canton, China, to England via Madras, India, with a cargo of 470,000 Dollars or Bullion.[45] Frank was fortunate, for the grateful East India Company subsequently presented him with £1,500[46] for his services. Charles and Frank not only had the same professional interests but were also close as brothers and friends. Thus, to discover that Frank was safely on his way to England would be satisfying news for Fanny even as she was assiduously hoping for Charles's speedy return to Halifax.

The practice of sharing personal information about the location and the well-being of fellow officers created a strong sense of membership in a wider naval family. It also fostered a communications network that reached out to include the wives, fiancées, and other family members of serving sea officers. Given this level of collegiality, it is not surprising that several of Charles's fellow captains took an interest in Fanny's welfare, especially when he was on a long and potentially dangerous mission. When they were in port, she could rely on the friendship of captains Edward Hawker, James, Lord Townshend, Fredrick Hickey, Henry Jane, William Byam, and Samuel Pechell. Edward Hawker was particularly close to Fanny and Charles. As Hawker was also one of Cassy's sponsors, he naturally took an interest in Charles's wife and young daughter.

Sometime in the summer of 1810 an unlikely but true event occurred within the Halifax naval community. It concerned the late Captain Shortland's favourite dog, a very handsome, mid-sized terrier named Pandore. She had "constantly attended him during those acute sufferings which preceded his death, licked his hands, and displayed every mark of affectionate attachment."[47] A seaman who had been Shortland's servant on the *Junon* had cared for the dog after her master's death. He had taken the terrier to England, planning to reunite her with the Shortland family, who had raised Pandore from a pup. Unfortunately, the dog was stolen from the Elephant and Castle pub in Newington and taken on board a ship bound for Halifax. When, by chance, a former sailor on Shortland's ship happened to meet and recognize Pandore in Halifax, he sought to claim her from her abductor. The rogue refused and Admiral Sir John Warren was called upon to adjudicate. Pandore obediently performed her usual repertoire of tricks for Sir John at the sailor's command and Warren insisted the terrier be delivered up into his care. Pandore was taken back to England and delivered to Mrs Shortland, the late captain's mother, in London.[48] This was a happy ending for the dog and a tale that surely pleased Fanny, as she was a firm believer that loved ones – and Pandore was well loved by the Shortland household – should not be separated but belonged together.

During those long days of waiting and of watching Citadel Hill for a flag signalling the return of the "Lisbon fleet," Fanny busied herself making clothes for her nephews and Esther. Her very long letter continues.

[August] 14th. Two more days have elapsed without bringing us a Packet & to-day there is no chance of one, as it is raining most furiously – Yesterday I received another welcome letter from you my dear Sister, by Col: Orde[49] who is delighted, beyond every thing, at quitting Bermuda, he was graciously pleased, to call here, as soon as the Anchor was drop'ed, even before the Commander of the Schooner the Admiral invited him to dinner immediately which invitation he accepted & I never saw him more agreable. I wonder how Dr Territ[50] would like to hear of all this –

I am grieved to find by your letter, how much you are suffering from the heat, but it is a great consolation, that the dear Children are doing so well; to hear frequently of them, & from you all, my dear Sister, be assured, affords me the most heartfelt pleasure, _so you need not for the future be afraid of repeating, so pleasing a subject to me, whenever an opportunity offers_. I only regret not being able to answer your letters as punctually as I wish, from the few opportunity's that have offered for Bermuda since I have been here, (this will only be the second) – I endeavour by frequently speaking of you, to keep up Cassandra's recollection of you, (which I think she retains a little of still); when I ask her where you are, she says, gone to _Bermuda_ & calls the little strip'd frocks you gave her, _Pamu's_ – I have lately been making her some very tidy little Spencers⁵¹ which I shall send my dear Hamilton one of, by Mr Hinson they button behind, & I think you will find them very convenient – Tell my dear Palmer that his friend General Hodgson, applied to me, to know what _Toy_, would be most acceptable to him, & I told him, I thought he would like a Wheel-barrow better than any thing; however he did not mention it afterwards, & I conclude he was not fortunate enough, to meet with one. Lady Warren always enquires very kindly after you all & so did _my very great favorite Capt Pechell_ & several of the other Capt's yesterday, when they heard I had received letters – Adieu for today –

[August] 15th. I have just requested Charles, (the Admiral's Butler) to procure the 6 Baskets of Salt, & he tells me that loaf Sugar, is much cheaper here, than at Bermuda, & I should have sent you two or three loaves, had the Swiftsure been here, that I cou'd have had it properly packed; but I do not like to hazard a thing, that wou'd spoil from getting wet, unless I had _a Jones_ to sew it up in canvass nicely for me – Indeed I requested you in my former letter, to let me know, (which you have not) whether I shou'd spend the remainder of your [guineas] here, or in England; I shall not venture to [touch] them, untill you give me an answer which I hope will be soon –

[August]17th It is now three days since the Packet arrived, & I have not received one single letter either for you, or myself: altho' Mr Tucker was kind enough, to go to the Post-Office, & request Mr Howe⁵² to send me, any letters, directed to the _Attorney General_, or _Chief Justice Esten_, when the Bermuda Mail was opened, which he said wou'd be, in the course of that day, but I cannot help hoping there may still be one for some of you, if there is pray send it to me by the first opportunity –

[August]18th I have this moment learnt that the Schooner sails immediately for Bermuda & am very much provoked for I have not said one half of what I intended The little Spencer for dear Hamilton is not finished but I shall send

it, & you must put the frill, on the collar, yourself. The Tucker[53] *you will find
with it is for yourself, I hope you will like it.*

*I am now obliged to close this without once mentioning a subject which
engrosses my thoughts very, very much, you may guess what it is, when I tell
you Mrs Hodgson was my informer. I have now only to beg you will take very
great care of yourself.*

*Yrs in the greatest haste
F. Austen*

Fanny's last lines speak of a subject that is much on her mind. It presumably has to do with the physical and emotional health of James Esten.
Fanny is very concerned but hesitates to identify what she thinks the specific
complaint is. Perhaps she is responding to a level of secrecy on Esther's part.
She does, however, choose to convey Mrs Hodgson's recent opinion that
James Esten is "looking much better, & is so, in reallity," a remark that
suggests that at least he looks well to others. James Esten apparently had a
record of uncertain health. In an earlier letter to Charles on 26 July 1808,
Esther wrote that "Mr. Esten has been taking a course of Medicine, which
I think will be of great service to him."[54]

Fanny received a welcome letter from Esther, delivered in person by
Colonel James Orde. He may have seemed charming to Fanny on this occasion, but his amiable appearance proved deceptive. Two years later he was
court-martialled and found guilty of flogging and other acts of "tyranny and
oppression from the time he joined the regiment in December, 1807 to the
present period."[55] Luckily for him, he was pardoned through the intervention
of the prince regent and escaped with only a severe reprimand. A year before
the court martial, Orde had eloped with Margaret Beckford, daughter of
the eccentric William Thomas Beckford, novelist, art collector, and builder
of a huge and fanciful gothic-revival mansion, Fonthill Abbey. He was said
to be the richest man in England. Apparently Beckford did not approve of
his daughter's choice, as he disinherited her on learning of the wedding.
At the time of this marriage, Jane Austen ironically wrote Cassandra that
she thought "too well of an Orde, to suppose that she [Margaret] has not a
handsome Independance of her own."[56]

Fanny, as the Warrens' guest, was most likely included in any entertainment taking place at the admiral's quarters. On such occasions, it would

be a courtesy to invite the Warrens' nearest neighbour of rank, Captain John Inglefield, commissioner of the Naval Yard. In 1799 Earl St Vincent, Admiral of the Fleet,[57] described him as "honest and sufficiently intelligent, but pompous, flowery, indolent and wrapped up in official forms, stay-tape and buckram,"[58] words that suggest an unattractive personality and a fussy administrator. Fanny may have been told that Captain Inglefield's naval record was marred by the circumstances surrounding the loss of his vessel, the *Centaur* (74 guns), which had foundered in a hurricane in September 1782 near the Newfoundland Banks. As she was slowly sinking, Inglefield, his sailing master, a midshipman, and nine seamen escaped in the ship's pinnace, a small boat with sails and oars, and reached the Azores sixteen days later. Some 400 men left on the vessel perished. Alexander Croke in his poem "The Inquisition" casts aspersions on this aspect of Inglefield's past. He wrote:

When from the shipwrecked vessel's side, he flew,
A bright example to the sinking crew.
And taught old tars, who every danger brave,
That precious thing, a Captain's Life to save.[59]

We don't know what Fanny thought of Commissioner Inglefield. That summer in Halifax she encountered a diversity of naval personalities, some charming, some much less so. One hopes that the variety within this social milieu distracted Fanny's attention from worrisome thoughts about Charles's safety. Fanny was delighted and immensely relieved when the *Swiftsure* sailed into port on 3 September after a thirty-seven-day voyage from Portugal. Now that he was back in Halifax, Charles awaited his new orders. He and Fanny must have discussed their possibilities at length. Would he be taking the *Swiftsure* home to England with Admiral Warren, or did the Admiralty have something else in mind for him? When Fanny next writes Esther, she can only hint about this matter until Admiral Warren officially informs Charles.

In the interim, on 7 September Charles had the pleasant task of collecting a portion of prize money still owed him. It had been five years since the capture of the American ship *Ocean*, but only now, after extensive court proceedings, did his agent, the Honourable Andrew Belcher, pay the final instalment of prize money. This late windfall materialized as a happy Charles was reunited with Fanny. Perhaps he purchased some special little luxury for her from a Halifax shop to celebrate their reunion.

Halifax 23d Sepr. 1810

Since writing you last my dear Sister I have been made happy by <u>the return</u> of my beloved Charles, <u>which</u>, after the arrival of the July Packet, I quite despaired of – He had a most tedious passage back, which was rendered doubly unpleasant, by his great apprehension, that the Admiral would have left Halifax before he arrived; but he is, thank God, perfectly well tho' if possible, thiner than ever – I need not say how delighted we both are, at the prospect of soon seeing you, shou'd this exchange be effected which I believe there is little doubt of.

Our dear little Girl improves daily: indeed I am quite astonished to see how fast she grows, I am going to put her into short frocks & pantaloons for she is such a romp, that <u>it is quite necessary</u>. I am sorry to find by your letter of 27th Augst. that poor little Hamilton has been so teazed with eruptions but as they are no doubt the effects of the warm weather I hope he will soon get the better of them. My uncle gives me a very good account of Palmer but none of you mention, whether he ever speaks of me –

We shall send you a part of our Brother Frank's China present & hope it will prove acceptable viz. A few Hams some Sugar Candy & preserves & part of a piece of India Crape which I have had made up into a gown for you by Miss Johnson who had <u>your</u> measure and 2 pieces of Nankeen[60] for the Boys – In the Box containing the latter articles is a Bundle of Furniture Callico for Mrs Dickenson the amount of Mr. Fowle's Bill, <u>within one Dollar which</u> you'll be so good as to pay her for me. Tell her I shou'd have written her a few lines had I not been very much hurried, & that I hope she will approve of the Pattern, it is quite a new thing –Shou'd I not be able to procure your Cambric Muslin & Stockings in time for this Oppy [opportunity] they shall be sent by your friend Capn. Byam[61] who is to call at Bermuda on his way to the West Indies.

The August Packet has arrived & as usual both Mails have been searched & no letter found for any of us, which makes me very unhappy as Harriet[62] never used to allow a single Packet to escape her, & this is the third that has arrived, since I have been here without a letter from any part of the family & I am the more astonished at their silen[ce] as they must have received a letter from me in

*July, which ought certainly to have been acknowledged before this —Mr Mends
met with Mr. Butterfield at Fayal, on his way to Bermuda & he gave him a letter
for me, from Harriet; but for that, I shou'd have been miserable about them,
I shall enclose it to you — We have never been able to forward Mrs. McKellar's
Arra-Root, from not knowing exactly where to direct to her, & there is now I
fear little chance of her getting it, as they are gone to Minorca —*

*24th I have succeeded in getting you some very good jct[63] Muslin (for there
was no cambric muslin to be had at the shop where I deal) & the black stockings
for Mary & as there were a few shillings change, left, of one of your <u>guineas</u>,
(<u>of which we have now 12</u>) I have sent Toddings to get dear little Hamilton
2 pr. Shoes with them —*

Yrs Ever most affectionately

    F.F. Austen

*P.S. Mr. Fowle has passed his examination for a Lieut. with great credit.
Remember me most kindly to my Uncle & say every thing affectionate for me
to my dear <u>Brother</u>.*

Fanny makes sure to tell Esther about seventeen-year-old Lieut. Tom
Fowle's recent promotion. He was a close Austen family friend who had
begun his naval career as a midshipman on the *Indian* under Charles's
command in 1808. His father, Rev. Fulwar Craven Fowle, the vicar of St
Mary's Church, Kintbury in Berkshire, had been one of Rev. George Austen's
pupils at the Steventon Rectory; and his uncle, another Tom Fowle, had
been engaged to Cassandra Austen but had tragically died of yellow fever
in 1797. Fanny and Charles felt a close connection to this younger member
of the Fowle family. Their care of him and their interest in his naval career
had led to a friendly communication between his parents in Kintbury and
Fanny's Palmer family in London. The Fowles and the Palmers exchanged
news about their loved ones in Bermuda and on board the *Indian*, and the
Fowles arranged for items to be sent out to Tom on the North American
station by way of the London Palmers.[64]

On 25 September Admiral Warren reassigned the captains of three of his
vessels. He posted Charles into the *Cleopatra* (32 guns); Robert Lloyd, an
officer senior to Charles, was given the *Swiftsure* (74 guns); and his friend
Sam Pechell moved from the *Cleopatra* to HMS *Guerriere* (38 guns). Since

Fig. 17   Three views of HMS *Cleopatra* (32 guns), Charles's first frigate. Fanny travelled on her with Charles between Bermuda and Halifax and across the North Atlantic in 1811.

Charles's move into the flagship HMS *Swiftsure* was to fill a death vacancy, posting into his own frigate was a welcome advancement in his career. Admiral Warren would soon be returning to England so it was fortuitous that he made these changes when he did, for there was no guarantee that the next commander-in-chief on the station would be as supportive of Charles as Warren had been. The families in Bermuda and England were thrilled that Charles finally had a frigate. But he would now be paid at the scale of a captain of a fifth-rate vessel, which was rougly half of his salary on the *Swiftsure*. He would receive £22. 11s. 10d. per month.[65]

Launched in 1779, the *Cleopatra* was a two-decker, fifth-rate frigate carrying 32 guns (Fig. 17). Her overall dimensions were 126 feet 5 inches long, her breadth 35 feet 2½ inches at her beam (mid-point), and the depth in her hold, 12 feet 1¼ inch.[66] When fully manned, she employed 220 sailors compared to the *Indian*'s 120 men. According to Brian Lavery, a frigate was a "sleek, well proportioned ship … [that] could sail well in almost any weather" and was suitable "for attacking enemy commerce," thus allowing "officers and men to gain prize money from captured enemy ships."[67] The *Cleopatra* was also a vessel with a dramatic history. In February 1805 while sailing off Bermuda, she was captured by the French vessel *Ville de Milan* (40 guns) after a bloody sea battle resulting in considerable loss of life. Soon after this disaster, Charles contributed £3 to a fund that was set up to benefit the widows and children of the twenty-two British seamen killed and thirty-six men wounded.[68] The *Cleopatra* was subsequently retaken by HMS *Leander* (50 guns) and after extensive repairs was put back in service with the North American squadron. She had brought Charles out to Bermuda from England in January 1805. Now the *Cleopatra* would be Fanny's temporary home at sea whenever she travelled with Charles on the Bermuda–Halifax circuit.

At the time of their departure for Bermuda in early October, news had yet to reach Halifax that the first brigade of the 7th Fusiliers had joined the Anglo-Portuguese army, which had defeated the French at the Battle of Bussaco in the mountains of central Portugal on 27 September 1810.[69] By participating in the mission to deliver the fusiliers to Portugal, Charles had contributed in a small way to maintaining the supply of men and equipment necessary to Wellington's army in the Peninsular War, but with that task completed, it was time to resume his career at sea in his first frigate.

When Fanny and her family sailed on the *Cleopatra* to Bermuda in October, they carried a very special cargo on board. While they were in Halifax, Charles had commissioned companion pictures from the Halifax-based British artist Robert Field, who was considered the foremost portrait painter of the time in North America. He was renowned for his proficiency in creating convincing images "in the neoclassical portrait style of Henry Raeburn and Gilbert Stuart"[70] and received many commissions from people of note. In America he had done likenesses of George and Martha Washington.[71] In Halifax he painted Bishop Inglis, Lieutenant-Governor Prevost, Attorney General Richard Uniacke, the Honourable Andrew and Marianne Belcher, and Provincial Secretary Samuel Hood George, as well as various naval luminaries, including Admiral Herbert Sawyer, who would soon become Charles's new commander-in-chief on the North American Station; Captain Inglefield of the Naval Yard; Admiral Alexander Cochrane; and the ill-fated late Captain John Shortland.

The fine portraits of Charles and Fanny measure about 9¾ by 10½ inches and cost Charles approximately $70 each.[72] Field signed Fanny's portrait with his name "R. Field," though it was not ordinarily his custom to do so. Perhaps he particularly liked it and wanted to put his name to it. These splendid individual paintings capture far more than the subjects' physical features. Dark-haired Charles appears dashingly handsome and competently professional in his smart post-captain's uniform. Fanny's portrait shows a young, girlish face framed by reddish-gold curls. Her forthright gaze is serious. Fanny's eyes are blue, her complexion pink and glowing. She is fashionably dressed in a white empire-style gown, a red cloak, and blue scarf, her hair held in place with a bandeau. The visual effect is striking. Field's portrait is the quintessential image of Fanny, the writer of the Halifax letters and of more letters to come.

CHAPTER 4

Unsettled:
Bermuda and England,
1810–1811

BY 26 OCTOBER OF 1810 FANNY AND CHARLES had returned to Bermuda. While Fanny and her girls once more settled back into local life, Charles was soon at sea. At first no suspicious American merchant ships or enemy privateers came his way, but late in December, there was considerable excitement when Charles, together with Samuel Pechell, captain of the *Guerriere*, and Frederick Hickey of the *Atalante* captured the American brig *Stephen* and her cargo of turpentine, staves, cotton, and English dry goods.[1] This seemed to be a valuable prize vessel and cargo, but unfortunately it was not as lucrative as anticipated. The Bermuda Vice Admiralty Court granted only the cargo to the captors, and the case was appealed to the High Court of Admiralty in London.[2] Charles's prize money of £63 13s. 7d. was not paid out until May 1813.[3]

Although co-captures involving two or more naval vessels were fairly common, it was sometimes a matter of dispute before the court as to whether all the naval vessels of a cruising group were close enough to the point of capture to count as prize takers. The logbook for the *Cleopatra* suggests that Austen and his fellow officers had decided in advance to share equally in any prize taken while they were cruising together, irrespective of each vessel's closeness to the captured vessel. This arrangement was to hold "until the last day of February, 1811 at noon … [and] the agreement to cease with any one of [their] squadron on her arrival at Bermuda, previous to that time, unless she escort a prize in which case she is to have the benefit of sharing with the others."[4] It is unusual to find reference to such an agreement. Its existence suggests collegiality and concern for the financial well-being of fellow officers.

The *Stephen* was the only prize Charles took while in command of the *Cleopatra*. This modest result was surely disappointing. The year before, his friend Edward Hawker, captain of the frigate *Melampus*, had an impressive record of captures. He took two armed French vessels, the *Colibri* (16 guns) and the *Fantome* (18 guns), which were immediately commissioned into the Royal Navy. Hawker received more than £1,500 in prize money from these two vessels alone.[5] This figure represented nearly six years' salary for a frigate captain in the British navy at that time.

Before he had the chance to look for any other prize vessels, Charles's assignments on the station were halted abruptly when the new commander of the station, Admiral Herbert Sawyer, ordered him to take the next convoy of British merchant vessels home to England. It was current Admiralty policy that British ships were "allowed to trade as long as they sailed under British convoy for the whole voyage, ensuring that they went to or from a British or friendly port."[6] This policy was designed to limit the risk of war and so to keep insurance rates on well-used routes at a reasonable level. Four times a year a naval vessel escorted the convoy to Britain from Nova Scotia and New Brunswick. The *Cleopatra* was an obvious choice for this duty, as she required repairs that were best accomplished at the sophisticated facilities of the Naval Yard in Portsmouth. Since she might be laid up for about five months, Charles happily anticipated an extended time with his English family, and better still, they could get to know Fanny, Cassy, and Harriet. Fanny eagerly awaited a long overdue reunion with her parents and sister Harriet in London.

Charles prepared for the voyage across the Atlantic, not knowing that the Admiralty had already dispatched revised orders reassigning Captain Pechell to the *Cleopatra*. This change was not through any fault of Charles's but for reasons he would discover only when he arrived in England. As it happened, by the time Samuel Pechell arrived in Halifax on 11 June to take up his new command, he found he had missed the *Cleopatra* by eight days.[7]

Although it was exciting to be planning a new phase of their life together, Fanny's pleasure was mixed with pain. She was leaving behind her beloved island and her sister Esther, as well as other family members and valued friends. She would miss the tropical birds, the vibrant flowers and shrubs, the sweet-smelling cedars, things that had defined the natural features of her Bermuda home since childhood. Moreover, Fanny did not know how long she would be absent. According to the *Bermuda Gazette*, 11 May 1811, "HMS Cleopatra sailed, Wednesday, Captain Austen for Halifax. Passengers: Mrs Esten and family." It was Charles's prerogative to carry passengers between ports at his discretion. In this case Fanny's transition away from Bermuda was made easier by having Esther and her children along. Some of those whom Fanny loved best were at hand for a last farewell as she departed from North America.

Fanny undertook the transatlantic crossing knowing that a threatening situation could develop quickly. During the voyage, Charles's primary job was to protect the convoy. As Andrew Lambert put it, "when attacked by hostile ships escort commanders understood their role was to delay the enemy, often by engaging in one-sided battles with superior warships while the convoy dispersed."[8] As the convoy system was common knowledge, there was an obvious risk that the *Cleopatra* might be attacked. This was a reality Fanny could not ignore. Moreover, she was no stranger to the ways of the sea. She had grown up on an island where winter gales sent waves crashing over the reefs, and she had experienced the terror of a violent storm at sea when she had travelled on the *Indian* between Halifax and Bermuda in late November 1809 (Fig. 18). To make this long voyage to England, especially with two very young children, Fanny had to suppress her anxiety and summon all her reserves of courage and fortitude.

Some weeks before the *Cleopatra* sailed, Austen family members in England speculated about their arrival. Henry had heard that "Charles may be in England in the course of a month." Jane was told at a London party in April that "Charles was bringing the Cleopatra home, & that she was probably by this time in the Channel,"[9] but both these pieces of news were unduly optimistic. On the other side of the Atlantic, Charles marshalled the convoy first at Halifax and then at Saint John, New Brunswick. The *Cleopatra* was at sea by 18 June, crossed the Atlantic uneventfully and safely, and reached Spithead, the anchorage for Portsmouth, on 15 July.

On arrival, Charles learned that his friend Samuel Pechell was to supersede him as captain of the *Cleopatra*. The Admiralty wanted to put Captain

Fig. 18   HMS Cleopatra *in a Storm*. Fanny braved a horrific voyage from Halifax to Bermuda in desperate conditions on HMS *Indian* in November 1809.

James Dacres, a member of a well-connected naval family who had been on half pay since 1807, into Pechell's current vessel, HMS *Guerriere*. To accomplish this, they shuffled Pechell back into the *Cleopatra*. In terms of the Admiralty's priorities for postings, Pechell enjoyed several advantages over Charles. He had been made post-captain almost two years before Charles and so had greater seniority in rank. He was also Lady Warren's nephew and had entered the navy under Admiral Warren's protection. Since then, Warren had lent support to his nephew's naval advancement, even approaching Admiral Horatio Nelson in October 1803 for the purpose of promoting Pechell's career. Nelson replied that "nothing could possibly give me more pleasure than paying attention to any recommendation of yours. At this moment I see little prospect, having twenty-six lieutenants and sixty midshipmen on my list."[10] Nelson also noted that Pechell had already been "strongly recommended" to him by the Duke of Clarence and Lady Warren.

Amid all the joys of returning home, Fanny and Charles found they faced an uncertain future yet again, especially given Charles's reduced chances for acquiring a new commission. In the autumn of 1811 the British navy had 746 ships of war, including 169 frigates, in commission[11] but many, many more commanders and captains than these vessels required. The practice of promoting all the first lieutenants of the ships of the line that had successfully fought the major sea battles in the early 1800s and thus secured Britain's sovereignty over the seas, had created a surplus of unemployed naval officers on half pay on land.[12] As Charles was one of the newer post-captains and was no longer assigned to the North American Station, it was very unlikely that he would be commissioned into another frigate in the immediate future. Charles was now essentially unemployed and he, Fanny, and their family homeless. The situation must have alloyed the pleasure of their various family reunions.

From Fanny's point of view, her parents and sister Harriet in London had an immediate claim on her attention and affection. While Charles finished his duties on the *Cleopatra*, Fanny was happily reunited with her family at 22 Keppel Street, Bloomsbury. Her little girls, after the disorientation of moving about and crossing the ocean, were now in one place and enjoying the loving attention of their grandparents and aunt. At Keppel Street, Fanny was once more in her sister Harriet's company. They had been long-distance correspondents for years.[13] Now they were able to become more intimately acquainted.

At twenty-five, Harriet was still single and her prospects for marriage were somewhat uncertain. In the opinion of the day, she would before too long "approach to the years of danger"[14] beyond which she would be less likely to attract suitors, if at all. As it was, there was a scarcity of suitable men because of wartime casualties and the absence of so many of them on military service. There was also the matter of eligibility; certainly her parents would expect a suitor to be of an appropriate social standing. Moreover, her "delicate constitution" appears to have limited her range of activities. Fanny later speculates that Harriet's ill health was "in a great measure owing to her residence in London, which certainly never did agree with her."[15] Fortunately for Harriet, John Grove Palmer appeared happy to maintain his middle daughter, and thus for her, marrying to ensure long-term support and protection was not a necessity. She was to take her duties as an aunt very seriously and became genuinely fond of Fanny's little girls, caring for them diligently when they stayed at Keppel Street. Fanny's brother Robert John, an army officer, was not yet back in England. He had been serving in the European theatre until he became a prisoner of war in the fortress town of Verdun in northern France.

Fig. 19   Chawton Cottage as it appears today. Here Fanny first met the resident members of the Austen family: Jane, Cassandra, and Mrs George Austen.

Fanny found 22 Keppel Street, with its walled garden and close proximity to fashionable Russell Square and the British Museum, a congenial place for the Palmer family home. During this initial stay she may have met some of the young mothers and children who lived close by.[16] Barrister Thomas Trollope, his wife, another Fanny, and their four children lived at nearby number 16. Fanny Trollope, née Milton, was "by nature gay and vivacious, with an irrepressible sense of humour and a gift for happiness."[17] She appears to have been the sort of amusing and cheerful person whose company Fanny would enjoy. She also had children very close in age to Fanny Austen's girls. Another mother, the accomplished flower painter Eliza Abraham,[18] née Brown, and her architect husband Robert and their family lived at number 1. By the time she died at the age of forty in 1818 she had produced ten children.

Even though Charles had duties as the *Cleopatra*'s captain until 27 August 1811, he was keen to take some leave and introduce Fanny and his little daughters to his immediate Austen family. On 8 August they went to Chawton, a small village in Hampshire about fifty-two miles southwest of London, for a week's visit. After travelling through lovely countryside with "beech woods, sheltered valleys, commons, hopfields, hollow lanes, hedgerows, downs and sheepwalks,"[19] they arrived at their destination, Chawton Cottage (Fig. 19). Originally an early eighteenth-century farmhouse, it had

Fig. 20   The only known full-face image of Jane Austen, drawn from life, by her sister Cassandra, c. 1810.

been more recently renovated by its owner, Charles's brother Edward. To the eye of the visitor, the red brick cottage looked inviting, set off by an attractive garden, composed of "the existing field hedgerows ... made ... into shrubberies by adding ornamental plants, such as syringa [lilac] ... and herbaceous plants to the thorns and evergreens."[20] This was where Fanny met the widowed Mrs Austen and her two unmarried daughters, Cassandra and Jane (Fig. 20). The novelist was by then thirty-five, and although she had been writing since childhood, she was not yet published. The women immediately warmed to Fanny and the children, and they were absolutely delighted to welcome Charles after an absence of over six and a half years.

Charles's oldest brother, Reverend James Austen, rode over from nearby Steventon to greet them. Other brothers were elsewhere. Edward was at his estate, Godmersham Park in Kent, but he would be inviting them to visit later. Henry Austen was presumably occupied with business interests, but his stylish and beautiful wife, Eliza, Charles's first cousin,[21] was visiting at the same time and added to the spirit of the party.

Charles must have told Fanny about Eliza's interesting history. Born in India in 1761, where her English father was a doctor, Eliza was educated in France, and at nineteen she married the handsome young Jean-François Capot de Feuillide, an ardent French royalist and a captain in the Queen's Regiment of Dragoons. He became a victim of the French Revolution, suffering death by guillotine in Paris in 1794. As the owner of lands at Nérac in the province of Gascony, de Feuillide had styled himself as *comte*, although there is doubt whether this was his authentic title. Eliza, nonetheless, continued to encourage the public recognition of her former title of *comtesse*. She did so even after marrying her first cousin, Henry Austen, in 1797, for she felt the title gave her a certain cachet and sophistication.[22] According to Maggie Lane, Jane Austen "appears to have been fascinated rather than disapproving of [Eliza], since Eliza mentions 'her kind partiality for me' in a letter to another cousin."[23] Unfortunately, Fanny's impressions of this lively, pleasure-loving, and fashionable sister-in-law have not survived.

Frank Austen and his wife Mary missed this reunion. He was in command of HMS *Elephant* (74 guns) at Portsmouth, and even if Mary and her three young children had managed to get to Chawton, the cottage was too small to accommodate any more guests; in Cassandra's words, "our house [was] almost running over."[24] Fanny would have liked to become acquainted with the other naval wife in the family. However, it is unlikely that the two women met very often, if at all. During the next few years, Mary was in seaside lodgings at Deal or Portsmouth, and by early 1814 she was caring for five young children.

Even given the busyness of a family visit, there would have been time for Charles and Fanny to share some of their experiences in the North American naval world they had recently left. Austen scholar Brian Southam pictures the returned Charles as "regaling the Austens with stories of Bermuda and Halifax, his successes in the *Indian* and his experiences as Captain of Admiral Warren's Flagship."[25] Moreover, these "little narratives or descriptions which conversation called forth," as Jane Austen puts it in *Persuasion*,[26] surely included Fanny's perceptions about her life as a naval wife on the station. In one or two of her novels, Jane was to make good use of the information

she gathered from visits such as this one and the ones to follow in subsequent years.

Several days after this first visit to Chawton, Cassandra wrote about it
to her cousin Phylly.[27]

*Chawton Augt: 18 [1811] – My Brother Charles and his Family spent one
week with us during Eliza's visit and they all left us together last Thursday. After
an absence from England of almost seven years you may guess the pleasure which
having him amongst us again occasion'd. He is grown a little older in all that
time, but we had the pleasure of seeing him return in good health & unchanged
in mind. His Bermudan wife is a very pleasing little woman, she is gentle &
amiable in her manners & appears to make him very happy. They have two pretty
little girls. There must be always something to wish for, & for Charles we have
to wish for rather more money. So expensive as every thing in England is now,
even the necessaries of life, I am afraid they will find themselves very very poor.*[28]

Cassandra expresses a touching concern about Charles's financial state,
although it is probable that he and Fanny had some monies at hand, at least
for the very immediate future, and some longer-term prospects for more.
Charles was waiting for his share of prize money from the American brig
Stephen, but this could take some time, as the case had gone on appeal. He
may have saved some of his pay from the *Cleopatra*, although the Admiralty's
pay ledger shows that he did not receive the last £85 owing to him until 10
August 1812.[29] He may also have had some modest income from bonds had
he invested some of his prize money from recent years.[30] When Charles left
the *Cleopatra* towards the end of August, he would have gone on half pay of
about 10s. 6d. per diem, which amounted to £195 per year. This sum would
have been wholly insufficient for their needs, and since half pay was only
distributed every six months, he would have received about £95 twice a year
but no payments in between. Cassandra wrote her letter to Phylly at a time
when Charles would soon be unemployed. Thus, she had real grounds for
concern about her brother and his wife's future economic stability.

After Charles left the *Cleopatra*, he joined Fanny's family at Keppel Street.
He went on his own for a short visit to see his brother Edward Knight at
Godmersham Park. According to his niece Fanny Knight's observations,
he arrived for dinner on 1 October and was away early on 5 October.[31] In

mid-November Fanny and Charles accepted an invitation to the Steventon rectory, the home of Reverend James Austen, his wife Mary, and their three children, Anna, Caroline and James Edward.[32] Steventon was familiar and well-loved territory for Charles, as Steventon had been his home until 1801, when George Austen vacated his position as rector of St Nicholas Church and James succeeded him. Charles was familiar with Fanny's girlhood haunts in Bermuda. It was his turn to introduce her to the charms of Steventon, a hamlet tucked away in the chalk hills in the northeast corner of Hampshire. It would have given him pleasure to show her the rectory itself, "surrounded by sloping meadows dotted with elm, chestnut and spruce fir trees, at the end of a small village of about fourteen cottages."[33] Caroline Austen, James's daughter, later remembered this visit: "I was much charmed with both [Fanny and Charles] – but thought they looked very young for an aunt and uncle – though she must have been the mother of two children. She was fair and pink, with very light hair, and I admired her greatly."[34]

Although Steventon was only twelve miles from Chawton Cottage, it is unlikely that Charles and Fanny met with Jane, Cassandra, and Mrs Austen during their three-day visit with James and his family. Had they managed to get to Chawton, they would have found Jane in fine spirits because *Sense and Sensibility* had been advertised for sale on 30 October in the *Star* at 15s. for three volumes and also in the *Morning Chronicle*, 31 October. This was Jane's first novel in print. James marked this important occasion with a poetic tribute, which he wrote in a disguised hand and sent anonymously to his sister in the form of a letter. It read:

> To Miss Jane Austen the reputed Author of Sense and Sensibility a
> Novel lately publish'd
> On such Subjects no Wonder that she shou'd write well,
> In whom so united those Qualities dwell;
> Where 'dear Sensibility,' Sterne's darling Maid,
> With Sense so attemper'd is finely pourtray'd.
> Fair Elinor's Self in that Mind is exprest,
> And the feelings of Marianne live in that Breast.
> Oh then, gentle Lady! continue to write,
> And the Sense of your Readers t'amuse & delight.
>   A Friend.[35]

In the months to follow, one copy from that initial print run of 750–1,000 copies was given to Fanny, purportedly by Jane herself. Volume 1 is inscribed "Mrs. Charles Austen, given by her sister in law," and volume 2 is inscribed "F.F. Austen."[36] Thus, Fanny was connected to Jane not only as a sister, but also as an early reader of her fiction. Since the winter, Jane had been revising an earlier manuscript, initially called "First Impressions," and turning it into the novel *Pride and Prejudice*. But Fanny would have to wait until January 1813 to see it in published form.

The visit to Steventon ended rather abruptly on 19 November. According to their host, Mrs James Austen, "Cap and Mrs CA went off in a hurry."[37] There was good reason for their haste. Charles had received word that the Admiralty was prepared to commission him as flag-captain to Sir Thomas Williams in HMS *Namur* (74 guns), the guard and receiving ship at the Nore.[38] With this new employment on offer, Charles needed to go to London immediately to accept the appointment.

Admiral Sir Thomas Williams was well known to Charles as both a patron and friend. He had successfully served on three of Sir Thomas's previous vessels: as a midshipman in 1794 on HMS *Daedalus* (32 guns), then on HMS *Unicorn* (32 guns), and subsequently as second lieutenant on HMS *Endymion* (32 guns), where he remained until the spring of 1801. In 1792 Sir Thomas had married the beautiful Jane Cooper, Charles's first cousin.[39] Sadly, Sir Thomas lost his wife, aged twenty-seven, in 1798 when her gig collided with a runaway dray horse and she was thrown to her death. Two years later Sir Thomas married a Miss Wapshare of Salisbury, the current Lady Williams, but he was still considered part of the extended Austen family. Fanny became fond of Sir Thomas when she got to know him. She described him to Esther as possessing a "warmth of manner which you rarely meet with in [England]."[40] A man of generous spirit, the childless Sir Thomas founded in 1840 the Naval Female School for the daughters of naval officers with a donation of £1,000.

In his post as commander-in-chief at the Nore, Sir Thomas had jurisdiction over some of the naval operations in the Thames and Medway rivers and at the Buoy at the Great Nore Anchorage. Situated in the Thames estuary, the anchorage was a stretch of water roughly half a nautical mile wide and about three nautical miles northeast of Sheerness, Kent, at the point where the river meets the North Sea. It was the main assembly point for those naval vessels "blockading the Dutch coast and protecting the Straits of Dover"[41] and doing convoy duty.

Admiral Williams's flagship, HMS *Namur* (74 guns), was an old vessel that had seen much valiant service but was now employed in a stationary capacity and ordinarily rode at anchor at the Great Nore. One of her current functions was to provide floating accommodation for men waiting to be assigned to ships that were fitted out in the Thames and Medway rivers. She was also a guard ship, watching out for smugglers, spies from the continent, and any foreign shipping, and presenting the first line of defence against any enemy ships that might attempt to attack the Sheerness Naval Yard or advance against London further up the Thames. Additionally, she was part of a sequence of signalling stations that passed classified naval information along the coast.

Built in 1756, the *Namur* was originally a three-decker ship of 90 guns, but in 1804 her upper deck was removed and she was cut down to a 74-gun two-decker.[42] According to the National Maritime Museum, "the primary aim of this alteration was to improve her speed and sailing qualities although with some reduction to her gun power."[43] She continued in active sea service until 1807. By the time Charles came aboard, there had been further changes to adapt her for use as a receiving ship. When first built she measured 174 feet 11½ inches long, breadth 48 feet 7½ inches, depth in the hold, 20 feet 6 inches, with a tonnage of 1,779.[44]

The *Namur* had been famous in her day. For over fifty years at the height of the age of sail, the *Namur* was a leading ship of the line in important sea battles. She had performed with distinction during the Seven Years War between England and France (1756–63). As Sir Edward Boscawen's flagship, she was party to the capture in 1758 of Louisbourg, the French fortress on Isle Royale, now Cape Breton, Nova Scotia, built to protect access to Quebec by way of the St Lawrence River (Fig. 21). She fought in the Battle of Lagos, off the coast of the Algarve, Portugal, 18–19 August 1759, which saw the destruction of the French Mediterranean fleet, as well as in the Battle of Havana in August 1762, when British forces captured Havana, Cuba, the Spanish Caribbean fortress, together with a fifth of the Spanish navy. The *Namur* also saw action during the Napoleonic Wars at the Battle of Ortegal on 4 November 1805 off northwest Spain. She was part

Fig. 21 HMS *Namur*, then a second-rate ship of 90 guns, is the largest vessel in Halifax Harbour in this painting by Dominic Serres, 1762.

of Sir Richard Strachan's squadron that chased and captured four French ships of the line that had escaped after the Battle of Trafalgar.

The *Namur*'s story has a modern twist. In 1995 a large number of ship's timbers, as much as 25 per cent of the original hull, were discovered supporting the floors of the Wheelwright's Shop at the Historic Dockyard, Chatham, Kent. In 2005 they were conclusively identified as part of the *Namur*. Some 245 giant timbers are now on display[45] in a new sunken gallery at the Dockyard, forming part of the exhibit "Command of the Oceans." Thus, the *Namur* has risen to prominence again, some 260 years after her launch at the Chatham dockyard in March 1756.

With Charles once more employed, the next question was where Fanny and the little girls would live. Economics were one relevant factor. A gentleman could support his wife and a small family in modest comfort on £500 a year. This is the sum available for Mrs Dashwood and her daughters, Elinor, Marianne, and Margaret, when, in *Sense and Sensibility*, they are forced to leave their grand family house, Norland, for Barton Cottage in rural Devonshire. With this income, they will need to live economically but they will be able to afford the services of two maids, a boy and an occasional gardener.[46] Within the Austen family, Charles's brother Frank, already married with one child and with his family living on shore, "[limited] himself [in 1807] ... to four hundred [pounds] a year."[47] Since Charles's gross pay while on the *Namur* was to be £571 per annum, less a standard deduction of £57 5s. 6d. for taxes and naval charitable funds,[48] he could provide reasonable comfort for the time being for his family. His salary would be roughly equivalent to between £50,000 to £75,000 in modern buying power.[49]

What were the available choices for the family's accommodation and which might be most suitable? The comfortable Palmer home at 22 Keppel Street, Bloomsbury, offered the company of Fanny's parents, her sister Harriet, and presumably some of the services of their household staff in an airy and spacious part of town close to cultural centres. Fanny and the little girls would be able to pay short visits aboard the *Namur*, which was about fifty miles away by land or by sea, and would welcome Charles to Keppel Street whenever he had leave. Yet even if Fanny's parents encouraged such a plan, Fanny did not, for she had no desire to be even briefly separated from her beloved Charles. Moreover, his official leave averaged six weeks a year,[50] days best saved for visits to Jane, Cassandra, and Mrs Austen at Chawton Cottage, to the Edward Knight family at Godmersham Park, or for holidays with the Palmer family.

Locating in Sheerness would mean that Fanny was only a few nautical miles away from where the *Namur* lay at anchor. However, this option was unattractive because of the scrappy and undesirable state of the town. Sheerness was built on reclaimed marshland that was bleak and windswept, and the town lacked the fine stone houses and attractive officers' quarters of the nearby Chatham Naval Yard. The bulk of its inhabitants were naval yard labourers who lived in Bluetown, a jumble of rough dwellings in narrow alleys, painted in blue-grey paint of naval issue and situated close to the walls of the yard. This "seething, brawling atmosphere ... with closely huddled wooden houses, every one of which was a tavern and every third one a brothel,"[51] was no place to situate Fanny. The Royal Fountain Hotel was the only building of any note in the town. Although it was described as "a spacious hotel fitted up in a very superior style,"[52] it would hardly serve Fanny and Charles's budget or their purpose.

As a genteel woman, Fanny would have sought, in Deborah Kaplan's view, to create a home that would be a place of "physical contentment and intimacy." Home was to be not only a place to experience the comforts of one's physical surroundings but also a "space for leisure, pleasure and piety," where family members spent time together and forged "strong emotional attachments." Kaplan contends that this ideology of domesticity "achieved widespread acceptance in the upper and middling ranks of society by the second half of the eighteenth century."[53] If Fanny were to achieve these goals, she would have to do something quite out of the ordinary. To keep the family together, to foster intimacy and attachment in an atmosphere of acceptable comfort, Fanny and Charles decided that adapting his quarters aboard the *Namur* and employing sufficient servants to assist Fanny was the most emotionally satisfying as well as financially viable solution. This was the very project Fanny would soon undertake. Although the Admiralty discouraged the practice of officers having their families living with them on warships, the *Namur* was considered a different case. She was not expected to see action, as she was ordinarily anchored close to Sheerness.

Meanwhile, before they would settle on board, Fanny, Charles, Cassy, and Harriet Jane spent Christmas 1811 with the Palmer family at 22 Keppel Street. Sometime during this holiday or some other time when she was in London, Fanny had her silhouette made at the fashionable shop of Meirs and Field, 111 The Strand (Fig. 22). Silhouettes or profiles were very popular in the eighteenth century, being a quick and relatively inexpensive form of small portraiture. Fanny's profile is finely painted in black on an oval of plaster with the details of her head, hair, and shoulders enhanced by touches of gold paint. Meirs's trade label affixed to the back of the silhouette claims that he "executes likenesses in profile with unequalled accuracy which convey the most forcible expression of character."[54] Fanny's silhouette shows a profile of a young woman with a short neck and rounded features, but it is not nearly as revealing of her appearance and character as her portrait previously painted by Robert Field in Halifax. The silhouette cannot convey Fanny's face in all its detail, her serious and candid expression, her splendid red-gold hair, her pleasing figure, or the vibrant colour of her dress, all features that the Field painting so richly captures.

Although Fanny would be living mostly at sea in the following years, 22 Keppel Street would become an important place for her. There, her company was always appreciated and she was able to receive Bermuda friends as well as other naval wives of her acquaintance. While in town Fanny also

Fig. 22 John Meirs made this silhouette of Fanny in his London studio of Meirs and Field sometime between 1811 and 1814. It is now part of the Chawton House Library Collection and hangs in the Oak Room.

joined her parents' social circle, which included her father's cousins the Strangways, members of the aristocratic Yorkshire branch of that family. Such relationships were considered important in English circles, since family connections were a means to establishing one's place in genteel society.

Jane, Cassandra, and Mrs Austen welcomed "Charles and his pretty little wife [back to Chawton Cottage] early in the winter." According to Cassandra, "Charles and his Fanny came to us for a few days previous to taking possession of their aquatic abode."[55] Their stay was a chance for Jane and Cassandra to hear about the couple's plans for domestic life with their children at sea, and to enjoy a farewell visit before the family became much less accessible. Their choice to live on board the *Namur* represented a brave new venture for Fanny, who had never lived on board a working warship, as opposed to temporarily travelling in one. Jane, who retained such an avid interest in naval life as well as in the family's well-being, may have wondered how successful this plan would be for Fanny and Charles.

CHAPTER 5

Afloat and Ashore,
1812

SOMETIME IN LATE DECEMBER 1811 OR EARLY JANUARY 1812, Fanny and Charles boarded the *Namur*'s tender and sailed out to the vessel's anchorage, located about three nautical miles northeast of Sheerness, Kent. What might Fanny have seen as she approached her future home? Another observer, Douglas Jerrold, dramatically described his first impression of the *Namur* as he perceived her several years later from a small boat coming alongside. To him she was a "towering [two] decker looming above, … a great floating mass" with all "the pomp and power of a kingdom about it."[1] Likewise, Fanny must have been struck by the sheer size of the vessel. She was to make a small part of that "kingdom" their own, and she set about the exacting but exciting task of transforming the captain's quarters into a home, the first home of their own.

Due to the configuration of the vessel, they would be living in the stern on the quarterdeck under the poop deck. The quarterdeck was above the upper deck and reached from the stern halfway forward; the poop was a raised deck about half the length of the quarterdeck, forming the roof of the captain's cabin (Fig. 23). The family would occupy the full width of the ship, but the apartment included the captain's day cabin, which would be used by Charles for meetings with his officers. Thus, Fanny had to determine the best possible arrangement of the space allotted to them while taking account of these official requirements.[2] Their new accommodation was to

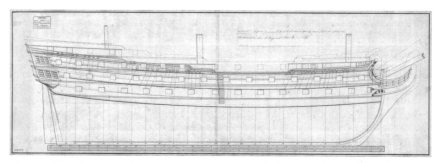

Fig. 23   The plan to cut down HMS *Namur* to a two-decker, 74-gun, third-rate ship. It shows the captain's quarters on the stern section of the quarterdeck, which Fanny transformed into her family's "aquatic abode."

become a comfortable place with as much privacy as possible for family life. How might she proceed?

The captain's day cabin was the finest room, its large windows over the ship's stern making possible a panoramic view of the anchorage. Existing walls likely marked other defined areas: a state room or sleeping cabin on one side of the vessel and a dining cabin on the other. From the remaining available area, Fanny could establish additional "rooms" by arranging movable wooden panels. Fanny appears satisfied with the results of her organization, for she accommodated her father, her sister Harriet, and a family friend during their visit in March while still providing sleeping quarters for her daughters and their nurse.

There were trials to face in the course of moving in and setting up house. The Admiralty supplied cots, which were essentially small canvas beds. However, since a typical cot was only three feet wide and swung suspended by cords from the ceiling, feeling secure enough to sleep in such a bed must have required a period of adjustment. As for comfort in cold weather, the Admiralty ordinarily provided each captain with a single coal-burning stove. With a two- and a three-year-old living on board, Fanny, who was used to the warmth of Bermuda, might feel that they needed more than one stove to make their quarters comfortable. Likely the greatest drawback of their accommodation for Fanny over time would be the isolation of her location. She had very little freedom of movement. The only place she could go to outside the apartment was a small part of the quarterdeck and the poop deck over the captain's quarters. She had no female company of her social class. She faced the danger of loneliness and cabin fever.

It fell to Fanny to identify and acquire the necessities needed for shipboard life. Mattresses, pillows, and bedding, cooking utensils and cutlery were all priority items, as were china, glassware, and table linen. There were personal possessions to assemble and then stow in limited storage facilities: all the clothing, toys, and childhood essentials belonging to Cassy and Harriet; Charles's regular and dress naval uniforms, cocked hats, civilian clothes, and Masonic regalia. For herself, Fanny had an even longer list of personal items, including her shifts, muslin and dimity dresses, pelisses, spencers,[3] and shawls, assorted bonnets, caps, gloves, purses, silk stockings and shoes, her needlework, sewing supplies, pocketbook, writing paper, and personal seal. This was a family that valued books and wanted them to be shelved and accessible. We know that Charles had a copy of *Buffon's Natural History* on board, and their collection of Jane Austen's novels was destined to grow, with *Pride and Prejudice* and *Mansfield Park* joining *Sense and Sensibility.*

A captain was responsible for providing his own furnishings. Presumably Fanny and Charles had brought a minimal amount of furniture with them from North America, for they did not know at the time that they would be staying in England. In addition, a home aboard ship presented Fanny with special challenges regarding interior decoration. The constant movement of the ship spelled disaster for loose ornaments and other fragile decorations, and a damp environment was no place for the fine oil portraits of Fanny and Charles. When a newly recruited tradesman, John Manning, painted the captain's cabin and its surrounds that summer, Fanny may have objected to the insipid blue-grey paint commonly favoured by the Admiralty and begged Charles to request a colour that would at least better complement the attractive appearance she hoped to achieve in their living quarters.[4]

Affixing some favourite prints and drawings to the wall panels would at least make their quarters look less austere, and to achieve this end Fanny had some avenues of choice. Cassandra Austen was a dedicated amateur artist who favoured pleasing country scenes and portraits, which she executed in pencil or watercolours. On request, or even voluntarily, she could be expected to contribute some of her sketches (Fig. 24).[5] There were also numerous inexpensive prints available of famous sea battles. For example, the dramatic depiction of HMS *Unicorn* taking the French frigate *La Tribune* (44 guns) in 1796 would be of particular interest (Fig. 25). Charles had been a midshipman on the *Unicorn* at the time of the capture and had participated

Fig. 24   This drawing by Cassandra Austen, titled *Loosing the Hawk*, probably after a similar image by German artist Johann Elias Reidinger, would have been a suitable choice when Fanny decorated the family quarters on HMS *Namur*.

in the ten-hour running chase and subsequent close combat, which lasted for half an hour. Fifty years later the Admiralty awarded the seven remaining survivors of this action, who included Charles, the Naval General Service Medal with a clasp inscribed "Unicorn 8 June 1796."

In the Georgian period, a woman of the gentry, reports Amanda Vickery, "turned her house into a home. Your home reflected your taste, your character, moral values and even the state of your marriage."[6] Would Fanny attempt to conform to such attitudes and expectations given the unusual features of her abode on the *Namur*? Because of the remoteness of their location, Fanny and Charles's visitors were either family or close friends, individuals who understood their current situation and did not expect to find stylish elegance and fine decor on a working ship. Such individuals were unlikely

Fig. 25   An artist's impression of the capture of the French frigate *La Tribune* (44 guns) by HMS *Unicorn* (32 guns), 8 June 1796. Charles was involved as a midshipman aboard the *Unicorn*. Sir Thomas Williams, her captain, was knighted for this action.

to criticize Fanny's taste and lack of fine possessions. For now, her goal was to make the family quarters as snug and comfortable as possible. Developing her decorative taste and setting up a home that reflected her personal style and values would have to wait.

Even so, as Deborah Kaplan notes, "according to domestic ideology, it was [a lady's] duty to maintain a well-ordered, well-stocked residence."[7] This was a role Fanny undertook with enthusiasm. As her letters from the *Namur* will show, she became an astute shopper who discovered the best sources for fresh meat, fish, eggs, and good-quality butter and cheeses, on shore at Sheerness or at Southend across the River Thames, on the nearby Essex coast. She accumulated baskets, canisters, a frail, and a butter crock for transporting food back to the *Namur* or for despatch to the Palmers in London. By the terms of naval policy, wives and families of officers serving on board had no claim to the standard rations of beef, pork, biscuit, oatmeal, pease, sugar, cheese, butter, and beer. Charles must have shared his rations of these staples with his family, whereas Fanny went about acquiring their other fresh foods and delicacies.

Fanny had some assistance in planning her family's meals. A captain was entitled to a staff of servants, including a cook and a steward to "take charge of his sea stock," an expression that referred to managing a captain's rations as well as his private supplies of items such as teas, wines, and spirits. An officer's cook ordinarily had the use of "the forward part of the ship's galley stove, with such sophisticated fittings as an oven, a grill and a spit."[8] Presumably Charles made good use of his domestic staff, including his cook, whom he might ask to prepare meals for his family. He sometimes dined in the wardroom or officers' mess with the lieutenants, marine officers, master, surgeon, chaplain, and purser.[9] It would be a courtesy to invite Fanny, the captain's wife, to eat with them occasionally.

Fanny kept the family's household accounts. She needed to plan her purchases in accordance with when and how Charles was paid. Given the Admiralty's policy regarding remuneration of officers, Charles had ready access to some of the money he earned, and the amounts he withdrew were recorded in the Admiralty's pay ledger as "abatements." For example, Charles earned £513 14s. 6d. net between 16 December 1811 and 15 December 1812, but he had £264 4s. deducted during that period as abatements, presumably to offset his family expenses.[10] The remaining portion of his salary for that period, £249 11s. 6d., was not paid out until 16 March 1813.[11] The delay in actual payment of an officer's salary meant that naval families could sometimes find themselves cash-poor even though significant monies were owed to them and would eventually be received. At least with this system an officer had something in reserve in the event that his commission ended and he was cast ashore on half pay.

Fanny was vigilant about her daughters' well-being and determined to provide them with a healthy and happy environment. The poop deck was a convenient place for exercise in the fresh sea air and a prime location for watching the life of the vessel unfold. Fanny and the little girls regularly spied sailors aloft working on the masts and sails or observed the *Namur's* tender, the *Nile*, coming alongside to deliver groups of recent recruits, some of them pressed men, or to transfer sailors to their assigned ships. Periodically the lighter, a barge-like vessel from the Sheerness Dock Yard, unloaded bulk shipments of food and drink; occasionally red-coated marines could be seen drilling on the upper deck. If the timing was right, the children got a glimpse of their father returning from a consultation with his superior, Admiral Sir Thomas Williams, in Sheerness.

Although life on board the *Namur* entailed periods of noise and commotion, the family quarters provided some measure of quiet and seclusion. The quarterdeck was reserved for the officers who worked there; ordinary seaman went there only when their duty required it. A marine sentry permanently guarded the doors to the captain's apartment, a precaution that must have increased Fanny's sense of security. Fanny rarely had prolonged contact with the ordinary seamen except when attending Sunday service and at the periodic entertainments arranged by Charles for the men.

Warrant or standing officers, such as the master, the master shipwright, the boatswain, and the carpenter, were allowed to have their wives and children live aboard with them. It is not known how many of these family arrangements were in place on the *Namur*, but there must have been some, for in May 1814 Fanny and her girls removed to London because the "odious meazles have got amongst the Children belonging to the Ship."[12] Fanny apparently wanted to avoid sources of contagion, so it is evident that she and her girls were sometimes in the company of other mothers and children on board. She was to employ the services of at least one of these women from time to time. But apart from these encounters, Fanny was virtually cut off from female company, especially any association with those of polite society. She had no companions of her class to discuss topics of common interest and everyday concern, be they issues of domestic management, remedies for illness, child care, or the latest fashions in dress and needlework patterns.

Several individuals have left accounts of life on the *Namur*. Tradesman John Manning, who signed on in late June 1812, was employed "painting the captain's cabin and all around the sides of her." Writing to his brother in early August, he enthusiastically declared, "[I]f I should be fortunate enough to belong to the Ship I shall be happy as if I were on Shore for it is a very good living we have nothing to drink but grog and wine." Manning's perspective was, of course, affected by the terms of his employ. He was aboard in the capacity of a tradesman, and as he cheerfully told his brother, he had the luxury of going to bed "any time he [liked] after 8 O'clock at night and [could] lay til 6 or 7 in the morning."[13] Yet, his narrative suggests an orderly vessel with a good atmosphere.

In contrast to Manning's experience, the lifestyle of the regular sailor was much less comfortable and free. A young Scot, Clarkson Stanfield, arrived on the *Namur* in 1812 after he was unluckily taken by a press gang on Tower Hill in London on 31 July. The resourceful Stanfield identified himself as Roderick Bland, because, should he manage to escape from the *Namur*, he hoped to elude detection and reclaim his real name and identity. Nineteen-year-old Stanfield had already been to sea in a collier, or coal-carrying vessel, so working as an able-bodied seaman was not an entirely new experience. A brief letter to his sister, an actress in Edinburgh, tells of a young man doing his job and taking his turn on watch. He wrote about the occasion of a visit by the Duke of Clarence, the future King William IV, to Sheerness in August 1813 to witness the departure of the Russian ambassador, describing it as a "grand sight" when "every ship had her yards manned."[14] But over time Stanfield became increasingly angry and frustrated by his enforced stay on the *Namur*. In the spring or early summer of 1814, he went ashore to "do a painting for the admiral's ball room." Stanfield already had the makings of an accomplished artist, and he "worked day and night at the commission for three weeks."[15] The results greatly pleased Commissioner Lobb of the Sheerness Naval Yard, who promised to get him a discharge from the navy and a situation in the dockyard. Unfortunately, the commissioner died unexpectedly in late July and Stanfield was forced to remain on the *Namur*. His letters reflect his extreme disappointment, for he had been so hopeful of finding satisfying work on shore away from the strict naval discipline aboard the *Namur*.

While Fanny was living on board, she could not completely escape a much darker and more violent side to naval life. She was situated in a world where misdemeanors were punished swiftly and brutally. The Admiralty required, without exception, that any instances of mutinous language and conduct, disobedience of orders, theft, interpersonal violence, drunkenness, or riotous behaviour on the part of the men must be punished by public flogging. This, it was ruled, was necessary to maintain the authority of the officers, who were by far the numerical minority, and to ensure the effective performance of a vessel in war or peace. Flogging was also considered a deterrent against desertion, a serious threat to a navy that could only operate efficiently if its vessels were adequately manned.

The *Namur*'s population of non-permanent seamen fluctuated. Some had short stays because they were quickly assigned to another vessel; others remained longer, like Clarkson Stanfield, who was kept on the *Namur* for more than two years. Fortunately, these seamen, as well as the crew of the *Namur*, were not prone to excessive violence and crime. The ship's logbook identifies a spectrum of misdemeanors requiring disciplinary action that occurred at times when Fanny was on board. For example, in January 1813 there were three cases of punishment for theft: John Bailey received thirty-six lashes, while James Taylor and John Blinkensop were given twenty-four lashes each. In addition, Benjamin Douglas was punished with thirty-six lashes for "attempting to stab Serjent Mons."[16] These statistics, together with the record of other punishments for 1812 and 1813, confirm that Charles was not a flogging captain. He avoided making excessive use of the cat o' nine tails, or cat, which was a short stick with nine strands of two-foot-long knotted rope attached.[17] In fact, sometimes Charles chose to lecture delinquent seamen instead of punishing them and on one Christmas, he pardoned "at least a dozen offenders ... in honour of the day."[18]

Nonetheless, public punishment by flogging was a formal and grisly affair during which all the officers, lieutenants, and a full muster of the crew stood together with the armed marines assembled on the quarterdeck above. The victim was stripped to the waist and lashed securely to a grating as the boatswain's mate administered the prescribed number of lashes. Piteous cries rent the air. There was a temporary stay or termination of the flogging only when the attending surgeon made the order.

During Fanny's tenure on board, there were five occasions of the cruellest sort of punishment, known as "flogging around the fleet." The offender was "tied to the capstan bars erected in the ship's launch and rowed from one ship to another, accompanied by a drummer playing the Rogue's March."[19] On 5 March 1813 seaman John Crossley, "belonging to HMS *Starling*," was brought to the *Namur* and received "200 lashes being part of 300 for deserting his post."[20] The additional 100 lashes were administered in equal portions by the other naval vessels at the anchorage at the time.

Charles was ordinarily able to warn Fanny in advance when a flogging was about to occur. Perhaps he sometimes arranged for her to be on shore in nearby Sheerness. Yet inevitably there must have been times when there was no ready escape from the distressed cries of the punished. How, one wonders, did Fanny manage to cope with the cruelty of flogging when she heard the unmistakable sounds of suffering and the ominous pulsating of the drums, all terribly disturbing noises for her and her children, should they be aboard. Another naval wife of the Napoleonic period, Betsy Fremantle, who lived with her husband, Captain Thomas Fremantle, on his vessels HMS *Inconstant* (36 guns) and HMS *Seahorse* (38 guns) for a period of seven and a half months during 1796–97, spoke of her horror of floggings and her distress when she could "'distinctly hear the poor wretches cry out for mercy,' something which 'broke my heart.'"[21] Perhaps Fanny tried to deal with the brutality of flogging by cultivating the belief that this practice ensured naval discipline and, by extension, her own and her family's safety while they were living on a working naval vessel.

Fanny was spared one source of distress. Although it was a fairly common occurrence, in fact an ancient naval tradition, to allow prostitutes on board when a ship was in port or just off shore, the *Namur* did not follow this practice. It would be contrary to Charles's conception of right behaviour, especially when Fanny was living on board. Some years later their friend Edward Hawker, a strongly evangelical Christian, argued vehemently against allowing prostitutes on ships. As the author of a pamphlet, published anonymously, entitled *Statement Respecting the Prevalence of Certain Immoral Practices in His Majesty's Navy*, he commented on "a case that has lately occurred, [when] the captain and his wife were actually on the quarterdeck on a Sunday morning while seventy-eight prostitutes were undergoing an inspection of the first lieutenant to ascertain that their dress was clean."[22] Such a situation would have horrified Fanny, had she been that captain's wife.

During his captaincy of the *Namur*, Charles tried to counterbalance the more violent aspects of shipboard life. Luxuries such as beer and tobacco were for sale, although tradesman John Manning complained in his letter to his brother that he could get both these items cheaper and of better quality on shore. Charles's background in family theatricals stood him in good stead in the matter of entertainment. The Austen family had performed dramas in their barn at Steventon from about 1782 to 1790. According to Paula Byrne, "it is tempting to think that either [Jane] or little Charles took on the role" of the diminutive hero Tom Thumb in the family's theatrical *The Tragedy of Tom Thumb* (1787–89).[23] Irrespective of his earlier experiences, the adult Charles was a great supporter of lighthearted amusements for his men and he had a skilled scene painter available in the person of seaman Clarkson Stanfield.[24] Fanny also mentions a band, already in performance by March 1812. It was most likely composed from the *Namur*'s marines, who included a clarinetist, albeit a mediocre one according to the assessment of her father, John Grove Palmer. Fanny, who enjoyed music and theatricals, valued these artistic diversions, which encouraged a civilized atmosphere on board.

Fanny was not confined to the ship all the time. She periodically travelled to nearby Sheerness in search of fresh food and other household needs. She had access to the *Namur*'s tender, the *Nile*, on occasions when she wanted to travel up the River Thames to visit in Keppel Street or to move her children there for stays with their aunt Harriet and their grandparents. On these excursions Fanny had the protection of Hancock, the master of the *Nile*, whom she described as "a very excellent Man."[25] Moreover, this mode of travel into London was particularly interesting and enjoyable. Just before Greenwich, the *Nile* passed the density of masts and the great busyness of the East India Docks. On reaching Greenwich, they came close to the impressive Royal Hospital for Seamen situated at the water's edge and could spy the striking Royal Observatory, designed by Christopher Wren and built in 1676, high on the hill behind. As they approached London, the *Nile* sailed past a hodgepodge of wharves and warehouses on both the north and south banks of the Thames before reaching the Royal Naval Yard at Deptford, known for its large Victualling Yard, which supplied food and other provisions to the navy. This trip on the river gave Fanny an impressive profile of the might of England, notably its vibrant commerce and famous institutions, which contributed to Britain's dominance as a seagoing power. There was a vast difference in the scale and scope of industry on the Thames compared with the very modest marine and commercial business Fanny had grown up with in Bermuda.

Once she was settled on board the *Namur*, Fanny resumed her transatlantic and local family correspondence. In the opinion of Amanda Vickery, genteel young women's letters "virtually never canvassed [the topics of] spirituality and sex,"[26] but they did exchange detailed information on "local news, servants, prices and fashions, recipes and remedies, child-bearing and child-rearing."[27] Fanny regularly discussed these latter topics in her letters from Halifax to her sister Esther, and the same themes are prevalent in her correspondence from the *Namur*. Yet, from 1812 to 1814 her letters are richer and more complex. They express the thoughts and feelings of a more mature Fanny whose life now entails many more tasks and responsibilities. She speaks of the uniqueness of her situation, the difficulties of being a wife, a mother, and the mistress of an establishment which, though often in sight of land, was essentially at sea. Her circumstances dictate that her experiences, duties, and obligations differ from those of other young women of her age and class.

Fanny realized that certain features of her life as a naval wife had changed for the better. She was freed from anxiety about Charles's safety, as he would not be off cruising at sea. She was no longer the sole parent of tiny children for long stretches of time. Moreover, she would not be sailing through rough and potentially hazardous waters, a situation not infrequent during her later days on the North American Station. Best of all, she and the little girls would have the pleasure of Charles's regular company. He would be at hand to help with the children's education, to play with them at bedtime, and to celebrate the milestones of their development.

An early assessment of the success of Fanny's "aquatic abode" comes in a letter from Cassandra Austen to her cousin Phylly. She writes: "[Fanny and the] children are actually living with [Charles] on board. We had doubted whether such a scheme would prove practicable during the winter, but they have found their residence very tolerably comfortable and it is so much the cheapest home she could have that they are very right to put up with little inconveniences."[28] Yet over time Fanny's own letters indicate how the domestic and personal challenges of life aboard the *Namur* test her inventiveness, patience, and even her physical strength.

Her letters for 1812 begin with a short note to James Esten in Bermuda, written from the anchorage at the Great Nore. The ship's log records it was a breezy and cloudy day with a NNW wind.

Great Nore Namur, 21st Jan. 1812
My dear Brother
    I have just seen by the paper that a vessel has arrived at Deal, from the river, for Bermuda; & as the Belona will sail in the course of an hour or two for the Downs,[29] *I have determined to drop you a few lines, as I am sure it will be a great satisfaction to you to hear that my dear Sister is* quite recovered, *& all your friends in* Keppel Street *as well as those on* board the Namur *in high preservation.*

Mama & Palmer have been staying with us, since the 15th & we mean to keep them as long as the Holidays will permit: they are very much pleased with our habitation, which, now that we have got things to rights, we find extremely comfortable. I have been endeavouring to prevail on Sister Het,[30] to come to us for a little while as I think change of air will be of great service to her, but she puts off coming untill the days are longer & the weather warmer –

Capt. Douglas[31] has this moment come into the Cabin & tells me he shall sail immediately therefore I hope you will excuse this scrawl & accept our united love for yourself & offer it to all who you know we value and esteem. Palmer desires his best love & desires me to say he has had one of his front teeth drawn to-day by Uncle Austen.

> *Adieu yours most truly*
> *and affectly.*
> *F.F. Austen*

Fanny's letter is shorter than she would have wished, but she does not want to miss the chance to have it sent on its way. On this occasion and on others when Fanny is pressed to write quickly, this was no mean feat, as she is using a goose quill pen that needed to be periodically sharpened. Although she signs it rather formally as F.F. Austen instead of Fanny, this is merely a convention of letter writing and does not signify anything about her relationship with the person she is addressing. Jane Austen followed a similar practice, signing letters to her sister Cassandra sometimes as J. Austen or just J.A.

Fanny's letter is very cheerful in tone. She gives priority to family news about Esther and Palmer. Her sister is in London with her younger son Hamilton. Palmer, her older boy, is in a residential preparatory school in Kentish Town, an area that was losing its rural character as it was absorbed into London. The school was probably the Gordon House Academy, an establishment for "young gentlemen," whose headmaster was a Scot, A.A.M. Mensal. Palmer has made an early visit to the *Namur*, where his "Uncle Austen" (Charles) has fulfilled the roles of both ship's captain and emergency dentist. The novelty of life on the *Namur* was of a style to intrigue both Fanny's mother and her seven-year-old nephew. The ring of the ship's bell signalled the watches and marked the time. At night, the sounds of the sea entered the sleeping cabins, and the movement of the waves and the creaking of the ship's timbers lulled the visitors' sleep. By day, there was a fine view of the shipping traffic approaching and passing the anchorage, since the navigable channel of the Thames lay just to the north and the approach channel of the Medway to the southwest. Fanny's situation, however, was not the same as that of a visitor, who, with no particular duties and responsibilities, was free to enjoy the uniqueness of shipboard life. Her subsequent letters to Esther in early March provide a somewhat mixed opinion and nuanced account of her circumstances.

Namur 5th March [1812] –

Your kind offer my dearest Sister of Polly's³² services has relieved my mind very much for I quite despaired of getting any person to assist me in Nancy's³³ absence, which will I fear be at least one Month, tho' she persists in saying, it will only be three weeks. If you <u>can conveniently</u> spare Polly she will relieve me from a great deal of fatigue & we will send the Nile on Monday either to the Tower or Greenwich, if the weather will permit, & Hancock the Master (a very excellent Man) will escort her to the Tender; Papa at present talks of going up in her, on that day; he is very much pleased with our accomodations & enjoys sleeping in a Cot extremely.

I am truly thankful that our dear Hamilton is not here, for the Surgeon has reported another, doubtful case, today. Tell my dear Mama that we do not think it worth while to remove our children as, from our situation here, they may frequently be exposed to the same, & many other disorders of that nature; therefore, we must make the best of it, but you may depend, when any thing of the kind happens, on hearing of it in time to prevent either of your children from running any risk in coming to us Do not let it frighten you my dear Sister from sending Hamilton as soon as we are free from apprehension, for I assure you my children never enjoyed better health, than since they have been living on board. Nancy is going in the Cherokee Sloop of War [10 guns] to Leith, she is expected to sail on Saturday next & will lie too, when she comes within hail & one of our boats will take Nancy on board.

We sent you a Leg of Pork by the Town Tender yesterday & Little Harriets straw bonnet with directions what to have done with it. We are going to Southend³⁴ tomorrow or next day to look at a house which Papa thinks will answer for you *all, & if we approve of it, I believe he will take it. The moment Papa heard <u>our</u> <u>Band</u> he discovered that one of the Clarionets was defective, what an excellent ear he has for musick!*

Will you be good enough to let me know if you approve of our plan of sending for Polly? Harriet & Charley[35] *both desire me to thank you for your kind letters & the former will be gla[d] of another Morning dress & a pair of [Si]lk Stockings when the Nile returns.*

We all unite in best love to Mama yourself and your Children & I am ever yours most affectionately

F.F. Austen

Fanny writes Esther again early the next day, this time expressing a personal plea.

Namur Friday Morning 6th [March 1812].

My dearest Sister

Nancy has this morning determined to wait untill April before she visits her Mother, <u>as she has just found out</u>, that March is the very worst month in the year for travelling by Sea: therefore I shall not take Polly from you at present, & hope when I do require her, there will be nothing to prevent dear little Hamilton's coming with her.

I am grieved to find my dear Sister that you have not recovered your appetite yet; do let me entreat you to come down to us when Papa returns for I am sure that change of air will restore it sooner than any thing. Harriet will go up in the Tender with Papa & you will not certainly refuse to leave Hamilton with Mama untill he can come to us without fear or apprehension. Will you just write two lines tomorrow to say whether you will agree to this arrangement? <u>I think you will not refuse</u>. If you are determined to be obdurate, I must beg Harriet to relinquish her intention of going up with Papa on Monday – The two Gentlemen of our party are going on Shore this morning to call on the Admiral & shou'd to morrow be fine we shall go to Southend.

Thank my dear Mother for her joint letter which we received this morning & tell her that Grand-dad[36] *appears very happy & that I have not heard him cough these two days; he is now shaving and beautifying in Charley's dressing room. I fear we shall have lightend your purse a little this Week with the postage* *of our letters, and wou'd fain have <u>this</u> charged in Capt. Austen's Postage Account but Harriet will not allow me.*

 Papa has just completed his toilette & I assure you, without exaggeration looks infinitely better than when he came to us; this will I hope be an inducement to you. Charley desires me to tell you that he shou'd have written you himself to-day had he not [been] very much engaged. [Do not] plague yourself to wri[te] [a] [le]tter tomorrow but just drop me a line in answer to our entreaties.

 Our united love to Mama & yourself

Ever your most affecte.
F.F. Austen

In this short, succinct letter Fanny urges Esther to visit her on the *Namur*. She makes her case in a polite but insistent manner, using the underlined sentence, "<u>I think you will not refuse,</u>" to convey the seriousness of her invitation. Fanny gives Esther several reasons for a visit that she hopes are persuasive, as she very much wants her favourite sister's company. This plea is perhaps more urgent because Fanny is pregnant for the third time in four years, a situation that may explain her need for relief from a "great deal of fatigue." If Esther cannot stay, Fanny will "beg" Harriet to remain on the *Namur* a bit longer. She seems to need psychological as well as physical support to manage her two young girls while she copes with the weariness of pregnancy. This expressed desire for the help of a sister is a theme that resurfaces in the future.

These two letters suggest that the smooth operation of Fanny's domestic arrangements will depend on her securing adequate domestic staff. Although Nancy was working for Fanny in March 1812, she was the first of many servants who found reasons to leave. The fault could have lain with Fanny as an employer but more likely lay with the job itself. A domestic in Fanny's employ could expect only a modest salary, would be living primarily at sea, and would thus be isolated from friends and family on shore. Although it was customary for a domestic servant to be employed for a year, it was not the practice for the parties involved to sign a contract. Fanny had only verbal agreements with her servants, who apparently did not hesitate to break them. Her uneven success in retaining staff sometimes frustrated Fanny, making her anxious about her ability to cope with household arrangements.

Fig. 26   J.M.W. Turner painted the turbulent waters at the Nore anchorage c. 1807.
HMS *Namur* can be seen faintly in the left background, the seaport of Sheerness appears
in the distance. Turner called the painting *The Junction of the Thames and the Medway*.

Fanny now weathered some chilly and inclement weeks in late March
and April when the Sheerness marine area was notoriously subject to strong
northwesterly winds and high spring tides (Fig. 26). It was not a comfortable
location, swinging at the end of an anchor at every tide's change and rolling
with the shifting currents. By June, the scene changed. John Grove Palmer
decided to treat his wife, three daughters, four grandchildren, and son-in-
law, Charles, to their first English seaside holiday together at Southend, an
ideal location about six nautical miles from the *Namur's* anchorage by water
and a manageable forty-two-mile journey by land for the London Palmers.

By the early nineteenth century, seaside spas had become popular des-
tinations for relaxation and sociability among the gentry class. With access
to the Continent off bounds for British visitors during the Napoleonic
Wars, new resorts around the British coast rapidly developed and attracted
increasing numbers of visitors. The lure of fresh air and the vogue for sea
bathing were motivating factors, together with the provision of facilities
for refined entertainments, recreations, and diversions. By 1813 the local

Chelmsford Chronicle was enthusiastically describing Southend as a "very pleasant and delightful little watering hole, rendered so popular of late years, as being the fashionable resort of the beau monde." This claim stemmed from the visit of the Prince of Wales's[37] estranged wife, Princess Caroline, who in 1803 stayed for a period on the Grand Terrace,[38] with her entourage thereby lending a royal cachet to the young resort. The newspaper declared that the town is "most beautifully situated on a fine rising ground, and commands a very extensive and picturesque view of the Isles of Sheppy and Grange [Grain] the Great and Little Nore [anchorages] and the town and harbour of Sheerness, to and from which packets and pleasure boats sail daily." In addition to "the peculiar advantages it affords for the comforts and conveniences of sea bathing, the rides and walks are numerous, and for beauty, and variety of scenery, can scarcely be equalled."[39] The summer of 1812 was the first of two extensive periods that Fanny, her little girls, and the London Palmers spent together at Southend.

In her letter of 5 March, Fanny mentions an expedition to Southend for the express purpose of viewing "a house which Papa thinks will answer for you all." No extant letter subsequently describes the accommodation they eventually secured, but the *Chelmsford Chronicle* regularly carried advertisements for the kind of properties available, such as: "HANDSOME HOUSE ... well adapted to let for lodgings to one or two families, ... four rooms on a floor, the good kitchen fitted with all conveniences, large garden, commanding and extensive views of the Kent coast ...let when furnished for Ten Guineas per week."[40] This sort of establishment would have suited the tastes and needs of the Palmer and Austen party. Fanny's parents were used to a well-appointed living space with an adjacent garden. On most days the *Namur* could be seen at her anchorage; her proximity was an important consideration, since Charles had only three weeks' official leave that summer. Wherever it was they stayed in Southend, Fanny was content. She was surrounded by a profusion of summer plants and flowers, and she had a view of the sea from the solidity of the land. Her girls were joyfully reunited with their affable Esten cousins, and she had the congenial companionship of both her sisters and her parents.

Fanny and her extended family entered into the spirit of the place. The facilities of the Royal Hotel in the New or Upper Town (which had developed along the elevation of the cliff top) included a coffee room and

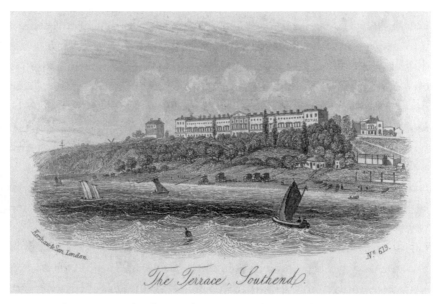

Fig. 27 *The Terrace, Southend*, 1808. This engraving shows the elegant Georgian terrace of the seaside resort, with its shrubbery leading down to the beach and five bathing machines ready for clients on the shore. Fanny and her daughters had two happy summer holidays here with her Palmer family in 1812 and 1813.

a handsome Assembly Room, with adjoining music gallery and supper and card rooms. The nearby lending library offered a wide range of books as well as London and provincial newspapers and periodicals; it also served as a morning lounge and location for evening raffles. The hotel advertised "Bathing Machines with proper Guides," and the proprietor, D. Miller, promised that "dinners [were] dressed and sent out to private homes at the shortest notice."[41] On fine days visitors walked on the broad gravelled promenade along the Royal Terrace or in the attractive shrubbery where criss-crossing paths invited access to the shingled beach (Fig. 27). By 1812 Southend had about 2,000 inhabitants. It tended to attract the "wealthy, quiet and cultured sort of visitor,"[42] but it was also a popular destination for shore-based naval families and officers whose ships were repairing at the nearby Sheerness Dock Yard. Thus Fanny and Charles were bound to meet people they knew in naval circles.

Southend had a theatre that offered a summer season in July and August. Built in 1804 by actor-manager Thomas Trotter near the Castle Inn, in the

Lower Town, it was described as "a very small house, but neatly divided into boxes, pit and gallery."[43] There had been memorable performances during Trotter's tenure as manager. The eminent actor Edmund Kean had on one single bill "played Shylock, danced on a tightrope, took the part of Apollo in Midas, singing all the music, – afterwards set up with Belasco, the Jewish pugilist, and wound up the whole with Harlequin."[44] By 1810 Samuel Jerrold, another actor-manager, had taken over the theatre and developed a reputation for fully mounted productions. He presented the Byzantine melodrama *Adelgitha: or the Fruits of a Single Error*, by Monk Lewis, in which patrons were promised the sight of "Rocks, and a Water-Fall, *Grand Gothic Palace*, Subterranean Cavern, and Grand Banquet."[45] As Fanny and Charles greatly enjoyed the theatre, they no doubt seized the opportunity to see whatever was on the playbill during their stay. They may have met and talked with Samuel Jerrold.[46] They would get to know his young son, Douglas, much better in the future.

Southend's New Town advertised the use of eight to ten bathing machines fully equipped with awnings. These contraptions were like small beach huts on four wheels and were used chiefly by women. Once inside the hut, the bather put her clothes on a shelf and changed into her bathing costume. Most resorts employed "dippers," strong women who pushed the bathing machine into the water. The dipper then assisted the bather down steps into the sea, and back out again when the dip was finished.[47] There were warm salt water baths for the less adventurous. These were available in a facility built in 1804 by an enterprising Mr. Ingram who used a pony to pump water from an artesian well. The Warm Baths were located on a site below the Royal Hotel.[48]

There is no record of how many of the Palmer-Austen party explored the relatively novel pleasures of sea bathing. Fanny, who was four months pregnant, likely demurred, although an aunt possibly accompanied young Cassy, who was a prime candidate for salt water therapy after a difficult spring aboard the *Namur*, where she often suffered from seasickness. In later years, sea bathing became an established pastime among the Austen children. After a holiday at Broadstairs in Kent in 1815, their grandmother, Mrs George Austen, pronounced the little girls to be "better for the sea air and bathing."[49] Their aunt Jane was a self-confessed aficionado, describing an occasion of sea bathing as "so delightful this morning & Molly so pressing with me to enjoy myself that I believe I staid in rather too long."⁵⁰ One of Jane's favourite poets, William Cowper, was not immune to the popularity of sea bathing. He wrote, somewhat facetiously, in his poem "Retirement":

But now alike, gay widow, virgin, wife,
Ingenious to diversify dull life,
In coaches, chaises, caravans and hoys,
Fly to the coast for daily, nightly joys,
And all, impatient of dry land, agree
With one consent to rush into the sea.⁵¹

On 4 July Edward Knight escorted his sister Cassandra to Milton (near Sheerness) so she could, as her niece Fanny Knight reports, "visit Uncle Chas. on board the Namur."⁵² Fanny must have returned briefly to the ship to welcome Cassandra and show her around their quarters. Jane did not accompany Cassandra on this visit. Their niece, Anna Austen, had recently arrived at Chawton Cottage for a three-month stay, and by this time Jane and Cassandra did not leave their mother alone without one of them there to assist. Moreover, Jane was probably hard at work on the manuscript of *Pride and Prejudice*, which she subsequently sold to Thomas Egerton, the publisher, in late November for £110.⁵³ Her brother Edward's goodwill made Cassandra's visit to the *Namur* possible. She was already visiting at his estate, Godmersham Park, and from there he escorted her to a location where Charles met her and took her to the *Namur*. On the strength of Cassandra's subsequent report, Jane could picture the details of Fanny's situation, the family's accommodation, the positioning of the *Namur* at her anchorage, and the general feel and climate of Sheerness and the Nore.

Later that month Fanny paid her first visit to Godmersham Park, Edward Knight's handsome country estate situated eight miles south of Canterbury, Kent, in the Stour River valley and about twenty-six miles southwest of Sheerness. The mansion was situated in a fine landscaped park, with wooded downlands rising in folds behind it to the west. The harmony of the setting was enhanced by the sheep grazing in the meadows and a herd of 600 fallow deer browsing in the parkland (Fig. 28). Charles's older brother, Edward,

Fig. 28   Godmersham Park, Kent, the primary seat of Edward Knight. Set in an idyllic park, here Fanny enjoyed the luxury of "carriages and coachmen, fine wines and ice, late dining and lady's maids."

had been very fortunate. Adopted in his teens by his father's childless third cousin, Thomas Knight, and his wife, Catherine, Edward was made their heir with the expectation of later inheriting not only Godmersham Park, but considerable property in Hampshire, including Chawton Great House and estate and additional lands at nearby Steventon and Winchester. In 1798 Mrs Knight decided that Edward should take possession of his inheritance during her lifetime.[54] Thus Edward and his family moved into Godmersham, but it was only after Mrs Knight died in November 1812 that he formally inherited the estate and officially changed his family's name to Knight.[55]

Fanny had been in England for over a year, but it is unlikely she had encountered the calibre of architectural and decorative refinement she now found at Godmersham. On the approach through the park, she caught sight of the impressive red-brick, eighteenth-century Palladian-style house, built in the 1730s by Thomas Brodnax and enlarged in the 1780s. On arrival, Fanny entered the house through an elegant hall decorated with fine white plaster work, beautifully carved wood ornamentation, inset statuary, and a magnificent white marble fireplace. High on the walls was a decorative frieze that incorporated medallions of Roman emperors and coats of arms of the May and Brodnax families. The ceiling was wonderful to behold, being "divided by beams into rectangular compartments enriched with stucco fruit and flowers. The floor had its original stone flags with insets of black marble."[56] The total effect of the room was of light, luxury, and refinement. If this was only the hall, Fanny must have wondered what grandeur she would meet elsewhere. She was not to be disappointed.

The nearby drawing room was equally splendid, decorated with a "voluptuous frieze in which female masks alternate with scallop shells and acanthus leaves."[57] Elsewhere the design incorporated motifs of musical instruments, baskets of fruit, and flowers. A superb black and white marble fireplace completed the effect. The adjacent rooms also invited Fanny's notice: the bay-windowed breakfast room, the library, and the south drawing room with its unparalleled views of the park and the elevation of the North Downs. Visitors to Godmersham today can see the wonderfully opulent hall and drawing room much as Fanny did in 1812.

Charles must have already told Fanny about the pleasures of visiting Godmersham. Since 1798, he had enjoyed autumn shooting parties on the estate whenever he happened to be home in England at that time of year. He had been so engaged when, in the words of his niece, Fanny Knight, "Uncle Charles was sent for by the horrible abominable beastly Admiralty & was away at half past 2."[58] She is referring to the occasion on 11 October 1804 when Charles was summoned to London, having been commissioned into the new sloop *Indian* the day before. This was the fortunate posting that had brought him to Bermuda by the next January and made possible his fortuitous meeting with Fanny.

Charles's brothers and sisters greatly appreciated Godmersham and the fine welcome they always received there. Jane had earlier testified to the "Elegance & Ease & Luxury" of Godmersham, the place where she intended to "eat Ice & drink French wine, & be above Vulgar Economy."[59] Her brother Henry, always a grateful guest, expressed his thanks in verse. After one particularly enjoyable visit, he sent Edward a poem titled "Godmersham, The Temple of Delight." It read:

Gentle Pilgrim, rest thy feet,
Open is the gate to thee;
Do not doubt that thou shalt meet
Mirth and Hospitality.
Elegance and Grace shall charm thee
Reason shall with wit unite –
Sterling sense shall here inform thee
How domestic love can find
All the blessings, which combined
Make the Temple of Delight.[60]

Such a gesture no doubt pleased Edward immensely. His son, George, who was seventeen when Fanny first came to Godmersham, responded altogether differently. He created the following parody of his uncle Henry's efforts. It is known under the title "George Knight to his Dog Pincher."

Gentle Pincher, cock thy tail,
Open is the door to thee;
Enter, & there ne'er shall fail,
Mirth and Hospitality –
Partridge bones, & Pork shall charm thee
Mutton shall with Veal unite;
Sterling Beef shall then inform thee
How domestic Dogs can find
All the savings, which combined
Make the Temple of Delight –[61]

George, who later married the widow of Admiral Nelson's brother, was described by his nephew as "one of those men who are clever enough to do almost anything, but live to their lives' end very comfortably doing nothing."[62]

Jane Austen was also inspired to situate Godmersham in poetry. When her brother Frank and his new wife Mary, née Gibson, spent their honeymoon there in July 1806, she penned a short verse describing the bridal couple's arrival, written from the point of view of her niece, Fanny Knight. With a single change in name – (Uncle Francis) becomes (Uncle Charles) – and one change in rhyme the lines are charmingly apt for the first arrival of another sister-in-law, Fanny, on 21 July 1812.

Down the hill they're swift proceeding
Now they skirt the Park around;
Lo! The Cattle sweetly feeding
Scamper, startled at the sound!

Run, my Brothers, to the Pier Gate!
Throw it open, very wide!
Let it not be said that we're late
In welcoming my Uncle's Bride!

To the house the chaise advances;
Now it stops – They're here, they're here!
How d'ye do, my Uncle [Charles]?
How does do your Lady dear?[63]

While they were at Godmersham, a large attentive staff guaranteed every comfort for Fanny, Charles, and their children. Sadly, Edward's wife, Elizabeth, had died in childbirth four years earlier, but his eldest daughter, another Fanny, aged nineteen, proved to be a good hostess and an effective organizer (Fig. 29). During their fortnight's visit from 21 July to 5 August, she arranged an outing to the nearby cathedral town of Canterbury and she walked with "Uncle Chas. & At. F.," as her pocketbook names them, "to the top of the [North] Downs"[64] so they could admire the fine views in every direction. The surrounds of the house were very pleasing. Fanny could choose to walk in the gardens, through the lime tree avenue and shrubberies, or within the wooded plantation on Canterbury Hill. Just outside the park, she could climb "a small rounded hill on top of which, within the woods, was a summer house which had been built by the Knights earlier in the eighteenth century as a Grecian temple in the Doric style with a portico entrance of fluted columns and marble steps, and a fine grassy walk leading up to it."[65] Family tradition says that Jane Austen liked to take her current

Fig. 29   Fanny Knight, as drawn by her aunt, Cassandra Austen, was the young chatelaine of Godmersham Park during visits by Fanny and Charles.

manuscript to the summer house, as it was a place of welcome seclusion. Fanny Knight may have introduced Fanny Austen to other routes on the estate, known as the "River Walk" and the "Serpentine Walk."[66]

On 27 July, Edward Knight drove Fanny to nearby Eastwell Park, home of George Finch-Hatton, the former member of Parliament for Rochester, Kent. The Knights were very friendly with the various generations of the Finch-Hatton family, so Fanny would be very welcome to tour their attractive Park. This was a property widely admired for its deer herd, its fine oaks, beeches, and ancient yew trees. On the top of a high hill in the northwest part of the Park was an octagonal-shaped clearing where eight avenues, known as the Star Walks, had been cut. From this high vantage point, on a fine day it was possible to see the course of the river Medway all the way to Sheerness, and, in the far distance, the area of the Nore anchorage.

The hilltop viewing point would be an obvious place for Edward to take Fanny. As she gazed toward Sheerness, she was looking right towards the place where the *Namur* was riding at anchor. What might she be thinking if she paused to contrast her cramped, makeshift accommodation there with the luxuries that Godmersham offered? Fanny's letters to date give the impression that she had accepted their shipboard quarters as home, their own private family preserve, at least for now. Fanny had the gift of making the best of a situation. For the time being, it would be delightful to enjoy the luxury of the "carriages and coachmen, the [fine] wines and ice, late dining and ladies' maids"[67] that the Knights were so willingly providing.

Once back on the *Namur* Charles faced a serious challenge. The Admiralty had set up a series of signal stations at various prominent locations along the coast. These facilities were required to observe ships' movements in adjacent waters, to warn any merchant ships if enemy activity was detected, and to inform the local militia should the enemy attempt a landing.[68] The *Namur* was a key link in this chain of signal stations. Early in September it was claimed that a message had been sent from the *Namur* stating that "the enemy have sailed from the Texel" (one of the string of West Friesen islands in the Netherlands that provided protection for the Dutch naval base at Amsterdam). If authentic, this message would have been of the greatest military importance, indicating that the enemy fleet had exited the Texel channel from the Dutch mainland and had entered the North Sea. Charles objected vehemently and insisted that no such message had been sent from the *Namur* to the next station, Wakering Stairs, on the Essex coast. He produced the complete semaphore log for 2 September as proof of the innocence of his officers and men in this matter.[69] Sir Thomas Williams stood by Charles,[70] and the Admiralty eventually dropped the issue. Whether there actually had been such a message sent or, if so, by whom, is unknowable. The crucial point is that Charles was cleared of any wrongdoing. This was important, for in order to advance his career, he had to avoid any marks of censure on his service record. Even so, the period of uncertainty before his name was cleared was surely stressful for Fanny, especially as she was entering the third trimester of her third pregnancy.

In October 1812 Fanny's father decided it was time to liquidate his real estate assets in St George's, Bermuda, and thus arranged for the sale at auction of his "commodious dwelling house" with two large gardens.[71] Thus, a very personal link with Fanny's past was severed. For someone who had yet to establish her own permanent home, the loss of a beloved family property, where she had been happy and thrived, must have been bittersweet. Although her uncle Alexander Ball still lived in Casino, her mother's original family home in St George's, this house did not mean nearly as much to Fanny as the property where she had lived with her parents, and later with Esther and her family, which was now for sale.

Sometime in November Fanny took Cassy and Harriet to her parents' home on Keppel Street for the weeks preceding her confinement. Fanny was grateful for the company and support of her mother, who had herself experienced nine births, the presence of her sister Harriet, and access to a midwife to manage the birth if deemed necessary. As Amanda Vickery has commented, "a crescendo of anxiety and hope was almost invariably experienced by the family of the labouring mother,"[72] not to mention the mother herself. Fanny was spared any complications with the baby's delivery, and her namesake, Frances Palmer Austen, to be known as Fan, joined the family on 1 December 1812. Now they were five.

CHAPTER 6

Carrying On:
Challenges and Choices,
1813

FANNY AND HER GROWING FAMILY welcomed the New Year at 22 Keppel Street. Her confinement and lying-in were now events in the past, but the comforts of her parents' home had their attractions nonetheless. Freed from household responsibilities, she was able to regain her strength after the rigours of giving birth. She could attend to the needs of little Fan, while others willingly cared for Cassy and Harriet. On 20 January Charles requested seven more days leave, perhaps because of business in London but more likely because he wanted to see Fanny fully recovered before her return to the *Namur*. Whether in person or by letter, Charles was also seeking another appointment, this time in the active sea service.

In light of current British naval policy, Charles had grounds to be hopeful he would get such a commission. Britain had declared war on the United States in June 1812, and by September his former commander, Admiral Sir John Warren, was once more in North America, where he was commander-in-chief of the consolidated North American and West Indies squadrons. Warren's first instructions from the Admiralty were to broker a peace with the Americans. When that overture failed, he vigorously lobbied for more frigates and smaller cruisers to defend the convoys of British merchantmen against the relentless attacks of American privateers. Warren also needed vessels to form a blockade of portions of the 2,000-nautical-miles-long Atlantic coast of America, not an easy job given its innumerable harbours and inlets. This proposed blockade was a key piece of a strategy designed to wage economic warfare on the Americans and to prevent privateers and American warships from leaving port.[1] Charles hoped to become part of this action.

Jane Austen empathized with Charles's continuing disappointment. On 24 January she wrote to Cassandra with a characteristic touch of irony: "Poor Charles & his frigate. But there could be no chance of his having one, while it was thought such a certainty."[2] It did not improve his spirits that his current job made him responsible for manning some of the frigates that would be crossing the Atlantic while he was stuck back in England on the all but stationary *Namur*.

While Charles was irritated by the lack of front-line naval activity, his sister Jane was active and happy. She was deeply involved with her writing and already about halfway through *Mansfield Park*. To her great delight the first edition of *Sense and Sensibility* was sold out by June, and she was particularly thrilled by the very favourable reception of *Pride and Prejudice*, the novel she called "my own darling Child."[3] Her elder brother, Henry, despatched pre-publication copies to Charles and Edward, although for some reason Jane had wanted the very first copies to go to Steventon (for James) and Portsmouth (for Frank). With an early copy in hand, Charles and Fanny were in a position to read what was considered "the fashionable novel for the spring of 1813."[4] Perhaps Charles read it aloud to her, since reading to others was a highly favoured practice within the Austen family. Aboard ship, any shared reading in the evening took place in the evocative atmosphere of flickering candle-light and against the background sounds of wind and water.

As the weeks dragged on, Charles grew increasingly frustrated by the restriction of the anchorage at the Nore and the task of supervising all the naval recruits and pressed men under his control. As he was in charge of a perpetually circulating population of sailors, some of whom were in service against their will, it was difficult, if not impossible, to establish an enduring sense of community aboard the *Namur*. On his other vessels he had fostered an esprit de corps that he found very satisfying. According to Henry Wilkinson, "Captain C.J. Austen ran a good ship [during his five years on the *Indian*] and could count on his men."[5] Nonetheless, Charles struggled on. He was a diligent officer who kept his men busy with their usual duties, and he continued to instruct midshipmen and candidates for the lieutenant's examination. Fanny was taxed with the management of their family, including a new baby on board. It must have affected her spirits when, as the weeks went by, there was no new commission in sight for Charles. They were a close couple and Fanny shared the realities of his disappointment, although given her more recent experience of togetherness on the *Namur*, she would not have wanted their inevitable separation.

By 1813 the charm of living at sea had paled for Fanny. She felt captive when fog confined her to the vessel for long intervals. Her eldest daughter, Cassy, suffered horribly from seasickness, and Fanny hated to have any of her children on the *Namur* when gales raged and the damp chill penetrated and persisted. She periodically found it necessary to send one or more of her daughters to the more congenial quarters of her parents' home on Keppel Street or to Jane and Cassandra at Chawton Cottage in Hampshire. Thus, her family group was often incomplete.

Unmarried aunts were expected to help with the care and education of nieces and nephews, should their services be required. Fanny was fortunate that her children had three aunts who could be reached within a day or two's journey. Each aunt had a different style of mothering. The diligent Harriet Palmer was scrupulous with her charges' health, yet probably little given to imaginative play. Fanny's mother, Dorothy Palmer, also helped with child care on some occasions, even coming aboard the *Namur* in November 1813 to assist with baby Fan. Essentially, however, the children were Harriet's responsibility when they were at Keppel Street.

When the children went to Chawton, however, Cassandra and Jane Austen looked after them. According to Caroline Austen, James Austen's daughter,[6] when Cassy stayed at Chawton she was "under the special tutelage of Aunt Cass."[7] In 1813 Jane Austen was finishing the final draft of her manuscript of *Mansfield Park*,[8] so Cassandra organized the children's daily routines. She did most of their caring and nurturing, although Jane was also somewhat involved. Cassandra particularly encouraged her godchild's literacy skills and the development of good manners. Perhaps she introduced Cassy to the family copy of the moral and educational story *The History of Little Goody Two Shoes.*[9]

Jane excelled at keeping children entertained and was known for her "power of telling amusing stories to [her] nephews and nieces."[10] She had her own resources for entertaining Cassy, if she chose to use them. While unpacking family possessions after the move to Chawton Cottage in 1809, Jane is thought to have found her earlier manuscript notebooks.[11] *Volume the First* included "Sr William Montague" and" Memoirs of Mr. Clifford," which had been expressly written for Charles Austen when he was a little older than Cassy. What better vehicles for his daughter's current edification? For example, "Sir William Montague" addresses the multiple and sequential love interests of the sporting seventeen-year-old hero, Sir William, and the convoluted relationships that ensue. There is plenty of action, a funny place name, the mock-Irish "Kilhoobery Park," and much to laugh about. Jane discussed and may have even edited several of her early stories between 1809 and 1811 at Chawton in the company of Anna and James Edward Austen, who were themselves interested in writing.[12] Now that Jane had revived her juvenilia, perhaps she liked the symmetry of retelling to the visiting Cassy stories she had written for Charles.[13]

Recalling Jane's gifts for entertaining, Caroline Austen commented that "we often had amusements in which my Aunt was very helpful."[14] Caroline remembered that if her two cousins Cassy and Mary Jane, Frank Austen's eldest daughter,[15] were at Chawton, Aunt Jane "would furnish us with what we wanted from her wardrobe, and *she* would often be the entertaining visitor in our make beleive[16] house. She amused us in various ways – *once* I remember in giving a conversation as between myself and my two cousins, supposed to be grown up, the day after a ball."[17] Jane's imaginative interactions with her nieces may have been intended to achieve more than amusement. Children were expected to display good manners in social situations. Jane's invented dialogues with her nieces may have been a way to show them how polite conversation could be expected to proceed.

When their mother died suddenly in 1808, Jane comforted her young nephews, George Knight, aged thirteen, and Edward, aged fourteen, by keeping them occupied with their favourite games: bilbocatch, spillikins, paper ships, riddles, conundrums, and cards.[18] Bilbocatch is played with a wooden cup with a handle and a ball attached to the cup by a string. The object is to flick the ball upward and catch it in the cup. Jane Austen was particularly proficient at bilbocatch; her nephew George was described as "indefatigable" at this game. Spillikins, or pick-up-sticks, involves tossing a number of thin sticks in a random heap and then trying in turn to remove one stick at a time without moving any of the others. Though simple, both games demand dexterity and concentration, and they continue to be played for their fun and challenge.

Fanny was very grateful to Harriet, Cassandra, and Jane for their help, but at the same time she bitterly regretted the necessity of separation from her children. She missed her older girls terribly, thought of them constantly, and wrote about them in detail in her letters. For example, in an October letter to James Esten, she describes Harriet, at three and a half, as "grown quite out of your remembrance & is thought like me" and "my last little Pet Fanny," now aged ten months, as "a very fine Child, she has got three Teeth & begins to trot about nicely, but is not yet weaned."[19]

An unexpected event broke the tedium of the winter naval routine when Charles claimed involvement in a prize capture. According to the entry in the *Namur's* logbook for 22 February 1813, HMS *Scipio*, bound for Ostend, Belgium, with a cargo of cotton, together with her prize capture, a privateer named the *Courier*, was found by the *Namur* stranded on the Middle Sand about a mile from the Nore anchorage. Now, a British vessel, the *Scipio* had been a Dutch corvette (20 guns) captured by the British in 1807. Once the vessels' nationalities had been identified and the situation assessed, Charles sent a message to the *Scipio* that "a claim would be laid in from the Flag Ship at the Nore as joint captures"[20] on the part of the *Scipio* and the *Namur*. Unfortunately, the outcome of this claim is not known.

On 11 May Fanny, Charles, and their two youngest children joined a large family gathering at Chawton. It was early summer and the cottage's garden was a delight. Peonies, pinks, Sweet William, columbines, and syringas were coming into bloom in the shrubbery boarder, and the Orleans plums and greengages were setting in the orchard.[21] Fanny and her family slept at the cottage but were often at Chawton Great House, which was currently occupied by Edward Knight and his immediate family while Godmersham was being painted.

Chawton Great House had its origins in Elizabethan times but had been subsequently altered by generations of Knights (Fig. 30). Here was a house that retained some of its original sixteenth-century features, such as a fireplace backed with herring-bone brickwork and richly carved oak

Fig. 30   *Chawton House and Church*, 1809. Fanny would have attended services here when she visited Charles's relatives at Chawton.

panelling in many rooms, including the Great Hall and the dining room.[22] In the ground floor library hung a family treasure, the Lewknor armorial table carpet. Created in 1564, this magnificent tapestry records the pedigree of the family by incorporating into its design the heraldic arms of generations of Lewknor marriages.[23] It was an impressive record of family alliances and itself beautiful to behold. It is now in the collection of the Metropolitan Museum of Art, New York.

Fourteen-year-old Fanny Knight, on first seeing Chawton Great House in 1807, described it as "a fine large <u>old</u> house." She was struck by the layout, noting there were "such a number of old irregular passages &c &c that it is very entertaining to explore them, & often when I think myself miles <u>away</u> from one part of the house I find a passage or entrance close to it, & I don't know when I shall be quite mistress of all the intricate, and different ways."[24] Perhaps on the occasion of Fanny Austen's visit, Fanny Knight offered her a tour of the warren of passages of the Great House for the sheer amusement of them both.

At this time the Austen family was in mourning for Henry's wife, Eliza, who died aged fifty on 25 April and was buried in London on 1 May. At Henry's request, Jane had been with her in London during her final days. Eliza would be remembered in the family for her vivacity, her style, and her adventurous spirit. This sad event, though, did not put an end to sociability. Mary, James Austen's wife, and her daughter Caroline stayed at the Great House for twelve days; Henry Austen spent five days with the family before he drove Jane to London in his curricle on 19 May. Fanny's own party was complete when Cassy and her nursemaid Betsy arrived at Chawton the next day.

The Knights' hospitality maintained its usual high standard. On 17 May, Fanny, Charles, Jane, Cassandra, and Martha Lloyd dined at the Great House and enjoyed games in the evening. Perhaps those assembled played charades, a favourite pastime within the Austen family. On an earlier occasion, Charles had contributed one of his own:

Without me divided, fair ladies I ween
At a ball or a concert you'll never be seen
You must do me together or safely I'd swear
Whatever your carriage you'd never get there

Charles's solution was a light.[25] Fanny was surely impressed, if not a little overpowered, by the display of wit and intelligence whenever she observed Charles, Cassandra, and Jane exercising their creative powers at charades. Before she and Charles departed, they dined at least two more times at the Great House. One evening they played a parlour game known to the Austens as "jeu de violon," although it is a puzzle what it involved.[26] Their hostess, Fanny Knight, described the occasion as "merry."[27]

Two and a half weeks after their arrival at Chawton, Fanny and Charles collected little Fan and returned to the *Namur* but left Cassy and Harriet with their Austen aunts for most of June. On this occasion Jane found Cassy, now almost four and a half, to be very trying – observing that she "ought to be a very nice Child – Nature has done enough for her – but Method has been wanting." In contrast, little Harriet, who was just over three, was declared "a truely sweet-tempered little Darling."[28] Jane was pleased when

Fanny and Charles later judged their recently returned daughters to be improved in health (Harriet) and in manners (Cassy). We know that Jane Austen espoused firm principles concerning child rearing and that she subscribed to the necessity of bringing children up "with a proper sense of what was expected of them."[29] Thus it is not surprising that she was particularly attuned to the quality of a child's manners and standard of politeness.

A critical undercurrent persists in some of Jane's subsequent references to Cassy's public and private behaviour. Just prior to Fanny and Charles's visit to Godmersham in October 1813, Jane feared that Cassy would "disappoint me by some immediate disagreeableness" and that a "cross Child" will limit Charles's enjoyment of his visit.[30] Cassy was, even from her mother's description, a sometimes obstinate, head-strong girl.

In many families, adults periodically find a child's behaviour both irritating and disappointing, but at the same time they still love those children for who they are as individuals. Jane's thinking reflects this attitude when she observed that although Frank Austen's children are "sometimes very noisy & not under such Order as they ought and easily might, I cannot help liking them, & even loving them."[31] In the course of her 1813–14 letters, Jane speaks as if her attitude towards Cassy is on balance an affectionate and even understanding one. In July 1813 she related to Frank that "Charles's little girls were with us about a month, & had so endeared themselves that we were quite sorry to have them go."[32] By November 1814 Jane refers to her niece as "that puss Cassy,"[33] words that have an affectionate tone.

While she was staying at Chawton Cottage in March 1814, Cassy received an unexpected message from Aunt Jane in London, carried in a letter to Cassandra. It read: "I hope she found my Bed comfortable last night & has not filled it with fleas,"[34] a joke that continued a week later with the follow-up message that "if Cassandra has filled my Bed with fleas, I am sure they must bite herself."[35] The reference to fleas is surely a jest on Jane's part, for Cassy has come to Chawton from the attentive care of Aunt Harriet at 22 Keppel Street and is unlikely to be harbouring bugs. In early January 1817 Cassy received a charming ten-line puzzle letter from Jane in which each word is spelled backwards.[36] It begins with a traditional greeting, expressed as "I hsiw uoy a yppah wen raey." A curious Cassy was left to decode her aunt's message of "I wish you a happy new year."[37]

The meaning of Jane's remarks about Cassy's looks is a matter of some speculation. Writing to Cassandra in October 1813, she decries her niece's "very Palmery" features, adding that she "never knew a Wife's family features to have such strong influence."[38] Perhaps Jane simply meant that Cassy did not have the dark looks that characterized so many of the Austens. Although Cassy might be said to look like Fanny, who was very blond and pretty, dark colouring, in Jane's view, was the superior attribute. Yet, there may be, in Jane's remarks, a pejorative tone that goes further than the mere matter of hair and eye colouring. Other members of the Palmer family, whom Jane had already met, had indifferent looks. Harriet was plain; Fanny's father, John Grove Palmer, according to a likely portrait of him, had a jowly face and a severe mien. Does Jane fear that Cassy is coming to resemble her Palmer aunt or grandfather? At the time, Cassy was not yet five and her adult appearance was yet to become obvious. It was rather too early to judge how attractive Cassy would turn out to be. In fact, a watercolour sketch of her in adult life shows a very attractive young woman with brown hair.

Between July and September 1813, Fanny and her girls, together with her parents, sister Harriet, and nephew Palmer spent another holiday at Southend. The *Namur* was visible to them anchored at the Nore, and Charles joined them from the ship when he could. His presence was duly noted by the *Chelmsford Chronicle* for 13 August, which listed "Captain and Mrs. Austin" [*sic*] among the "fashionable arrivals," a category that included "The Right Hon. Lord Petrie, Mr Alderman Aikins M.P. and family, the Miss Bryants, Mr Salt and Mr Champerdowne."

The many amenities of Southend that they had discovered the year before were still available to be enjoyed. Fanny may have particularly benefited from membership in the thriving circulating library. This would entitle her to borrow books on a wide range of subjects, including the latest novels, biography, poetry, and history. After periods of isolation on the *Namur*, going out to select a book of one's choice with the prospect of later returning it for another was surely a pleasure. More than simple pleasure, the introduction of circulating libraries around the country gave genteel woman, like Fanny, an opportunity to step outside the limitations of their domestic spheres and exercise a new independence of choice in what they might read. Access to circulating libraries was a means to the intellectual liberation of women.

Jane Austen identified the importance of the circulating libraries in women's lives. In *Mansfield Park*, the fictional Fanny Price feels quite empowered by her membership in the Portsmouth library. In the novel, some of her wealth "found its way to a circulating library ... She became a subscriber ... a renter, a chuser of books!"[39] This freedom amazed and delighted her and, in addition, greatly pleased her because she could share her choices in the improvement of her sister Susan's education and taste.

Fanny's letters from 1813[40] continue to address practical matters, but at the same time her tone becomes increasingly more personal. She reflects with some passion about the sort of life she is leading. Fanny often sees the irony in her situation, and says so. She expresses frustration when her servants are unsatisfactory, and she registers concern when she perceives that Charles is unhappy with his current posting. Apart from sometimes admitting to tiredness, there is a certain stoicism about Fanny. She never complains – at least in her letters – if she feels ill, anxious, or depressed because of her pregnancies.

Just before the family leaves the *Namur* for another visit to Godmersham, Fanny writes a long and candid letter to James Esten in Bermuda. This letter, like some of her others, bears a clear imprint of her name "Fanny" in the red wax with which she sealed it.

Namur 4th. October [1813]

My dearest Brother

How truly thankfull must we all feel for my beloved Sisters preservation from that tremendous hurricane, which by the papers, appears to have done incalculable mischief in your part of the World; I am glad however to find that you have individually suffered very little: it afforded you a good opporty. of trying your new purchase (Belvidere) which my Sister writes word [of,] stood the gale uncommonly well. Tell her she must write me a particular account of the house, viz: which she makes sitting & dining rooms of &c: & whether she has a nice garden & who keeps it in order, a letter of this kind will be very interesting to Capt. Austen & myself both; for we often very often think & talk of you all; & shall I say, sometimes wish ourselves amongst you again; thus it is you see, with us fickle mortals we are never satisfied –

We came on board on the 20th Sepr. after spending 3 Months pleasantly enough at Southend; we had the comfort of our Keppel Street friends society &

but for the illness of my Nurse should really have been very happy. Your dear Boy enjoyed himself thoroughly, he made several friends who were very kind & attentive to him, but notwithstanding all this, he did not shew the smallest reluctance in returning to School: he is a sweet, interesting Boy & promises fair to be every thing you cou'd wish; our accounts of him from Town are very satisfactory, but of course Harriet will give you a more particular account of him than I can do —

How does dear little Hamilton get on with his reading? Cassandra begins now to read very prettily, but I have had an amazing deal of trouble with her not owing to a dulness of comprehension; but a dislike to learning; she grows tall & thin, but I do not think her countenance has changed at all since you saw her; she remembers the names of many of her Bda. friends & beg'd me when she heard me reading your letter, to send her love & a kiss to Uncle & Aunt Esten, Hammy & Uncle Ball. Harriet is in Town with her Aunt, she has grown quite out of your remembrance & is thought like me. My last little Pet Fanny is a very fine Child, she has got three Teeth & begins to trot about nicely, but is not yet weaned — Tell Sister Het that I am again reduced to one Servant[41] for I was obliged to send my Nurse home to her friends poor thing, she was an excellent Servant & I have sustained a great loss in her, but her health was not equal to the situation

Capt. Austen has given up all expectation of a Frigate for the Present, Coquette is paid off, wherefore nothing more is to be expected from that quarter & I rather think we shall remain here some Months longer, for Lord Melville does not seem disposed to give our Admiral[42] any thing better the only two commands that were vacant have just been disposed of, viz, the River, & Cork.[43] Dear Admiral Sawyer has the command but I am sorry to hear that Mrs. Sawyer is not well enough to accompany him there, at least for the present. We often receive letters from Lady Warren to enquire about the Bermuda convoys from which it appears that she has not yet given up the idea of going out there; she is like some <u>other Ladies of our acquaintance</u> never happy but when she is with her husband.[44]

I am afraid that three years indulgence have quite spoiled me, & do not know how I shall reconcile myself to Capt. Austens going to Sea again: he is very anxious to be in active service just now & I am of course obliged to acquesce in the propriety of his wishing it but something tells me that we are much happier in our present situation: however that being only a temporary one, it is but right that he should endeavour to be in the way of making a little Money while there is an opporty. I look forward with great pleasure to the prospect of again visiting dear little Bermuda for shou'd he be fortunate enough to get a Frigate before the American War is over he will certainly endeavour to get out on that Station & has promised that I shall accompany him.

Pray remember me very affectionately to Mrs. Dickenson & her children tell the former that either Capt. A. or I mean to write her in a few days; & say to Catharine that it will give me great pleasure to receive a letter from her. One of us will write to my Uncle by the same conveyance. Say every thing kind for me to dear Mrs. Holliday[45] I hope soon to be personally acquainted with her Husband, whom I have heard spoken of by all who know him as a most amiable deserving Man. I should like exceedingly to hear from her, but do not know how to make such a request, as I ought to have written to her many months ago, but you can answer for my being a miserable correspondent. How does David[46] go on? is he in want of Cloathes? pray tell him I have been very much pleased with the good accounts I have had of him & give my kind remembrances to poor Catharine & the rest of her children & also to my old Sert. Molly. I shall not teaze you with enumeration of my friends but beg you to mention me to all you know I value & esteem

Adieu my dearest Brother & now you must divide what of my love remains between yourself Wife & dear little Boy, believing me always your most affte.

F.F. Austen

Fanny is thankful that the Estens have survived a recent tremendous hurricane in Bermuda. She is interested to hear more about their new mansion house, Belvidere, located on a desirable ten-acre site situated off the Cut Road just outside of St George's, where there was a good view of the vessels entering the harbour. Her desire to know more about its amenities reflects a strong sisterly interest, yet this is a poignant request, given that Fanny has no assurance that she will ever return home to Bermuda or when she will have her own home on any shore. Her letter continues with references to the children dearest to her. She praises her nephew Palmer's mature behaviour; she makes queries about his brother Hamilton; and she proudly reports on the progress of her own girls.

Yet above all, Fanny is very concerned about Charles's stalemated career. Expectations regarding the *Coquette*, a sloop of similar size and guns to the

Indian, have come to naught. It may seem puzzling why Charles even found her desirable: she was so much smaller than the vessels he has become used to commanding – the *Cleopatra* and the *Namur* – and a commission into her would cause him a substantial reduction in his rate of pay. Yet there may have been several reasons why he should try for the *Coquette*. Perhaps the attraction derived from the assumption that she would be remaining on the North American Station where Charles would see truly active service once again, the bonus being a chance to capture a valuable prize vessel, and Fanny might return with their children to revisit her "dear little Bermuda," a consoling prospect for her if she must be temporarily separated from Charles. In addition, he already knew his time on the *Namur* was coming to an end in 1814 and Sir Thomas Williams himself had no new commission in sight that might require a flag-captain. Charles must also have been aware that too many officers were competing for the few ships available, so that any vessel, even one as small as the *Coquette* – typically a craft for a first-time commander – would be better than half pay on land. That would be a double disappointment, offering much less pay and no naval activity at all. As it turned out, the *Coquette* would soon be taken out of service altogether.[47]

With great candour, Fanny articulates the dilemma she now faces. If Charles stays on the *Namur*, she will be happy to be living on board with him even though not very comfortably accommodated at sea. Yet Charles's captaincy of the *Namur* will finish in a year, and meanwhile his service on her conflicts with his great desire to be more actively engaged. Fanny is struggling to be a dutiful naval wife who, in her own words, is "of course obliged to acquesce in the propriety of his wishing [to be at sea]." This comment is revealing. It is quite appropriate and makes good sense for Charles's career, and also for his family's well-being, that he should seek command of a ship in the active sea service. But Fanny seemingly responds out of a sense of duty contrary to her private sensibilities. She does not feel sufficiently empowered to protest; she feels obliged to comply without objection with Charles's stated intentions. At the same time, Fanny does not know how she would "reconcile herself" to Charles's absence. She wants so much to retain and sustain family intimacy, and his departure would destroy the sense of close togetherness that she is trying so hard to perpetuate. In this moment of introspection and self-realization, Fanny displays a new maturity of character and of judgment about her situation. She determines to exercise self-control, so she does not betray to Charles her real ambivalence about his hopes and their mixed consequences for her.[48]

As Fanny frames her concerns, she identifies with the plight of other naval wives who are left on their own. She mentions two in particular and thus highlights the realities of all naval wives far away from their husbands. She empathizes with Mrs Sawyer, who is regrettably too ill to join "dear" Admiral Sawyer on the station at Cork, which is the home base for the Irish squadron. Fanny knows Admiral Sawyer well, as he was Charles's commander-in-chief in Halifax and Bermuda, in 1810–11.[49] She understands Lady Warren's determination to find a way to join Sir John as he commands the North American Station for a second time. As she observes, Lady Warren is like herself: she is "never happy but when she is with her husband."

While Fanny reflects on her feelings and fears, she admits to the "rightness" of Charles's making money when there is an opportunity. A posting back to the North American Station would give Charles the chance to earn prize money while the American war ran its course. Many of their naval friends, including James, Lord Townshend, of HMS *Aeolus*, Samuel Pechell, now captain on HMS *San Domingo* (74 guns), Admiral Warren's flagship, Frederick Hickey of the *Atalante*, Henry Jane on the *Indian*, and Philip Broke on HMS *Shannon* (38 guns) were there and regularly making prize captures. Captain Broke,[50] a former classmate of Charles's at the Royal Naval Academy, Portsmouth, achieved both fame and fortune when he challenged, fought, and took as prize the prestigious American vessel USS *Chesapeake* (44 guns) on 1 June 1813.[51] He received prize money amounting to £2,449, roughly equivalent to between £250,000 and £375,000 in today's currency.[52] Between 1812 and 1814 the Halifax and Bermuda Vice Admiralty Courts awarded 845 vessels to their captors and restored only 90 to their owners.[53] No wonder Charles felt he was in a backwater and missing the action.

Fanny and Charles must have spent a good part of 1813 discussing his career options, his chances for a favourable posting, and the possible consequences for her should he receive a new commission. She wrote to James Esten that if Charles "shou'd be fortunate enough to get a Frigate before the American war is over he will certainly endeavour to get out on that Station & has promised that I shall accompany him." This seemed her best hope in the situation. There is a measure of bravery in Fanny's willingness to go back to

North America with her three little girls in the middle of a war being fought in those waters. Admiral Sawyer, the commander on the North American Station until autumn 1812, had earlier left his wife at home in England, since he did "not want to expose her to the chance of American warfare."[54]

In the midst of their speculations and hopes, Fanny and Charles were most likely thinking that Charles's warm relations with Admiral Warren and his close acquaintance with the American coast increased the likelihood that he would be given a commission that would take him back to his previous station. Unknown to them, circumstances were not in Charles's favour. Admiral Warren's earlier influence was now limited owing to his strained relations with Robert Dundas, Lord Melville, the powerful First Lord of the Admiralty since 1812. Neither man liked the other; moreover, they had differing political bases of support. According to Andrew Lambert, Lord Melville had his own agenda. He spent "time and effort managing his extensive patronage interests, providing Warren with a list of promotion candidates on all three American stations and the precise order in which they should be promoted."[55] As Melville's political power in Scotland depended on his effective use of patronage, he was ill-disposed to granting any personal requests that Warren might make. In consequence, Warren had limited input in decisions about which vessels would be assigned to his command. The fact that Lady Warren was never given permission to join her husband in North America is perhaps more evidence that the Admiralty was not supportive of Warren's wishes.[56]

Charles was probably not privy to the depth of animosity between Melville and Warren, and for some months he retained the hope that a vessel would be forthcoming. In addition, Charles's chances for a North American deployment were limited by the small number of frigates allotted to the station. As of 1 December 1813, there were only nineteen ships – four frigates of 40 guns, eight of 38 guns, four of 36 guns, and three of 32 guns.[57] Most, if not all, of these vessels were captained by officers who had greater seniority than Charles.

In mid-October Fanny, Charles, Cassy, and little Fan paid a week's visit to Godmersham. According to the other family guest, Jane Austen, it was "by her own desire [that] <u>Mrs</u> Fanny is to be put in the room next the Nursery, her Baby in a little bed by her; – & as Cassy is to have the closet within &

Betsey William's little Hole they will be all very snug together."[58] Who better than Jane to describe the family's arrival and reception at Godmersham on 13 October 1813? In the first sentence, "the Woman and Girl part of us" refers to herself and her niece, Fanny Knight.

> We met them in the Hall, the Woman & Girl part of us – but before we reached the Library [Cassy] kissed me very affectionately – & has since seemed to recollect me in the same way. It was quite an evening of confusion as you may suppose – at first we were all walking about from one part of the House to the other – then came a fresh dinner in the Breakfast room for Charles & his wife, which Fanny & I attended – then we moved into the Library, were joined by the Dining room people, were introduced & so forth. – & then we had Tea & Coffee which was not over till past 10. – Billiards again drew all the odd ones away, & Edward, Charles, the two Fannys & I sat snugly talking.[59]

Jane gives the impression of a lively arrival, a late dinner for the travellers, and an enjoyable family chat in the library to end the evening.

Fanny and her family were late arriving at Godmersham because their journey had been long and complicated. The sea had been very rough that morning, making it tricky to transfer tiny children to the waiting tender. Once on shore, it was ten miles to Sittingbourne, where they were expected to pay a courtesy call on Lady Williams, wife of Sir Thomas, who was staying at the Rose Inn. The length of their visit there was most likely dictated by Lady Williams's whims and not by their preferred schedule of travel. Lady Williams was said to be difficult. Jane Austen certainly thought so. Earlier in the year she had written Cassandra that Lady Williams had "taken to her old tricks of ill health again & is sent for a couple of Months among her friends. Perhaps she may make <u>them</u> sick."[60] By the time Fanny and Charles had journeyed the additional sixteen miles to Godmersham, the others had already dined. Fanny could look forward to a more leisurely pace in the days to come.

Jane's early observations provide warm descriptions of both Fanny and Charles. She wrote to Cassandra: "[H]ere they are safe and well, just like their own nice selves, Fanny looking as neat & white this morning as possible, &

dear Charles all affectionate, placid, quiet, cheerful good humour."[61] Note that Fanny's choice of white clothing was in keeping with the custom of ladies of the gentry class. This was a practice well-known to Jane, whose fictional character Miss Tilney in *Northanger Abbey*, "always wears white."[62] In *Mansfield Park*, Edmund Bertram advises Fanny Price that "a woman can never be too fine while she is all in white."[63]

Fanny welcomed the week's visit to Godmersham, especially after her confined and isolated quarters at sea. She appreciated the civility, luxury, and good company that a family party at Godmersham provided. She gladly took part in a variety of planned entertainments and outings, such as "Late dinner, & Billiards German Tactics Chess" on the first full evening, courtesy calls on various neighbours[64] with her niece Fanny Knight and a "bustling day" in Canterbury where she and Fanny took Fanny's younger sisters, Louisa and Cass Knight, to try on new stays.

At first a patch of windy and blustery weather adversely affected the men's shooting parties about the estate. Nonetheless, Charles continued to go out with his gun after game birds – pheasant and partridge – even though, in the words of his niece Lizzy Knight, he "has come home half drowned every day."[65] Such inclement weather discouraged the ladies from walks along the nearby River Stour, climbs to the Doric temple, or longer rambles to the top of the North Downs, which were now rich in muted autumn colours. Instead they opted for the warmth and elegance of the Godmersham library, where they were happy to chat about absent friends, share family news, and occupy themselves with needlework and sewing. Jane was presumably in a good mood, as her publishing projects were progressing favourably. Several days before she had written to Cassandra that "I dined upon Goose yesterday-which I hope will secure a good Sale of my 2nd edition [of *Sense and Sensibility*]."[66] Jane had in mind the proverb that "[he] who eats Goose on Michael's Day/ Shan't money lack, his debts to pay,"– an apt sentiment for an author ambitious to do well financially.

Both Fanny and Jane were dedicated needlewomen. Jane was apparently "a great adept at overcast and satin stitch,"[67] whereas Fanny Austen was an inveterate netter[68] of purses and maker of clothes for her three girls. The women shared another activity of importance. According to a description sent to Cassandra, "we are now all four of us young Ladies sitting round the

Circular Table … writing our Letters."[69] Although this account comes from Jane's letter of 16 September, it could just as easily describe the endeavours of the current foursome. Once fine days returned, the ladies were at leisure to enjoy outdoor pursuits. We know that Jane Austen favoured long country walks, an activity that may have appealed to Fanny as well, since she had so recently left their cramped quarters on the *Namur*.

The women at Godmersham were a small party: Jane Austen, Fanny Austen, their young hostess Fanny Knight, and Fanny Knight's aunt, Harriot Moore. It is unlikely they would be together all the time. For instance, on 19 October Fanny Knight records that she and her "Sweet [Aunt Harriot] Moore … had a nice snug drive to Eastwell [Park] & spent near 3 hours there very comfortably,"[70] an outing that left Jane and Fanny behind. This week at Godmersham was one of the longest periods that Jane and Fanny were in the same household, but neither was distracted by domestic responsibilities. Jane was exempt from the morning household duties and social obligations that ordinarily occupied her at Chawton Cottage; Fanny's maid Betsy was caring for Cassy and Fan, whereas Harriet was with her aunt and grandparents at Keppel Street. So Fanny and Jane must have found opportunities for further private conversation, a chance for a "snug talk" on their own. Fanny's letters within her immediate family show her to be thoughtful, articulate, and willing to express her opinion. She would not be afraid to engage in a conversation of substance with Jane.

There is reason to think that Jane liked to spend time with Fanny. She appreciated her gentleness, her unswerving commitment to making a home for her family on board the *Namur*, and her utter devotion to Charles and the little girls. Notably, Jane's current letters from Godmersham speak of Fanny in familiar language. Fanny is dubbed "<u>Mrs.</u> Fanny," one of the "two Fannys," "Fanny Senior," "[Cassy's] Mama," and part of "the Charleses."[71] Jane commends Fanny's choice of dress and appearance, but of greater significance is the claim that she appeared "just like [her] own nice [self]." Jane, it seems, had a warm and affectionate attitude towards Fanny.

Noticeably, Jane felt no obligation to speak well of other family members if this was not what she thought. Mary Austen, her brother James's wife, was a case in point. Jane's letters assert that Mary was, by times, petulant, sharp tongued, and indiscrete. She was notoriously unsympathetic to the needs of her stepdaughter, Anna, sometimes fancying that Anna had slighted her. Jane thought Mary cultivated the view she was being ill treated "for the pleasure of fancying it."[72] The fact that Jane spoke well of Fanny counts in her favour, given that Jane did not mince words when she felt criticism was merited.

For her part, Fanny was well disposed towards Jane. She was particularly thankful for her shared care of Cassy and Harriet during the children's stays at Chawton Cottage. Moreover, Fanny must have been proud to have such an accomplished sister-in-law and pleased to have been privately included in the knowledge of Jane's authorship of both *Sense and Sensibility* and *Pride and Prejudice*. Fanny did not have to keep this secret much longer. By September 1813, word of Jane's accomplishments was beginning to spread among her readers and more widely in the Austen family. Her brother Henry had blabbed to Lady Kerr and another lady in Scotland about it that September. As Jane put it, "a Thing once set going in that way – one knows how it spreads!"[73] When her fourteen-year-old nephew James Edward found out about Jane's authorship, he expressed his appreciation in verse:

No words can express, my dear Aunt, my surprise
Or make you conceive how I opened my eyes,
Like a pig Butcher Pile has struck with his knife,
When I heard for the very first time in my life
That I had the honour to have a relation
Whose works were dispersed through the whole of the nation ...[74]

Her identity as the author of the novels only became publicly known in December 1818 when *Northanger Abbey* and *Persuasion* were published post-humously with a biographical sketch of Jane by her brother Henry.

Jane Austen's letters testify to her strong interest in Charles's professional career, his commissions and promotions, as well as his private reactions to his assignments. Fanny knew of Jane's great love of her youngest brother, a situation that predisposed the two women to discuss his feelings about his current posting. On this occasion, Fanny likely shared with Jane her worries about Charles's progress in his career, his hopes for a North American assignment, and their increasing anxiety while waiting for a development in that quarter.

There was another bond between these two women in addition to their being "sisters," which was the term then in use to describe their relationship. Fanny and Jane shared a keen interest in the ways of the navy, so it is easy to imagine that their conversation touched on the naval materials Jane included in *Mansfield Park*, the novel she had just completed in June. Several of her naval references had known connections to Charles. In 1801 he had used £30 of prize money, with the expectation of £10 more, to buy "Gold chains and Topaze Crosses" for Jane and Cassandra.[75] Now, twelve years later, Jane's cross found a fictional counterpart when midshipman William Price gives his sister Fanny an amber cross as a token of his great affection. This parallel between Charles's generous act and William's gift to a beloved sister is the sort of echo that would surely please Fanny when she came to read *Mansfield Park*.

Jane had secured Frank's and Charles's permission to use the names of four of their former vessels in *Mansfield Park*, a gesture which paid tribute to the careers of both her sailor brothers. Of the four named vessels, Charles had served on the *Endymion* and the *Cleopatra*.[76] His career in the *Endymion* predated his marriage, but Fanny had strong associations with his more recent vessel, the *Cleopatra*. She must have been gratified when she found out that a vessel she knew so well was commemorated in *Mansfield Park*.

On the *Namur* Fanny was well placed to become acquainted with the vessel's young trainee officers. Jane had recently asked Charles about the progress of a particular midshipman known to her as "Young Kendall," who had joined the *Namur* in August 1813. She subsequently reported to Cassandra that "I have made Charles furnish me with something to say about Young Kendall. – He is going on very well."[77] Jane, too, may have wished to question Fanny about this young man's progress. Moreover, since Jane had recently created the character of William Price in *Mansfield Park* and was so scrupulously accurate with the naval details in her novels, it would not be surprising that she sustained a particular interest in the experiences and education of an actual midshipman.[78]

About this time Jane was probably thinking ahead to her next novel, *Emma*, even possibly making notes about details relevant to its content.[79] Once more Fanny was in a position to be a useful source of background information, this time about the seaside resort at Southend, where she had spent most of the last three months. In *Emma* the John Knightley family makes an autumn visit to "South End," an expedition "most strenuously recommended" by their apothecary, Mr Wingfield, who prescribed "for all the children, but particularly for the weakness in little Bella's throat, – both sea air and bathing."[80] Fanny was able to explain the amenities of Southend, extol the benefits of its sea air, and describe the modern sea-bathing facilities. One can only speculate about the topics Jane and Fanny may have discussed and, in particular, how much they involved naval life and the merits of Southend. But given Fanny's first-hand experience and Jane's literary interests, it would seem natural for them to do so.

During the visit to Godmersham, the well-being of Fanny's eldest daughter, Cassy, became a matter of concern. When the child arrived, Jane noticed that "poor little Cassy is grown extremely thin & looks poorly."[81] Fanny needed to decide where the child ought to go when the time came to leave. Should Cassy accept her Aunt Cassandra's invitation to Chawton Cottage or should she return to the *Namur* with her parents? Jane carefully notes how Fanny, together with Charles, came to a decision. As she tells Cassandra, "the cheif,[82] indeed the only difficulty with [Fanny] is a very reasonable one, the Child's being very unwilling to leave them … At the same time, [Cassy] has been suffering so much lately from Sea sickness, that [Fanny] cannot bear to have her much on board this winter. – Charles is less inclined to part with her."[83]

Fanny and Charles continued to monitor Cassy's inclinations and state of health. By 21 October Jane observed that "Cassy's looks are much mended … [yet she] did not look as if the idea of going to Chawton again was a pleasant one."[84] By the time of their departure, "Cassy had recovered her Looks almost entirely," and her parents decided not to send her to Chawton for now. According to Jane, Fanny and Charles "do not consider the Namur as disagreeing with her in general – only when the Weather is so rough as to make her sick."[85] This vignette gives some idea of Fanny's and Charles's attitudes to parenting and underlines how strongly they wished to keep their family together whenever possible.

The dynamics of Fanny's and Charles's roles as parents may also be reflected in a further observation by Jane, one that depends on what is to be understood by her remark that she has done a "good deed" and "extracted

Charles from his wife and children upstairs, and made him get ready to go out shooting, and not keep Mr Moore waiting."[86] Jane's comment could be taken to imply that Fanny is too dependent on Charles in matters of child care, but alternatively it may suggest nothing more than that he needs to get ready to go out with Mr Moore. Jane, who respected punctuality, could have "extracted" Charles because she thought he ought to be preparing for his shooting engagement. Jane knew that Charles was an involved parent, living as he did in such close quarters with Fanny and their very young children. It would be in his nature to step in and help Fanny when some child's immediate need arose, which is what may have delayed his appearance. Jane's remark need not be understood as an implied criticism of Fanny – that she demands more domestic support from Charles than is reasonable in their circumstances. It looks instead as though Jane is concerned only with her brother's promptness.[87]

Part of the family's journey back to the *Namur* was achieved with greater comfort and style than their travel to Godmersham a week before. They had Edward's carriage for the nine miles to Ospringe. After that, they travelled to Key Street, just east of Sittingbourne, where they stopped to dine and spend the night on the invitation of James Street, the purser of the *Namur*. From Sittingbourne it was only ten miles further to Sheerness. At about the same time, Mary Jane Fowle of Kintbury, sister of Tom Fowle, who was now a lieutenant on the *Namur*, "was very near returning with her Brother & paying them a visit on board."[88] However, Mary Jane went to Cheltenham instead, and so Fanny was deprived of the welcome company of a young woman, only two years younger, who shared many friends and family connections.

A month later Fanny wrote to her sister Harriet in London.

Namur, Tuesday Morning [22nd November 1813]
My dearest Harriet
I meant to have written you on Sunday, but an early dinner & various other occupations prevented me & yesterday I went on Shore & did not return untill near dinner time. Don't imagine that I left your Pet on board with Betsy for Mama was so good as to take care of her untill I returned. Betsy has had the headache regularly every night untill last night when Mr. Cather[89] gave her a

draught which composed her; & if the pain returns she is to have a blister behind her ear, as it is now ascertained to be the rheumatism; What a strange thing it will be for me to have a servant who is good for any thing without some ailment or other! do you think I am likely ever to possess so great a treasure?

Little Fan behaves uncommonly well now of a Night, she sleeps close to my Bedside in one of the small Bedsteads, with the side out, which I find much more convenient than her Cot, as I can hush her off to sleep without getting out of Bed; she is never fed before six o'Clock & sometimes 1/2 past; & now & then sleeps the whole night; her appetite continues very good indeed & she is in perfect health & quite the favourite with Joe & Tom Fowle. Joe and Mr. Fearon[90] *go to Town to-morrow in the Nile, he was to have left us yesterday (very much to our regret) but we persuaded him to stay for* the play *last night; however we were all disappointed for* the Theatre *was not finished, & consequently they were obliged to postpone acting untill next Monday.*

I shall send the Cannister up & will thank you to have it replenished with Tops & Bottoms[91] *& the Butter Crock with some of your friend Grammers nice fresh Butter I hope you keep an account of all these little things.*

I have been thinking that we must bring our dear little Harriet down with us when we return, as I am afraid she will forget us, what say you to this? If you find it quite impossible to live without one of them, perhaps I may indulge you so far, as to leave little Fanny. We have not heard from you yet but I hope we shall by & bye, there is a very thick Fog which has prevented Groves from coming out. Capt. Austen is obliged to go in to see the Adr. & is only waiting for this therefore I must say adieu

    Yours in great haste

      F.F. Austen

We all unite in love & regards.

Fanny's catalogue of domestic concerns is by now familiar: her usually reliable servant, Betsy, is ailing and she is missing little Harriet's company. Once more she is without adequate servants, which makes it difficult to cope with more than one child in the isolating circumstances of the *Namur*. However, Fanny has a specific solution in mind, which she phrases in a way that she hopes will prompt a positive response. As Harriet may "find it quite impossible to live without one of [the children]," she proposes leaving the nearly year-old Fan at Keppel Street. It is not a cheering prospect to be leaving her youngest in town, especially when little Fan is responding so well to her mother's maternal attentions and to the sessions of play with the affable Tom Fowle. Meanwhile Fanny requests some rusk-like cakes, which she identifies as "tops and bottoms," probably because the baby is teething.

As the year 1813 drew to a close, Fanny could anticipate the pleasure of being reunited with all her immediate Palmer family at Keppel Street for the holidays and perhaps the enjoyment of a short visit to Chawton Cottage, something that Jane happily anticipated would occur.[92] Even so, as she looks beyond Christmas and into the New Year, Fanny is justifiably concerned about Charles's career. Will he be getting a vessel in the sea service? Might he be relegated ashore on half pay? In any event, he will be off the *Namur* by October 1814. As usual, his professional situation will crucially affect Fanny and will determine when and where their family will relocate.

Fig. 1   Fanny Palmer Austen, painted in Halifax by British artist Robert
Field, 1810.

Fig. 2 Captain Charles John Austen RN, Fanny's husband, a companion portrait to hers, also painted by Field.

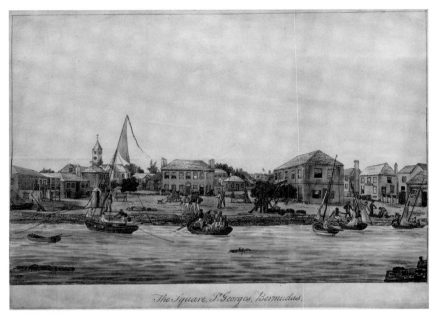

Fig. 3 *The Square, St George's, Bermudas* by Thomas Driver, 1823. King's Square looks very much as it did during Fanny's early years in St George's. The tower of St Peter's Church, where she married Charles in May 1807, can be seen towards the left.

Fig. 4 *St George's Harbour* by Thomas Driver, 1821. The artist effectively depicts the shape of the town in relation to the curve of the harbour and its busyness.

Fig. 5   Bermuda-built HMS *Atalante* (18 guns), sister ship to HMS *Indian*, which was Charles's first command, 1805–10.

Bailey sculp.

Sambro, Halifax N.S.

Fig. 7   Hon. Andrew Belcher, Charles's prize agent in Halifax, Nova Scotia, painted by Robert Field, 1808.

Fig. 10 Joseph Partridge provides a splendid view of the Grand Parade and St Paul's Church at the centre of Halifax, c. 1819. It was an area frequented by Fanny in 1809 and during the summer of 1810. The painting is titled *The National School at Halifax* to call attention to that institution, located across the street from the church.

Fig. 11 *Halifax, August 1848*, a fine watercolour by Lieut. Herbert Grey Austen RN, Charles's nephew, who also served on the North American Station, 1845–48. The drawing shows Halifax as seen from the opposite shore of Dartmouth.

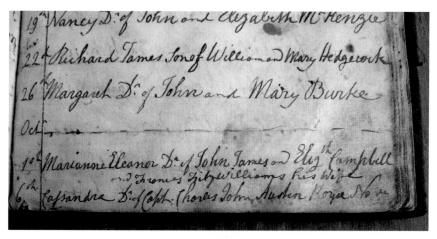

Fig. 12   Cassandra (Cassy) Austen's baptismal record in St Paul's Church, Halifax, 6 October 1809. Fanny's name in the register is the one public record of her presence in Halifax.

Fig. 15   *View from Fort Needham near Halifax* by G.I. Parkyns, c. 1801. The Naval Yard facilities stretch along the waterfront at the far left; Fanny lived in Admiral and Lady Warren's quarters there in the summer of 1810.

Fig. 16 *Government House from the S.W.* by John Elliott Woolford, 1819, showing Lt.-Gov. George Prevost's official residence, at which Fanny reported attending "a splendid Ball," seemingly "prefering a game of Commerce, (to Dancing), at which I won 9 Dollars."

Fig. 19 Chawton Cottage as it appears today. Here Fanny first met the resident members of the Austen family: Jane, Cassandra, and Mrs George Austen.

Fig. 20   The only known full-face image of Jane Austen, drawn from life, by her sister Cassandra, c. 1810.

Fig. 21   HMS *Namur*, then a second-rate ship of 90 guns, is the largest vessel in the harbour in this painting by Dominic Serres, 1762.

Fig. 22   John Meirs made this silhouette of Fanny in his London studio of Meirs and Field sometime between 1812 and 1814. It is now part of the Chawton House Library Collection and hangs in the Oak Room.

Fig. 25   An artist's impression of the capture of the French frigate *La Tribune* (44 guns) by HMS *Unicorn* (32 guns), 8 June 1796. Charles was involved as a midshipman aboard the *Unicorn*. Sir Thomas Williams, her captain, was knighted for this action.

Fig. 26   J.M.W. Turner painted the turbulent waters at the Nore anchorage c. 1807. HMS *Namur* can be seen faintly in the left background, the seaport of Sheerness appears in the distance. Turner called the painting *The Junction of the Thames and the Medway*.

GODMERSHAM PARK in Kent, the Seat of THOMAS KNIGHT ESQ.

Published as the Act directs   May 4 1785, by W. Watts, Chelsea

Fig. 28   Godmersham Park, Kent, the primary seat of Edward Knight. Set in an idyllic park, here Fanny enjoyed the luxury of "carriages and coachmen, fine wines and ice, late dining and lady's maids."

Fig. 29   Fanny Knight, as drawn by her aunt, Cassandra Austen, was the young chatelaine of Godmersham Park during visits by Fanny and Charles.

Fig. 30   *Chawton House and Church*, 1809. Fanny would have attended services here when she visited Charles's relatives at Chawton.

Fig. 32   Kentish Town Chapel in the Parish of St Pancras, where Fanny's funeral was held and Charles placed a marble tablet in her memory.

Fig. 33   Portrait of Frances (Fan) Austen, youngest daughter of Fanny and Charles, as a young woman.

Fig. 34   Portrait of Cassandra (Cassy) Austen, eldest daughter of Fanny and Charles, as a young woman, probably contemporary with her sister's portrait.

Fig. 35   Portrait of Charles Austen in the 1840s in his post-captain's uniform. He was promoted to rear admiral in 1848.

CHAPTER 7

Family Obligations,
1814

THE BEGINNING OF 1814 WAS EXCEPTIONALLY COLD. The frost was so severe and the temperature fell so low that the River Thames froze between London Bridge and Tower Bridge, creating an ideal situation for celebrations on the ice. From the 1st to the 5th of February, Londoners flocked to the river for what was to be the last Frost Fair held on the Thames.[1] There was music and dancing, gambling and games, skittles and sports, and food and drink galore. Gin was consumed with gingerbread, and hawkers with baskets of hot apples circulated among the crowds. To the amazement of many, an elephant was led across the Thames alongside Blackfriars Bridge. Ten printing presses were in operation on the ice, printing souvenir cards and sheets of music. One press produced the following text:

NOTICE
Whereas you J FROST
have by Force and Violence
taken possession of the RIVER
THAMES I hereby give you
warning to quit immediately
A Thaw
Printed by S Warner
On the ICE FEB 5 1814.[2]

While Londoners were out and about celebrating the freezing weather, Charles was not in a festive mood. He was expected to return to the *Namur* but was stuck in London without transportation. The vessel to convey him to the Nore was frozen in the river. Charles requested further leave but was refused. The next day he wrote the Admiralty from Gravesend, describing the road as "impassable owing to the depth of snow, which between this place and Chatham is in places 20 feet. The coaches have been stopped & even the Royal Artillery weapons this night are unable to be moved."[3] He eventually reached the *Namur* but was anxious that the rest of his family should wait for better weather. Fanny was left to manage her girls' requirements at Keppel Street.

With a new year under way, Fanny began to write in her *Pocket Magnet, or elegant Picturesque Diary, for 1814*. Bound in red Morocco leather, with a tuck-in flap, it was a handy size for slipping into a purse and for jotting down incidental information. Fanny's little book also provided her with a wealth of practical details: a weights and measure table, a list of current fares for coaches and watermen, the lengths of major London streets, and a catalogue of "remarkable events" from 1813. For instance, on 7 July "Intelligence was received of the capture of the Chesapeake, American frigate, by the Shannon frigate, commanded by Capt. Broke." Fanny was aware of this event already from the publicity surrounding it at the time and Charles's long-standing friendship with Philip Broke.[4] The entry was a gratifying recognition of a major naval success. The pocket diary also contained small engravings of picturesque places at the head of some pages. These sketches, which included East Cowes Castle and North Lodge, both on the Isle of Wight, as well as Hastings and Glastonbury Tor, were meant to afford aesthetic pleasure for the book's owner. For Fanny, who had seen so little of England, these drawings introduced her to interesting and attractive locations yet to be visited.

Fanny used her pocket diary more as a notebook, a place for recording purchases and reconciling her monthly expenses. This was a common practice. In Jane Austen's novel *Northanger Abbey*, Catherine Morland receives a pocketbook from her mother, who hopes its possession will encourage her daughter to keep account of her expenses while in Bath. Studying the details of Fanny's purchases helps us to understand how she managed her domestic affairs. Some of the items mentioned are designated for particular members of her immediate family: "Captain Austen" (Charles), "Mrs. Esten" (Esther), "Betsy" (her maid servant), "Cassandra" (Cassy), and "Fanny" (little Fan). Other entries relate to domestic services such as laundry or washing and to articles and supplies that Fanny needed for her household.

Entries for January and half of February record a wide range of purchases, including "shoes for Fanny," who was about to walk. There are eleven separate entries for laundry: clothing belonging to the children, to Fanny's servant Betsy, to Captain Austen, and her own silk stockings. Fanny bought furniture cotton and bed ticking, brushes, toothbrushes, and ribbons. Perhaps the ribbons were for trimming a dress. Jane Austen approved of such fashionable touches and that March was "determined to trim [her] lilac sarsenet[5] with black sattin ribbon just as my China Crape is, 6d width at the bottom, 3d or 4d at top." In her opinion, "Ribbon trimmings are all the fashion at Bath."[6] Unfortunately, Fanny's entries for 1814 are incomplete as erasures mar the pages for March through July. It is unclear who did the erasing. The pages for the rest of the year have not been used.

Fanny carefully recorded each item and its cost. At that time British currency was counted in pounds, shillings, and pence.[7] Either as commissions or as gifts Fanny acquired a cap (£1 4s.) for Esther, a gown (12s.) for Betsy, and a waistcoat (12s. 6d.) for an unidentified recipient, ribbon (1s. 5d.), socks (7s. 8d.), stockings (6s.), gloves (3s. 6d.), brushes (2s. 9d.), and sundries (13s. 7d.). In the course of January and February, she notes expenses for postage (1s. 7d.) and packet letters (2s. 1d.), presumably for her Bermuda-bound letters, bookbinding (17s.) (books were ordinarily sold without covers), fresh fruit (4s.), sugar (2s. 10d.), several cakes (2s. 3d.), bulk tea (the cost is not decipherable), and washing (£5. 8s.). Coach hire in June cost 5s. 6d.[8] Jane Austen's expenses for certain items were similar to Fanny's. In 1811 Jane paid 4s. for gloves and £1 16s. for a cap.[9]

"Cassandra's expenses for Kintbury" in January came to £2. Cassy, aged five, must have accompanied one of her Austen aunts from Chawton in Hampshire to Kintbury in the neighbouring county of Berkshire to see old family friends. They visited Reverend and Mrs Fulwar Fowle at their rectory, which was attractively situated on the banks of the Kennet and Avon Canal and near woodlands and fields. Cassy knew their son Tom Fowle from his time as a midshipman on the *Indian* and more recently as an officer on the *Namur*. Tom was very likable and took an avuncular interest in the Austen children from their youngest days. His parents, knowing about this relationship, would make Cassy very welcome.

Fanny calculated her expenses in January to be £10 9s. 8½d. and for the first part of February, £4 2s. 11½d.[10] Some of the entries indicate acts of generosity. She writes that she "gave away" a shilling. On a separate line, she records: "lent Mr. RP £4" which was the third-largest individual expense recorded in her January and February accounts. The initials "RP" spark speculation. A possible candidate was her brother, army officer Robert John Palmer, known to his sisters as "John" but referred to as "RJP" in Charles Austen's journal. If RP does refer to her brother, she may think that he needs money while his incarceration at Verdun in France continues and she has thought of a way to get it to him. In later letters, Fanny shows a thoughtful concern for John. If he was the recipient, Fanny's liberality is evidence of her generosity. Although Charles's current salary is sufficient, given the uncertainty of his future employ, saving would be prudent.

Another entry in her pocket diary attests to Fanny's interest in fashionable accessories. As dress styles changed to a more flowing, classical look, purses became important as a way for a lady to carry her necessities, such as a small coin purse. Netted purses of great variety were very popular. The requisite supplies for making one's own purse could be had from one of the many purse makers' shops in London, which supplied netting needles, purse-twist, and tassels for trimming. The simplest style had the shape of a small bag and was closed with a drawstring.[11] On a back page of her pocket diary, Fanny listed the materials required to make a purse. Her pattern specifies that she needs "24 yds," although she does not state whether it calls for silk, cotton, linen, or wool thread. The recorded details of the pattern suggest that she knew how to net a purse, a skill that Mr Bingley in *Pride and Prejudice* thinks is an admirable achievement for young ladies.[12]

Fanny's pocket diary is her only surviving personal possession apart from her letters. As such, it is of special interest. Her notations reveal a mother carefully providing for her growing daughters' needs. They disclose how she budgeted to make available treats of fresh fruit, cake, and tea. Other entries tell of household needs, of books bound, laundry sent out, and coaches hired, all at recorded costs. Just as Fanny's letters provide a window onto her thoughts and feelings, entries from her pocket diary enhance the profile of a young mother running her household with organization and care.

Mothers of Fanny's era and class ordinarily began their children's education at home. At an early age a little girl was taught to read, to spell, to write grammatically, to gain competence in plain sewing, to understand the principles of Christian religion, and to display good manners and good sense. By 1814 Cassy was becoming the particular subject of her mother's educational efforts. By Fanny's own admission, Cassy had always been very active and determined; as a toddler she was described as "so riotous & unmanageable, that I can do nothing with her."[13] Fanny had recently, and tellingly, observed that "Cassandra begins now to read very prettily, but I have had an amazing deal of trouble with her not owing to a dulness of comprehension; but a dislike to learning."[14] These observations suggest that Cassy was a challenging child to teach. Moreover, there were further complicating factors. For the past three years, Cassy had lacked the continuity and security of one home and one neighbourhood. Since coming to England, she had been constantly shuttled between the *Namur* and the households of different aunts with very different personalities, Harriet in urban Keppel Street and Jane and Cassandra in rural Hampshire. This experience could be disorientating for any child, especially one of Cassy's temperament. At least by March and under Aunt Cassandra's watchful eye, Cassy managed to write a letter to Charles that was largely her own composition.[15] As it was the women who were most often the conscientious correspondents within a family, letter writing was a valuable skill to acquire and Cassy's early effort an encouraging development towards literacy.

In her pocket diary, Fanny lists books suitable for educating Cassy. The volumes she selects could either be used on the *Namur* or be lugged along when Cassy was staying with her aunts. Fanny includes Mrs Trimmer's *Little Histories*, in particular her *Ancient History*, *Roman History*, and *History of England*,[16] as well as *A Geographical Companion to Mrs. Trimmer's Histories*, together with printed maps, keys, and explanations. Mrs Trimmer's books were very popular choices for a Georgian schoolroom. Her *Geographical Companion* was a particularly good selection for Cassy, since she had already travelled extensively on her father's ships.

Mrs Trimmer's volumes also included pedagogical hints for the teacher. The *Geographical Companion* was "calculated to make the study of history of more interest to children." Mrs Trimmer believed that "as soon as they understand any historical relation children are pleased to know when and where every circumstance happened." She recommended that the teacher sketch an outline map and once the place or places in question were satis-factorily introduced and discussed, the corresponding names were to be entered on the outline map. In consequence, "every place with which a child is at any time made acquainted, may be introduced into [her] maps until all are found." Mrs Trimmer advised that the "separate maps, [created during the lessons] be hung up in some place where they will frequently be taken notice of."[17] Thus it would be no surprise if the *Namur's* private quarters were decorated with the results of Cassy's and Fanny's cartographic endeavours.

Mrs Trimmer's method had the virtues of one-to-one instruction, a con-versational approach, and a respect for the principle that children learn at different speeds and have different levels of interest. She tried to be topical and suggested linking places with well-known events. For example, the Scilly Islands and Rocks were notable because "three Men of War, under the command of Admiral Sir Cloudesley Shovel struck and were lost, together with the Admiral, west of Cornwall."[18] True as this was, such a description might induce fear and anxiety in a naval child, like Cassy, who already knew about the perils of the sea. Presumably Mrs Trimmer's pedagogical principles allowed a teacher to use her discretion, thus, for example, letting Fanny substitute some other event.

Fanny may have known some French; Charles certainly did, given his early lessons at the Steventon rectory where the family library contained a copy of *Fables Choisies*, a primer of ninety-nine fables with rules for gram-mar and vocabulary written by Jean de la Fontaine. When he undertook further studies of French at the Royal Naval College, Charles was rated as "very diligent."[19] For the present purpose, Fanny planned to supply Cassy's French instructor with *Brossert's first Grammar* and *St Quinton's first Grammar*. Perhaps Jane Austen recommended the latter volume, as its author, M. Dominique de St Quentin, had taught at the Reading Ladies Boarding School, which she had attended at age nine.[20] Charles was a father committed to assist with his daughters' education. Three years later an entry in his pocketbook describes him as "engaged as usual teaching the Children till noon."[21]

Fanny's list of books included religious material, such as *Dr Watts's Hymns in Verse* and *Mrs Barbauld's Hymns in Prose*. For a lighter touch, and because learning poetry was considered important, she chose *Original Poems for Children in two little vols.* and *Simple Stories in Verse*. The discipline of organized study and the examples of good behaviour conveyed in the chosen texts would, it was hoped, go some way towards further educating and civilizing Cassy.

Instead of returning to the *Namur* in February, Fanny was required to leave her three children behind and join Charles in Sheerness for an obligatory visit with Admiral Sir Thomas and Lady Williams. As Amanda Vickery suggests in her book *The Gentleman's Daughter*, there were certain dimensions of behaviour that a refined young woman was expected to value and aspire to achieve. "To be mistress of oneself was paramount – genteel ladies aimed to be self-possessed in social encounters, self-controlled in the face of minor provocations, self-sufficient in the midst of ingratitude, and, above all, brave and enduring in the grip of tragedy and misfortune."[22] Such a mindset was consistent with the "habitual self projection of ... upright strength, stoical fortitude and self-command."[23] Fanny has tried her best to follow this code, even when she felt stressed and irritated. She knows she must be pleasant and congenial for the sake of making a favourable social impression when she accompanies Charles to the Williams, but as her next two letters to Harriet show, she is growing increasingly thoughtful and dissatisfied with her lack of autonomy.

Sheerness, Saturday – [5th February 1814]

My dear Harriet-

We have this morning heard from Miss Austen[24] in answer to our queries about Anne, & I shall extract that part of her letter viz: "Anne says she is afraid on thinking the matter over, to undertake a place which might require her to be on board of Ship more than her health was equal to – It was a subject on which I could not attempt to persuade her I only told her therefore that your family were likely to be here in the summer & that if she were still out of Place, & Mrs. C.A. still unprovided with a Servant, she might then hear more particulars than I could inform her of. I suspect that neither Anne nor her friends wish her to go out again very soon as she asked me this morning, how early she should be wanted in your Place, & said Father was not in a hurry for her to go out again. The reason of her quitting Mrs. F.A., was only on account of wages." Miss Austen gives us a very good account of Dear Cassandra & speaks of her improvement in her studies.

I was in great hopes this morning that we should have gone off to the Ship to-morrow in consequence of a letter from Sir J. Yorke saying that he should set out on Sunday but Sir Thomas & Lady Williams both insist on our staying, & have requested Mrs. Lobb[25] *to accomodate us, untill Sir Joseph goes & then they wish us to return to them — tho' I receive every kindness & attention from them both, I cannot help feeling a great desire to be at home, however uncomfortable that home may be — but I must submit & pretend to like it. I believe Capt. Austen rather wishes to stay than otherwise. We all dine at the Commissioners today but we come back to sleep, & remove our trunks to-morrow.*

I was told yesterday that there are to be had in Holland very handsome Velvets at about 4 Guineas the dress, & also Sarsenets, but I do not know the price of them. If you & Mama can command the money I shall be very happy to forward your commission & am su[re] that Capt. Baldwin will have great pleasure in executing it; but there rests the difficulty for I am advised by all means to send Guineas, as the discount on Bills is very considerable & I know that we have not one in the World —

I was introduced to Capt. Wallace[26] *yesterday, & am happy to tell you that he gives our poor Brother*[27] *an excellent character, he says he is a very correct young Man keeps the best Company & is very intimate with a Col: in the Army, whose name I forget but he is an acquaintance of Lady Williams & a very respectable man, John is a good deal with this Gentleman, rides with him every day, but they both smoke, however this is a trifle, & I have no doubt he will soon forget it —*

Sunday — Thank you my dear Harriet for your letter. I am sorry to hear such a bad account of yourself & have just written to request Mr. Cather to make up some Medicines for you; this will prevent your receiving your Box so soon as you may expect as I think the Nile had better wait a day or two untill the Medicines are prepared[28] *— [I]shall not open the Box; indeed I am sorry to say, I shall have no opportunity of doing so, as it is on board the Namur & I am* *kept in delightful ignorance when I am to leave this; but I shou'd think it a pity, even had I an opportunity, to unpack it before it has finished its voyage.*

I do not like my little dear Fan's having a Cough at this inclement season as I fear she will have some difficulty in getting rid of it & I strongly recommend your beginning with the White Mixture at once, & continuing it untill she is quite well; don't let her eat Meat as long as it lasts, but if you can conveniently, have a little Pudding made for her of a day, as I do not think her Broth is substantial enough without any thing else untill four o'Clock. I shall endeavour to get a dozen Eggs from Southend & send you by Hancock, as I know they are a very dear article in Town just now –

We are still at the Admirals & are likely I find to continue here some days longer, as it is now undecided when Sir Joseph comes. Mrs. Lobb & the Commissioner are extremely kind about our going & not going to them, for we, or rather the Admiral & Lady W. have made a sort of conveniency of them, (so far as this goes,) that we are not to leave our present Quarters untill they are wanted for Sir Joseph, & then the Lobbs <u>must receive us</u>, but they are very friendly & Hospitable & seem to feel great pleasure in receiving us on any terms. This I think will make it necessary for me to spend a day or two with them when my visit here is finished I mean in case it shou'd not be requisite for me to pawn myself upon them now.

I shall desire Thomas to send you a Salt Fish when the Nile goes up but I am afraid you did not return the Frail to put it in nor my Baskets nor Capt. Austens Hat Box, this is very naughty of you – I am glad to find you going to a little dance I wish I cou'd get your Medicines to you in time to set you up for it, but you know Mr. Cather takes a long time to prepare them, however I have told him in my note that the Nile is going up in a day or two by way of hurrying him a little. Is Harriets birth-day on the 16th or 18th for I cannot remember!²⁹ it is necessary I shou'd know, as we mean to try & run up the day before, shou'd there be no Courts Martials in the way & the weather be settled enough to go by Water, these are the conditions, therefore you must not depend too much upon it –

Adieu³⁰ kiss my dear Children for me & give my love to Papa & Mama. If you can, write three times a Week as long as little Fannys cold lasts. Yours affly.
F.F. Austen

As Fanny undertakes the current visit to see Admiral and Lady Williams, her spirits are lower than usual. Staffing issues continue to oppress her, although there is some consolation in Cassandra Austen's efforts to help solve her difficulties. Apparently, a woman known as Anne, who might become available in the summer, had indicated she was "quitting Mrs. F.A. ... only on account of the wages." With this information in mind, Fanny may have felt sympathy for Mary Austen, the other naval wife of the family, who also had to run an economical household and was unable to retain a servant who desired a greater wage than she could afford. Noticeably, it is Cassandra who is advising Fanny on domestic issues. Although Jane was not uninterested in Fanny's problems, she was seriously absorbed in her own writing at that moment. She was in a state of great mental energy and creativity. She had begun *Emma* on 21 January and there was still work to be done to see *Mansfield Park* to press.

Although Fanny does not say so specifically, she may be finding Lady Williams's company trying and she is currently irritated by Lady Williams's manipulation of her guests. She intends to shunt Fanny and Charles off to Commissioner Lobb's house in the Dock Yard, when the priority guest of rank, Sir Joseph Yorke, the Senior Naval Lord of the Admiralty, arrives in Sheerness. This plan makes Fanny feel like a pawn. Worst of all, she hates the uncertainty; she wants to know how long she and Charles will be staying on shore in Sheerness. Nothing is said to suggest that Sir Joseph's wife, Urania Anne, formerly Lady de Burgh, the dowager Marchioness of Clanricarde,[31] will accompany Sir Joseph to Sheerness. Thus the females of the party will be restricted to the close company of three: Fanny, Lady Williams, and Mrs Lobb.

In times past Fanny happily accompanied Charles on the social round with his naval superiors. If Sir Thomas's plans for a richly decorated ball-room[32] were any indication of the style and the attractiveness of his mansion, Fanny would be in very pleasing surrounds. Moreover, Captain and Mrs Lobb lived within the walls of the yard in a fine-looking Adams-style house with a high walled garden. Yet the prospect of a period of ease and comfort was not enough to bolster Fanny's spirits. Although her children are safe with their aunts in Chawton and Keppel Street, Fanny "cannot help feeling a great desire <u>to be at home</u>, however uncomfortable that home may be."

At least on the *Namur* she is autonomous. She can run her family's daily domestic affairs as she wishes.

Fanny is trapped by social conventions and knows it. She feels required to acquiesce to her husband's wishes to remain in Sheerness and mask her own feelings of frustration about the current arrangements. With a touch of irony, she speaks of her "delightful ignorance" about when they will be returning to the ship. Although she has been conditioned to hide her irritation from Charles, this now seems much harder to do. Fanny perceives that there is a conflict between her obligation to support Charles, as he furthers his professional and social contacts, and her need to articulate her strong desire to return to the *Namur*.

The forcefulness of Fanny's emotional response is understandable. She has recently discovered she is pregnant again for the fourth time in six years, and this situation will complicate their choice of living quarters when Charles leaves the *Namur* in October. Moreover, her pregnancy makes it even more crucial that she acquire competent and permanent domestic staff. But apart from difficulties stemming from her health and her household, Fanny vents her feelings about what she perceives may, at the moment, constrain her choices. She is annoyed that she cannot even guarantee they will be able "to run up [to London] the day before" in time to celebrate Harriet's fourth birthday because Charles's naval obligations or their social obligations to the Williamses may intervene.

In this letter Fanny openly examines her emotional state with a degree of sophistication of reflection. She finds comfort in confiding in another woman, this time her sister Harriet. Fanny is also unashamedly thinking more independently about her own needs and wants, rather than, as previously, being singularly attentive to Charles's plans. Fanny is registering an understanding of what it would be like to have more control over family decision-making, and although she can clearly articulate what she thinks, she does not yet feel sufficiently empowered to verbalize her desires to Charles.

Fanny makes a passing comment about their finances, a remark that seems puzzling at first. She will not be ordering velvets from Holland, for, as she explains, "we have not one [guinea] in the World." This is not quite the gross exaggeration that it seems. Fanny probably means that although she does not have cash at hand, she could draw a bill on Charles's pay account. This, however, does not seem to be a wise choice, since, as she tells Harriet, "the discount on Bills is very considerable." She is referring to bills of exchange that were used as a form of negotiable and transferable credit.

News that Little Fan has a cough is a source of worry for Fanny. She sends Harriet very specific instructions concerning the avoidance of meat and regular doses of white mixture, directives that were considered appropriate treatment at the time and consistent with commonly held medical beliefs. A cough was regarded as a phlegmatic condition, and as such, an effort would be made to feed "dry and hot" foods. Since meat was thought to be "hot" and "wet" and would further imbalance one's bodily humours, it was believed to make a cough worse. The notion of the humours would be familiar to Fanny. The word "humour" was used to refer to what were described as the four chief fluids of the body: blood, phlegm, yellow bile, and black bile. (In modern terms these are very loosely related to the liver, lungs and brain, gall bladder, and spleen respectively.) Humours were believed to determine an individual's physical and mental well-being. It was important to have them in balance because imbalance was thought to be the source of all illness.

Fanny has great confidence in the restorative powers of white mixture, a preparation composed of magnesium sulphate, magnesium carbonate, and *aquae menthe piperitae* (peppermint water).[33] White mixture was prescribed as an aperient, something that would "open" the humours and cause them to flow and restore harmony or balance to the body. However, as magnesium caused diarrhoea, its use often had unhappy consequences for the patient.

Fanny is also concerned that Fan will become undernourished and recommends feeding her a pudding. This might be a panada, which was a mixture of bread and milk with tapioca or another powdered grain to thicken it, or a suet pudding. Fanny's quick response and her detailed instructions are further evidence of her motherly concern for her little girl's health.

Fanny writes another letter to Harriet ten days later.

Commissioners Wednesday 16th [February 1814]
You have I fear thought me very neglectful my dearest Harriet in not answering a part of your last letter to me, relating to my dear little Fanny, but it has entirely arisen from my not having written to you myself since, for Capt. Austen did not think of it when he wrote on Sunday – You have no doubt before this given her

a dose of Magnesia if you found it necessary, therefore I need not say any thing more on the subject except that I perfectly approve of your care on the occasion, & shou'd have done the same myself – I fear from your not mentioning your own health, that you do not feel any better, & yet there has been sufficient time too, I think, for your Medicine to have taken effect; mind & give me a particular account of yourself when next you write.

I am very much disappointed at being prevented spending my sweet little Harriets birth-day with her, but you well know the uncertainty of Naval people, & that their private arrangements must yield to public duty, indeed I find there is so little use in planing any thing of the kind, that I have now quite given it up – Your message to Mr. Cather shall be delivered as soon as I see him, & I sincerely hope you will <u>have reason to thank him</u> – When the Eggs are nearly out let me know & I will get some more up to you by the first opportunity. The Nile did not arrive untill Sunday evening & I received my Watch on Monday in very good condition for which I beg you will thank Papa –

We sent by our friend Capt. Baldwin, (who, by the bye is still here, detained by Easterly Winds) for fifty weight of Fresh Butter half of which we intend for you.[34] should it be as good as some Lady William[s] got from Holland at 8d. pr. lb. we shall have a very great bargain. I did not send for any velvet. I think I shall buy something here to make little Fanny shifts, for by the time her Sisters are made I am sure hers will not be worth transferring – They are not touched yet, nor do I expect they will be, untill I am quietly settled on board the Namur; not that I am very gay I assure you; but when you are visiting, you must do as other people do – Capt. Austen unites with me in kind love to you all & many kisses to our little darlings. We have not heard from Chawton since we last wrote you. Adieu.

Yours most Affectly

F.F. Austen

I hope you keep Betsy employed. I have not yet been able to send her work.

As the visit to the Williamses drags on, Fanny and Charles were transferred to the Lobbs, as she had predicted. She agonizes over her reduced independence, for, as a visitor, she "must do as other people do." A seminal comment captures her further sentiments exactly: "[Y]ou well know the uncertainty of Naval people, & that their private arrangements must yield to public duty, indeed I find there is so little use in planing any thing of the kind, that I have now quite given it up."

Fanny does eventually return to the Namur and in March she begins a very long letter to Esther in Bermuda.

H. M. S. Namur 8th March [1814]

Many thanks my dearest Sister for your very nice present to myself & little Girls by the Dolphin;[35] *we sent our Boat for the Box as she was passing the Nore, & as I knew the articles in it were most of them seizable, I unpacked it, & sent the parcels separately to Town by Hancock, who delivered them all safe in Keppel Street.*

We spent our Christmas in Town with our friends; Palmer's <u>holidays</u> commenced the day <u>before ours</u>, and our pleasure in meeting was mutual, for besides being very fond of his cousins, who he was of course delighted to see, his attachment to his Uncle & myself is, if any thing, encreased by absence – I cannot help regretting your being so averse to his following his Uncle's profession, for he shews such a decided fondness for the Navy or rather for every thing relating to Ships & Boats, that I fear you will have some difficulty in checking his propensity for it – Do not imagine that we, or his friends in Keppel St. encourage him in it, on the contrary, his Uncle always strongly recommends his being a <u>Chief Justice</u>; he says I must confess to you, his having done, <u>only one thing</u>, for which you can blame him, & that is, for having made Palmer a present of a very handsome Model of the Indian which was carved on board this Ship, & is now painting & rigging; when it is quite completed it is to be sent to Keppel St. & I suppose Grandpapa will treat him to a Glass case for it –

Cassandra is still at Chawton where she has been spending two Months we sent her the Cedar Box, for which she returns you her love and many thanks; she composed a very nice little letter to her Papa the other day (in answer to one he wrote her) which her Aunt Cassandra commited to paper & said that she had had very little assistance in the composition – Harriet is with us just now in high health & spirits & never fails to drink "dear Aunt & Uncle Esten's & Uncle Ball's health too" after dinner; she has grown very tall since you saw her, but still retains her <u>em bon point</u>[36] *which was not the case with Cassandra at her age, for as <u>she</u> grew taller, she became thiner, & still continues so, but I hear <u>she</u> is looking <u>very</u> well & has excellent spirits; tell dear Hamilton that*

Cassy begins to read very prettily & can work a little at her needle. Little Fanny (for she is no longer entitled to the appellation of "Baby" or even "little") is in Town with Aunt & Grandmama, indeed I did not wish to have either of the Children on board here as long as the Cold weather lasted, but our poor Sister has been so unwell lately with her old complaint that I was afraid the charge of two children would fatigue her too much, which made me determine to have little Harriet here for a short time.

I have no female Servant but Betsy, nor have not had since Symes left me, for our present life is so unsettled & we are so continually roving about, that I thought an additional Servant would rather be a plague than a comfort untill we are settled on Shore in some way or other – I left Betsy in Town to attend little Fanny & Mrs Jones is kind enough to come up of a morning & Evening to fit my Bed & other little &c's for me – I make no apologies my dear Sister for entering so largely into my domestic concerns, as I am sure you are too deeply interested in every thing relating to us, to consider it an annoyance; but I think you'll not be satisfied unless I tell you something more about my little namesake, you must picture to yourself, Cassandra, at her age, we think her excessively like what she was; she is a very engaging child, & trys hard to speak, in which she succeeds pretty well but we cannot persuade her to walk yet. Cassandra will be in Town about the end of this Week & will I suppose spend some time with her friends in Keppel St. I shall request Harriet to take her to Kentish Town to see dear Palmer, as I think it will be a great treat to them both –

On my return from our Christmas Holidays I stoped at Sheerness, and paid a long promised visit of a fortnight to Sir Thos & Lady Williams, which went off better than I had expected her Ladyships manners are exactly <u>those</u> of <u>an English Woman</u> but I shou'd be very ungrateful not to allow that she was very friendly & kind to me, & expressed a wish, that I shou'd prolong my visit; Sir Thos possesses a warmth of manner which you rarely meet with in this country and which <u>Bermudians know how to value</u> – We passed a week with the Commissioner & Mrs Lobb after our visit to the Williams's was over, & we found them excessively kind –

11th. Since writing the above we have received yours and my Brothers kind letters by the Diadem,[37] *pray thank him for mine and say I will answer it by another opportunity if not by this – You neither of you mention my friend Mrs. Holliday*[38] *of whom I am particularly anxious to hear, as you spoke, in a former letter, of her being in a bad state of health – Write me word whether she is likely to increase her family, if you think her happy, if she is likely to come to England & in short every particular of this kind; you cannot think how interesting it is to me to hear the most trifling circumstances relating to my old friends, particularly those who I considered more immediately my companions viz Mrs Moore,*[39] *Mary Hinson,*[40] *Jane*[41] *I hear is married but I forget the Gentlemans name & pray tell me whether Louisa Goodrich*[42] *is going to be married, and how Mrs Territt is going on, now I really must stop or I shall wear your patience completely out –*

We saw Lady Warren two or three times during our visit in London; she is just as you left her, her spirits very low, and her health much injured by her continual anxiety about Sir John. She has lately had one or two very severe bilious attacks in consequence of fretting. She always speaks most affectionately of you, and appeared much pleased with Palmer the last day she called in Keppel Street, indeed she had her arm round his waist the whole time she sat with us; I have received a very kind letter from her since my return here, in which she begs me to spend a few days with her when I next go to Town. I have been thus particular my dear Sister in mentioning Lady Warren to prove to those (of whom I believe there are several in your little Island) who are inclined to doubt her sincerity, that they have formed a very mistaken idea of her character; we know that Mrs T…t said all she could before we left B-da. to prejudice the minds of her most intimate friends.

I heard from Harriet this morning, she mentions having been at Kentish Town the day before yesterday and that she found your dear Boy very well and happy; she gives a good account of the Keppel St. party, except that Mama has an inflammation in one of her eyes; you will of course hear from her an account of Mrs. Palmer's[43] *death, and of her having sold the greatest part of my*[44] *Grandfather's old Plate.*

This prodigious letter of mine will I fear startle you a little when you first open it, but I hope you will have patience to read it thro' when you have nothing better to do – It goes by the Tonnant[45] *& will most likely be given to Mr. Tattnall who is one of her Lieutenants. One of her Marine Officers a Mr Macnamara formerly belonged to the Namur, and was a good deal on Shore at Southend last Summer when Palmer was there, and as he was excessively fond of your Boy and very kind to him, perhaps you would like to pay him some little attention, which I am sure he will feel very grateful for; I do not request you to do it on* *our account, as he is not a likely young Man to please Mr. Esten, being rather superficial and very unsteady, he is however a good hearted creature and if you won't mind his being a little silly, I dare say you will like him. Poor Tom Fowle who now belongs to the Elephant has been very ill with a complaint on his Chest but I trust they have prevented an inflammation by bleeding & blistering he has lost 90 ounces of blood, which as you may suppose has reduced him exceedingly; I received a letter from him about a week ago, he had then only begun to leave his Bed which he had been confined to for a week before, and was mending slowly, but very weak.*

Mr. Fearon heard me say I was writing to you & beg'd I would offer his best respects. Make our kind remembrances to Mr. Clarke (our old Marine Officer) should you see him again. My best love to your Husband, Hamilton, my Uncle, Georgiana,[46] *Mrs Dickinson, Kate, &c &c &c and believe me most affectionately your*

   F.F. Austen.[47]

Best regards to Mr. Butterfield[48] —

17th The Tonnant has been detained so much longer than we had expected that I feel very much inclined to burn this letter and [write] another, but Capt. Austen will not consent to it, as he says our dispatches really must go on board at daylight to-morrow morning & it is now eight o'Clock in the evening, therefore you must be satisfied with old dates – We heard from Keppel St. yesterday they were all well & mention having received a letter from my Uncle a day or two before dated 5th Feby. in which he complains that none of us write to him pray make our peace with him, & tell him I think he accuses us unjustly – Our expectations of peace are very much increased by the accounts in to-day's paper, & I trust the day is not far distant when our poor [brother] will be restored to his friends, we [have lately seen] a Capt in [the] Navy who escaped from Verdun & was intimate with John, he speaks in the highest terms of him & says [he is one of] the very few who will return to his Country and friends [as he left them the] only bad habit he has acquired [is that of smoking which I trust we] shall soon break him of. Adieu ever yours F. Austen.

In this letter, several topics of mutual interest to Fanny and Esther are particularly telling. Fanny knows that Esther longs for news of her son

Palmer, who has spent his Christmas vacation with other members of the family at Keppel Street. Fanny, who is a devoted and supportive aunt, speaks of the "mutual pleasure" of this time spent with her nephew and of his strong affection for herself and Charles, which is, "if anything, increased by absence." Fanny is appreciative of the nice presents Esther has recently sent. During wartime, goods coming in from North America were searched by customs and regularly impounded. However, the resourceful Fanny found a way to get around that eventuality by having the goods intercepted at the Nore before they reached the London docks where they would be examined.

Fanny's account of her stay with the Williamses and Lobbs is less negative than the narrative sent to Harriet a month earlier, and significantly, she does not allude to the anger, frustration, and sense of entrapment she felt when she missed little Harriet's birthday or to how she longed for the independence of her ordinary shipboard life when the visit in Sheerness seemed never-ending. How she felt may still be vivid in her memory, but Fanny may be concerned that if she describes her insights about her lack of autonomy, the much older Esther will think Fanny's attitudes are out of keeping with a dutiful wife's appropriate mindset. Fanny values Esther's good opinion and has no wish to appear as complaining and petulant. To avoid her disapproval, Fanny may have chosen to provide only a politely general description of her visit to the Williamses and Lobbs.

In the course of her narrative, Fanny shares her own insight about Lady Williams's character, describing her hostess's manners as "exactly <u>those</u> of <u>an English Woman</u>." Fanny implies that Lady Williams assumes a superior air in the company of those she deems her inferior in rank, though she has not made Fanny feel inadequate while she is a guest. Fanny's remarks have a critical overtone. She is not pleased with the attitude of condescension she detects in Lady Williams's conduct towards others of a lesser social standing.

Good manners and right principles matter to Fanny. In fact, she does not hesitate to intervene when an unfair judgment has been made about another's character. For example, Fanny reminds Esther of criticisms of Lady Warren, circulated in Bermuda by someone Fanny only names obliquely as "Mrs. T...t." This is most likely a reference to Mrs Territt, Lady Warren's niece by marriage. Mrs T was also known to Fanny in Bermuda, as they were both young mothers who gave birth to daughters in 1810, Frances Mary[49] and Harriet Jane respectively. Fanny has been in Lady Warren's company several times in recent months. She is convinced that Lady Warren is sincere in her personal relationships, and moreover, she abhors Mrs T.'s attempts to "prejudice the minds of her most intimate friends," who on the basis of false reports have probably "formed a very mistaken idea of [Lady Warren's] character." Fanny not only defends Lady Warren, she empathizes with her current unhappiness and low spirits, caused by her "continual anxiety about Sir John," who is still serving on the North American Station and is arthritic, overtaxed, and becoming frailer. Lady Warren has had "one or two very severe bilious attacks in consequence of fretting." As a naval wife herself, Fanny understands how long separations trigger anxiety.

When Fanny mentions Mrs Palmer's sale of "the greatest part of my Grandfather's old Plate," she is referring to Mary, the second wife of their grandfather John Palmer. On his death in 1801 the terms of John Palmer's will gave Mary Palmer the use of his plate, china, and household furniture "for her life."[50] In selling some of the silver, she appears to have defaulted on the arrangement. Fanny and her sisters received no direct bequests from their grandfather in 1801, and now there was probably little chance that they would acquire any silver tableware linking them to their Palmer ancestry. This is Fanny's only mention of a Palmer step-grandmother. She may not have been in any contact with her.

The very act of writing to Bermuda rekindles Fanny's interest in news about the girls she has known there: Mrs Moore, Mary Hinson, Jane, and Louisa Goodrich. She particularly mentions her friend Betsy, who had married Evan Holliday, a naval chaplain, on 12 April 1813.[51] Fanny's queries about her friend's health, plans for motherhood, and personal happiness reflect the triumvirate of her own abiding personal concerns.

Fanny's desire to remain connected to her earlier circle of female friends is a touching detail. She names some of the girls who frequented the same balls and entertainments in St George's, that coterie with whom Fanny shared girlhood confidences, laughter, and tears. For most of the last three years, Fanny has spent longish periods of time away from adult female company. While on the *Namur*, she could not, in the ordinary sense, make and receive calls from other refined ladies. Indeed, her relative separation from cultured society has prevented her from making new friends and acquaintances. In such circumstances, news of old friends in Bermuda is cheering and important to her.

Fanny's fourth pregnancy is not mentioned, although Esther may have known that another baby is due in September, since Fanny is in the habit of sharing so many personal details with her sister. At least Esther is assured that Fanny has some support; she can call on a Mrs Jones, presumably a warrant officer's wife, for assistance with small domestic chores. If Fanny is hesitant to write about matters of pregnancy, Jane Austen has no such qualms. She describes the pregnancy of her other naval sister-in-law, Mary Austen, in somewhat graphic terms, saying that "Mrs. F.A. seldom either looks or appears quite well. – Little Embryo is troublesome, I suppose."[52] Perhaps it was considered easier for a genteel young woman to talk about someone else's pregnancy when she was unmarried and did not expect to experience this state herself. Or possibly, in Jane's case, she simply felt she could be candid with Cassandra about such matters in a private letter.

Towards the end of her "prodigious letter," Fanny writes about Lieutenant MacNamara, a marine officer who joined the *Namur* on 15 January 1813 but was now serving on HMS *Tonnant* and would be soon bound for Bermuda. Marines had quite different responsibilities compared to the sailors. They were soldiers trained to serve on both land and sea. "On board they formed part of the gun crews, acted as sharpshooters, made up the landing and boarding parties and acted as sentries."[53] Fanny thought Lieutenant MacNamara was "good hearted and … a little silly" but likeable and suggests Esther might want to treat him sympathetically on account of his kindness to her son Palmer the previous summer.

Lieutenant MacNamara and Lieutenant Tom Fowle, who had recently transferred from Charles's command to Frank Austen's vessel, HMS *Elephant*, were only two of the young men that Fanny came to know while on the *Namur*. She befriended Douglas Jerrold, who was only ten years old when he came aboard as a volunteer first class on 22 December 1813.[54] Volunteers were boys who went to sea before they were old enough to become midshipmen. According to a 1794 order in council, volunteers first class consisted of "young gentlemen intended for the sea service … provided they are not under the age of eleven years; to be styled Volunteers, and allowed wages of six pounds per annum."[55] A captain decided who he would accept as a volunteer, choosing only some of the boys brought to his attention by their fathers or other relatives. Candidates had to be "young gentlemen," since they were destined, if they proved to be up to standard, to become members of the officer corps.

On board, a volunteer first class was the immediate responsibility of the captain, although he received his education under the schoolmaster and learned navigation from the sailing master. As Brian Lavery explains, after three years he could be "promoted to midshipman, and begin to take some responsibility, perhaps taking charge of a group of seamen for welfare and disciplinary purposes, commanding one of the ship's boats or a group of guns in action, or acting as a deputy to the officer of the watch ... After a total of six years, he was entitled to sit a stiff oral exam before three captains, which not everyone passed."[56] If he succeeded, he would be promoted to the rank of second lieutenant.

Douglas Jerrold's family was most likely known to Charles and Fanny long before he came on board, since his father, Samuel Jerrold, held the lease of the theatre in Sheerness from 1807 and also from 1810 in Southend. Although he was still aged ten, Douglas joined the *Namur* at Charles's invitation and was warmly welcomed into the Austen family circle. He read Buffon's *Natural History* for hours in the captain's cabin, and he was allowed to keep pet pigeons on deck and "loved to see his flight of birds sweeping around the fleet."[57] While on board, he played the character of "Robber" in *The Iron Chest*,[58] and his experience as a child actor[59] contributed an air of professionalism to the *Namur*'s theatricals. However, his early naval education with Charles did not lead to a career in the sea service. Instead, Douglas Jerrold became a journalist, a contributor to *Punch* magazine, a popular playwright, and a significant figure in the London theatrical scene.

Another recruit particularly encouraged by Charles and surely by Fanny as well was "Young Kendall." He was probably William Webb Kendall, the son of Edward Augustus Kendall,[60] a social campaigner, travel writer, and author of popular children's books. William joined the *Namur* on 1 August 1813, and by October he was, according to Jane Austen, who knew of him, "going on very well" and going "into the Office now every afternoon – still attending school in the morning."[61] As the *Namur* was a receiving ship, there was a lot of paperwork documenting the sailors' comings and goings and perhaps

Kendall was useful in assisting with this clerical task. It made sense that young Kendall's father would find Charles, who was a caring man with extensive literary interests, well suited to encourage his son and supervise his naval education.[62]

In addition to Douglas Jerrold and William Kendall, Barry Haines had come aboard on 8 August 1812 and was under Charles's tutelage until he was first sent to sea from the *Namur*. Twelve years later Charles was pleased to encounter Haines again when they happened to meet in port in St George's, Bermuda.[63] By then Haines was commanding the schooner HMS *Union* (3 guns). All three of these young men received some of their instruction in the captain's cabin, adjacent to the family quarters where Fanny could ordinarily be found. They must have benefited from her gentle feminine attention and their connections to her gave Fanny a sense of community within the navy of the quarterdeck.

Able seaman Clarkson Stanfield also mixed with the family, but probably not as closely, for he was not a trainee officer like the others. He initially came to Charles's attention as someone who could paint a toy wooden coach for the Austen children.[64] Stanfield, who had a background in the heraldic painting of coach livery, was subsequently employed by Charles for other artistic tasks, such as creating theatrical scenes. He would have been a natural choice for colouring the model of the *Indian* that Charles had ordered to be made on board as a Christmas gift for Palmer Esten. While on the *Namur*, Stanfield continued to sketch for his own pleasure.[65] Several of his earliest surviving drawings date from his time. They include a crayon portrait of his sister Mary and a male figure in a kilt, which may have been part of the design for Stanfield's decoration of Admiral Williams's ballroom in Sheerness. It would be nice to think he might have sketched some shipboard scene for Fanny, like his charming drawing of two midshipmen (Fig. 31).

Clarkson Stanfield later became well-known for his varied artistic achievements. In the 1820s, together with David Roberts, he created moving dioramas, an impressive form of public entertainment in which huge paintings were unrolled to the accompaniment of sound effects and lighting. One of these productions told the story of *The Battle of Navarino* (1827), which occurred when a combined naval force of British, French, and Russian ships destroyed an Egyptian and Turkish fleet during the War of Greek Independence. Stanfield earned praise as a scene painter in London, where

Fig. 31 This sketch of two midshipmen by Clarkson Stanfield is a charming example of the artist's early work, dating from the time when he served as an able seaman on board HMS *Namur*.

he designed and painted the sets for both *The Rent Day* and *The Factory Girl*, plays produced in London's Drury Lane Theatre in 1832 and written by his former associate on the *Namur*, Douglas Jerrold. Stanfield also illustrated books by the popular novelist Captain Marryat – *The Pirate and the Three Cutters* (1836) and *Poor Jack* (1840). He was considered "the chief rival of [J.M.W.] Turner as a painter of marine subjects in the years following the defeat of Napoleon."[66] His most famous canvases included *The Battle of Trafalgar* (1835) and HMS *Victory Bearing the Body of Nelson* (1853).[67]

Although Fanny showed a caring interest in Charles's young protegés, her connections to her parents and siblings were her most important personal relationships after her love for Charles and her children. She maintained an affectionate rapport with her parents, Dorothy and John Grove Palmer. She was grateful for her mother's periodic help with child care, and she appreciated her father's role in organizing and financing family holidays at Southend. John Grove Palmer also undertook small practical commissions for Fanny, such as the repair of her watch. She was thankful for his help with matters she could not attend to for herself because of her remote location on the *Namur*.

Fanny's only brother, John, is a somewhat enigmatic figure in the Palmer family. He was an officer in the British army, but the identity of his regiment and the extent and location of his active service during the war years is not known. At some point he had became a prisoner of war at Verdun, a fortified town of about 10,000 in the province of Lorraine in northeastern France and the central depot for the detention of British officers. The expanded population at Verdun included some of those unlucky individuals trapped in France at the resumption of hostilities in May 1803; this group of *détenus* was comprised of a wide spectrum of individuals – people of fashion, businessmen, tradesmen, invalids gone abroad for their health, and families, including children. Their presence, together with that of the officers, meant that commercial Verdun thrived, albeit with inflated prices.

The comfort and quality of life of a detained British officer was a function of his financial resources, his particular interests, and willingness to give his word not to escape. Officers on parole could live in town and even venture a short distance into the countryside. John Palmer apparently chose this option, as Fanny speaks of him riding out every day with a colonel. Additionally, John might be enjoying various amusements,[68] such as entry to one of several social clubs, which held balls and assemblies, or attendance at "theatricals, cock-fighting, duck- hunting, and picnics [held] in the summer among the woods within the two leagues limit" from the camp.[69] The readily available gaming tables and gaming clubs were pernicious and dangerous forms of entertainment. It would be hoped, on Fanny's part, that John had not succumbed to this temptation. She states her disapproval that he is smoking, a habit probably originating in the informal atmosphere of Verdun club life.

Just how John fitted into life at Verdun is not known. The other Palmers would have some idea of his possible lifestyle, as escapees from the camp shared stories of their experiences in Verdun when they returned to England. Since personal communications between France and England were highly restricted and often impossible, exact details about John's existence, including his financial well-being, were probably matters of speculation in the Palmer family. When Fanny refers to him as "poor John,"[70] she may simply mean that she empathizes with his loss of freedom, missed opportunities to further his military career, and whatever lack of money he may be experiencing. Fanny speaks of him with sisterly interest.

Fanny wondered when she would be reunited with her brother.[71] Military and political developments in France that occurred just after she had written in March 1814 augured well for his return to England before too long. Under a campaign spearheaded by Tsar Alexander of Russia and the King of Prussia, the combined Russian, Prussian, and Austrian armies took Paris on 31 March after an intensive two-day offensive. Napoleon's abdication followed on 11 April, and with Napoleon exiled to Elba and the Bourbon King Louis XVIII reinstated in France, peace seemed secured and John's detention at Verdun would soon come to an end. Indeed, according to Fanny's subsequent letter to James Esten, John had arrived safely back on Keppel Street by 8 July.

Fanny's other sibling of concern was the "delicate" Harriet. They were separated for nine years by the Atlantic Ocean, as Harriet left Bermuda in 1802 and Fanny came to England in 1811. But over the past three years, from 1811 to 1814, Fanny has seen much more of Harriet, both at Keppel Street and aboard the *Namur*. They have now grown closer as friends as well as as sisters. Fanny was very grateful for Harriet's willingness to care for her little girls. In return, she was solicitous of Harriet's seemingly continuous ill health. Was her sister asthmatic, the victim of something more serious, or just a perpetual complainer?[72] No precise information is available, but we know that the apothecary, Mr Cather, had business from Fanny on Harriet's behalf.

Some of Fanny's letters provide hints about Harriet, her lifestyle, and her personality. By 1814 Harriet was twenty-eight years old. She had a measure of social life, for Fanny speaks of her attending a little dance in London. However, she has not received an offer of marriage, nor is there any mention of actual suitors. Fanny's manner of writing to Harriet would give one no reason to think that this sister was amusing, was someone to tease, or was even particularly good company. Fanny's correspondence with Harriet primarily addresses concerns about the children's well-being and practical matters concerning household supplies and management. The lighthearted sharing of news that characterizes Fanny's letters to Esther is missing. Even so, Fanny wrote two personal, even confidential, letters to Harriet during her visit to the Williamses and Lobbs in Sheerness. Rather than these letters serving as evidence that Fanny and Harriet had become much, much closer, they more likely suggest that Fanny had felt a great need to vent her frustration and the sister at hand seemed the best choice. Fanny loved Harriet, but their level of intimacy never approached the feelings Fanny shared with Esther. Esther had been a second mother to her from the age of twelve. She was Fanny's chief confidante and Fanny loved her without reservation.

Fanny's next letter is to James Esten and is written from Sheerness Harbour where the *Namur* has been undergoing repairs since 22 May. She has a lot to say; in fact every page is crossed with red ink.

Namur Sheerness 30th June. [1814][73]
My dear Brother

I hope I shall have better success with this letter, than I had with one which I began & nearly finished to you last Month just before I went to Town. I left it open intending to take it with me & give you the latest account of your dear Boy after I had seen him, but unfortunately in the hurry & confusion of going my letter was forgotten, my protracted stay in Town made it of such an old date when I returned, a fortnight ago that I did not think it was worth sending; you must therefore give me all due credit for the intention, & not condemn me as an inattentive correspondent –

Palmer was at home only one day & a night during my visit & he appeared in high health & spirits & as usual very much delighted at seeing us; we had promised ourselves great pleasure in having him here with us for a short time during his present vacation, but the odious meazles have got amongst the Children belonging to the Ship & knocked up all our plans. I have been obliged in consequence to have my Children in Town for tho' I ardently wish they had all had it & got well over it, knowing it to be a disorder they must one day or other have, I cannot prevail on myself to expose them to it, & I think I can answer for <u>one other person</u>[74] in the World, who feels the same with regard to every contagious disorder – I am afraid that poor Palmer was not gratified any more than myself with a sight of the allied Sovereigns before they left Town, he has however still a chance of seeing Blucher & Platoff who I believe will remain in Town some time longer. My little Girls came home one day from walking, in ecstasies at the thought of having seen the King of Prussia; this will give you an idea how entirely these great Personages engrossed the thoughts of every description of people when even little children talked of nothing else –

I dined with Sir John & Lady Warren when I was last in Town & met Mr Kennedy[75] who by the time we parted must have been pretty well tired of answering my innumerable questions about Bermuda; he did not give me a very pleasing accoun[t] of St Georges for he & Sir John both think it is very much altered for the worse in consequence of the increase of population – I am glad to find that Toddings arrived so opportunely, my Sister would otherwise have been at a loss f[or] a Man Servant; he is better than none at all but I fear not equal to Matthew in any respect. However as you do not intend to entertain much company, it is of no great importance. I am as much teazed in my domestic concerns as you have been of late & am at this moment without a Nurse tho' I left a very nice Woman in that capacity, with the Children only a fortnight ago when I came down here, who I hired when I was in Town, but some Lady has in my absence most unhandsomely enticed her away from me, by holding out advantages which I cou'd not – & I am now obliged to go up again in search of another. I called on Mrs Byng[76] when I was last in London & had the pleasure of seeing my old servant Molly, or in more refined language "Mary" she appeared much delighted at the meeting & came to Keppel St. twice or three times to see Cassandra whom she still seems very strongly attached to.[77]

Tell dear Hamilton with my love that I am glad to hear he is so fond of his Book & agrees so well with Miss Richardson,[78] to whom I beg you will offer my best regards. Tell him also that Cassy is a very good Girl & reads very prettily; & that I hope he is as fond of Aunt Austen as Cassy is of his Mama; for she always says that next to Papa & Mama she loves Aunt Esten –

My other two little Girls you know very little about, indeed the last you have never seen but you may form a very good idea of her if you can recollect what Cassandra, was at the Age of 2 Years. They are nice healthy good-tempered children & of course by Papa & Mama are thought very pretty also.

Keppel Street July 8th. We have been here now exactly a week & are just on the point of returning to the Namur, as my good Mans leave is nearly expired. We found our friends all well except poor Harriet, whose health still continues very delicate, but I think her visit to Kintbury will set her up again, for I am persuaded that her ill health is in a great measure owing to her residence in London, which certainly never did agree with her, & is at this season very trying to a delicate constitution – The Children are all quite well notwithstanding

the weather is excessively warm, they have excellent appetites, good spirits, &
happy countenances; of course when I speak of <u>the Children</u> I include Palmer,
for indeed my dear Brother I know no difference when he is with my children,
his Uncle Austen & myself both consider him as one of our own, & I can with
sincerity assure you that he is highly deserving of the affection and attention
of all his friends. He attends regularly to his lessons, which he performs as well
as a child of his age can be expected to do; sometimes of course he is a little
careless, but his Uncle John[79] takes great pains with him & always points out
his faults & his behaviour on these occasions is very proper, he does not cry &
get sulky as I have sometimes <u>seen little folks do</u>, but goes into a room by himself
& endeavours to learn it more perfectly. His Aunt Harriet's Motherly care of
him you are fully sensible of, as well as of the great affection his other friends
feel towards him, therefore I need not say anything further on this subject, but
I am sure it will be a great satisfaction to you to hear that the Servants are all
very kind & attentive to him.

We were at Mr. Leonards[80] last evening where we met your friend Mr.
Richardson[81] & his Wife & her Daughters & as many Bermudians as the old
gentleman cou'd Muster, for he still retains his fondness for large parties &
only think of his having been to the Queen's Drawing room! he was highly
delighted with it I understand & means to go again — We have just learnt that
Mr Holliday is appointed Chaplain to the Dock Yard at Sheerness & are very
much pleased at the prospect of seeing our friend Betsy,[82] but I am almost afraid
we shall have left before they arrive however we shall at all events see them for
I will go down on purpose —

Capt Austen unites with me in kindest love to my Sister, Hamilton, my
Uncle & all other kind friends & I beg my Sister's acceptance of a Case which
I have requested Harriet to pack up with some things she is about sending &
at the same time beg to offer my best thanks for the 3 pair of Gloves she was so
kind to send me. I am

   yours affectionately
    F.F. Austen

Fanny regrets that a measles epidemic amongst the ship's children has
caused them to leave the *Namur* in "hurry and confusion." This swift removal
of her own children from a source of infection marks a change of policy

from 1812, when Fanny thought it desirable to provide early exposure to measles. Perhaps she is concerned about her own health, as her pregnancy is now in its seventh month.

Fanny understates her situation when she describes herself as "teased in domestic concerns." Her letters from the *Namur* tell the sad saga of many servants who have left her employ – first Nancy in 1812; an unnamed and sickly nurse who accompanied them to Southend in 1813; Symes; and more recently a nurse she had hired in London, only to have her lured away by a more attractive offer of employment. Betsy alone has shown some measure of loyalty by remaining in Fanny's service. Fanny told Esther in an earlier letter that she is postponing the appointment of new staff until they are on shore, but this sounds like rationalization on Fanny's part.

Although Fanny is frustrated by hired help repeatedly leaving her employ, she is solicitous in her enquires about servants in the Esten household whom she remembers from Bermuda. In this letter she mentions, Toddings, who was with her and Charles in Halifax in 1810, and Matthew. In her previous letter to Esther, Fanny had sent regards to "Georgianna" and "Kate." Other servants have been mentioned in other letters. Fanny ordinarily sends good wishes to particular servants at the point where she is closing her letter with affectionate greetings to her own family members. Fanny gives the impression that these named people interest her still; they are part of the Bermuda world she has left behind, but whether they were really servants or in fact were slaves is unclear.

When Fanny had joined Esther's household in the Palmer parental home in St George's in 1802, such slaves and freed servants her parents may have had likely became attached to the Estens' household. If so, Fanny would have had an extended relationship with domestic help whom she had known most of her life, including in the early years of her marriage. Virginia Bernhard observes that given Bermuda's maritime economy, many black slaves were sailors; this meant that "many of [Bermuda's slave women] shared with their white mistresses the hardships and anxieties of having men at sea. In Bermuda's small households the bonds of womanhood, of female companionship, ... undoubtedly transcended race."[83] Accordingly, Fanny may have received empathetic support from one or more female slaves of the household who, like her, became worried about the safety of their loved ones when they were away at sea. If some of these slaves or their descendants were still with the Estens, it would be natural for Fanny's letters to include them in her enquiries.

Fanny's unexpected sojourn in London in May and June meant she had a longer visit than anticipated at Keppel Street. Fanny's children were thrilled to be in London during the celebratory visit of foreign heads of state. Major figures responsible for the allied victory over France were enjoying a euphoric reception. They included Tsar Alexander I of Russia, King Frederick William of Prussia, Prince Metternich of Austria, the Prince of Liechtenstein, Field Marshall Blücher, and generals Platov and Count Barclay de Tolly. The dignitaries were showered with gifts and feted at the Guildhall, where 700 guests dined on gold plate. They were cheered wherever they appeared. Cassandra Austen was in London about the same time and received a teasing warning from Jane to "take care of yourself, & do not be trampled to death in running after the Emperor [Tsar Alexander]."[84] Fanny was not partial to celebrity worship, though she sounds amused that her children are caught up in the wave of excitement that the presence of the "great Personages" has triggered. Their ecstatic response to a glimpse of the King of Prussia may have occurred if he, like Tsar Alexander, visited the British Museum, which was located very close to 22 Keppel Street.

As it turned out, the prolonged war with France took more time to bring to a conclusion than expected. The multiple problems of the peace were tackled at the Congress of Vienna, which formally opened on 1 November 1814. The Final Act of the Congress of Vienna, signed 9 June 1815, would redraw the map of Europe for the next forty years. Meanwhile, Napoleon escaped from Elba and landed on 1 March 1815 in France, where he raised a large army once more and waged a new war until his ultimate defeat on 18 June 1815 at Waterloo. In the final battle, Napoleon launched a strong attack against the British and other forces led by the Duke of Wellington, but Field Marshal Blücher marched his remaining Prussian troops to Waterloo and made a timely assault on Napoleon's right flank. With a counterattack by Wellington on Napoleon's centre, the French army was routed. Napoleon surrendered to the Royal Navy on 15 July 1815 and was exiled to Saint Helena, a remote island in the South Atlantic. During this period, the War of 1812 between Britain and the United States, in which Charles had hoped to take an active part, was brought to a negotiated close with the signing of the Treaty of Ghent on 24 December 1814.

There was another important benefit arising from Fanny's visit to London in May and June 1814. Her arrival occurred soon after *Mansfield Park* was advertised for sale on 9 May. Jane ordinarily arranged for her siblings to receive advance copies of her novels. As Fanny was now in Keppel Street, she was well placed to take receipt of the one earmarked for Charles and herself. Her reaction is not recorded, although she must have noted that the heroine, Fanny Price, bore her own first name. Perhaps this was merely coincidental; after all, "Fanny" was a common name. Jane Austen had already used the name "Jane" in *Pride and Prejudice*, but it is hard to believe that in so doing she intended to make some personal connection between herself and Elizabeth Bennet's sister.

Fanny writes of her delight in seeing all her children and her nephew Palmer with "excellent appetites, good spirits & happy countenances." She has been an affectionate and caring aunt to Palmer and Hamilton Esten since their babyhood, and she has become particularly close to Palmer since he began school in Kentish Town in 1812. She tells James, with all sincerity, that she and Charles treat Palmer as one of their own. She closes with cheerful descriptions of their social engagements in London, such as evening parties with Bermuda friends and a reunion dinner with Lady Warren and Sir John, who has now returned from the North American Station.

As she looked ahead, Fanny must have continued to view the future with mixed feelings. Charles has yet to secure another seagoing commission, and with the arrival of peace he could expect a drastic reduction of frigates in active service. Thus, their perennial problems about his employment persist. Yet, Fanny has some good reasons for thinking positively about their relocation on shore. It will be less difficult to attract and keep servants and easier to see friends and family. Charles's brother Frank has recently left the *Elephant* and joined his wife and children ashore, so there will be greater opportunities for their two families to become better acquainted. Fanny also anticipates a reunion with her Bermuda friend Betsy Holliday. Above all, Fanny looks forward to having a home of her own where she can support, protect, and nurture the ones she loves best: Charles, the little girls, and the baby soon to be born. At that time, she will encourage the intimacy of family life in what she hopes will be much more congenial and attractive quarters than on the *Namur*, until at some unknown time in the future Charles's career will take him away from them once again.

The rest of the summer passed quietly. Since April there had been much less activity aboard the *Namur*, as there were fewer vessels in service needing sailors. A very faint entry in Fanny's pocket diary reports welcome news about a new servant from Mile End, who is "taken into my service at Jul 16, Gravesend," a port town on the Thames easily reachable by water from Sheerness. Sometime in July a heavily pregnant Fanny returned to the *Namur* to be with Charles. She was spared the discomfort of riding at anchor on a rough sea, since the *Namur* was still in Sheerness Harbour, but as she expectantly awaited the birth of her child, Fanny could not foresee the extent of forthcoming change.

CHAPTER 8

Death and Disaster:
1814 and the Years Beyond

ALTHOUGH FANNY HAD ALREADY GONE through three successful pregnancies, every birth is different and any birth can be problematic. She knew of women who had not survived childbirth or whose baby had succumbed. Her sister-in law Elizabeth Knight had died in 1808, soon after the arrival of her eleventh child. Fanny's own mother had lost a son, William, at birth. Fanny was expecting her fourth child to arrive in September 1814 and must have planned to leave the *Namur* for Keppel Street well in advance of her confinement. However, her labour began two weeks prematurely and a fourth daughter was born on board the ship on Wednesday, 31 August. At least one of her little girls was probably aboard with her; the other two were either at Keppel Street or Chawton Cottage. No mention was made in the *Namur*'s logbook of the birth. According to this record, it was a day of "light winds inclined to calm." Life went on as usual and included a scheduled morning court martial that required Charles's attendance. In the opinion of David Nokes, Fanny laboured and delivered in a "stinking between-decks cabin,"[1] but his lurid description has no basis in fact, given the amenities of the captain's family quarters on the *Namur*, which is where she would have been.

Initially all was well with the mother and baby. The joyful news spread quickly. Martha Lloyd heard from Jane that "Mrs. C. Austen is safe in her bed with a Girl."[2] At Godmersham, Fanny Knight received "a letter from

Fig. 32   Kentish Town Chapel in the Parish of St Pancras, where Fanny's funeral was held and Charles placed a marble tablet in her memory.

Uncle Chs. to announce the birth of his 4th girl."[3] Then disaster struck: Fanny developed unexpected post-natal complications. The nature of these difficulties is not known, but most likely Fanny was the victim of an infection, possibly the condition known as puerperal (childbed) fever. Six days after giving birth, she was dead.

Charles was stunned and overwhelmed with grief. Others helped him as they could. His brother Edward Knight rushed from Godmersham to his side. Some interim provision was made for the baby and whichever children were still aboard. The Admiralty gave Charles three weeks leave from the *Namur*. He never returned as her captain.

On 12 September Fanny was buried at the Kentish Town Chapel in the parish of old St Pancras (Fig. 32).[4] In the official records, her abode was listed as the parish of St Giles, a description that fitted with the location of the Palmer home on Keppel Street and reflected the family's connections to Kentish Town. Only the male members of the family were at the funeral. Attendance on such occasions was considered "too stressful for the female mind and body to bear."[5] The *Namur*'s former chaplain, Reverend Joseph Fearon,[6] was asked to read the funeral service.[7] He must have found this an immensely sad duty, as he had been a valued friend to both Fanny and Charles since their arrival on the *Namur* and until he left the ship in March 1814. The tiny baby was given the name Elizabeth, but she did not bear it for long. To add calamity to disaster, she survived her mother by only three weeks and was interred beside her on 23 September.

Charles was inconsolable. The Admiralty was apparently compassionate. On 1 October he was commissioned without a gap in service into HMS *Phoenix* (36 guns), which was being readied for service on the Mediterranean Station, although she would not depart England until 1 April 1815. In accepting this commission, Charles acknowledged his desperate need to be employed and thus distracted from his immense grief. At the same time, he bemoaned the fact he would be leaving behind his motherless children, his lasting connection to Fanny.

In the Kentish Town Chapel, Charles placed a white marble memorial tablet on a black marble surround. The inscription reads:

Sacred to the memory of
Frances FitzWilliams Austen
wife of
Capt. Charles John Austen
(of the Royal Navy,)
Who died in childbed, Septr. 6th 1814
Aged 24 years

The design of the tablet incorporates, above the inscription, the motifs of an anchor lying under a palm tree and, at the bottom, a small shield, whose right half appears to show three palmers' purses and a chevron, emblematic of the Palmer family arms. The details to the left are too faded now to be deciphered. The anchor and palm[8] are fitting remembrances of Fanny's naval connections, her beloved Bermuda, and her maiden name. The text of the epitaph is touchingly personal in tone. It captures her relationship to the important people in her life: her parents, siblings, husband, children, and friends, and it recognizes her standing as a Christian. It reads:

Stop Passenger[9] and Contemplate!
A Child whom Natures God had taught the Way,
Her Parents dictates ne'er to disobey,
A Sister, in whom Center'd every Love,
To Charm the Angels in the Realms above.
A Loving Wife, a Parent truly dear
A Pious Christian and a Friend sincere,
Reader! Example take, let you and I
Live as She liv'd, and like Her learn to Die,
Sleep on dear fair One, wait the Almighty's Will,
Then rise unchang'd, and be an Angel still.

Fanny's epitaph memorializes a young woman of many virtues. Might this have been Charles's composition, for who would be better suited than he to pen it? It is telling that Fanny's attributes celebrate Charles's particular connections to Fanny: she was "a loving wife," "a parent truly dear," "a friend sincere." It was a comforting and necessary inclusion for him that she be described as "a pious Christian." Fanny's epitaph suggests that her inherent goodness shone so brightly for all to see that she could "charm the Angels in the Realms above," until she joined them herself, an angel.

The Austen relatives responded to the news of Fanny's death in diverse ways. A cousin of Charles's mother, Elizabeth Leigh of Stoneleigh, noted on 20 September that "the Austin family have a great loss in the attach'd & beloved wife of Captn. C. Austin; who died (by a mistake) on board a Ship from whence she ought sooner to have removed."[10] Fanny's unexpected death was greeted with great sadness at Chawton Cottage. Jane Austen broke off a written commentary on her niece Anna Austen's manuscript novel and only returned to it on 18 September. In a letter that day, she noted: "I am very glad dear Anna, that I wrote as I did before this sad Event occurred. I have now only to add that your G. Mama does not seem the worse now for the Shock."[11] Jane's words suggest that in her present grief she has had little inclination for literary criticism and that her mother had been greatly upset by the news but is now better.

This was Jane's second sister-in-law to die in childbirth. It was a serious risk for married woman of those times, but one that Jane never faced. She did, however, use maternal language in relation to her novels as if they were her progeny. She called *Pride and Prejudice* "my own darling Child,"[12] and she could "no more forget [*Sense and Sensibility*] than a mother can forget her sucking child."[13] Whether she also reflected that her own three literary children to date – *Sense and Sensibility*, *Pride and Prejudice*, and *Mansfield Park* – may have owed their creation to her unmarried state is unknown, but when Fanny died as a consequence of giving birth, such a thought might have crossed her mind.

Fanny's own family did what they individually thought was best for Charles. Her brother John joined him on board the *Phoenix* and sailed on her as a passenger for some months. His presence afforded Charles supportive male company from his Palmer family. On two occasions John shared with Charles his negative feelings about his immediate relatives. Since his return to England in July, a serious rift had apparently arisen such that he was "totally estranged from his Father & Mother as well as from his sister Harriet." Charles's journal entry about this unhappy state of affairs continued: "[T]he part of his family in Bermuda are those only for whom he appears to have any affection; to my Children he is I believe much attached also, & I think to myself this is a sad thing."[14] John must have stayed with the *Phoenix* until at least late June 1815, as a journal entry by Charles again records "what sad feelings [John] has towards his nearest relations."[15] Charles does not identify what would explain John Palmer's intense feelings of disaffection.

Even in the midst of his unhappiness, John was not uniformly morose. When the *Phoenix* made a call at Brindisi, John waltzed with enthusiasm at a party on HMS *Garland* (22 guns) even though there was, in Charles's words, "a very poor display of females one or two only tolerable out of the six who were there."[16] In later years John Palmer chose to connect to his Irish roots.[17] By the terms of his grandfather's will, he eventually inherited the Palmer's Irish property in County Kerry, Banemore House, and its adjacent land.

The Estens in Bermuda heard the devastating news of Fanny's death some weeks later. James Esten had already replied to Fanny's last letter, little knowing she would never read his. Esther and Harriet carefully preserved some of Fanny's letters from the last four years. Although keeping family correspondence was a common practice, there was a special poignancy in this case. Fanny's letters became a very personal resource about a sister, wife, mother, and aunt who had loved them all so dearly.

Charles gave pieces of mourning jewellery to those female relatives closest to Fanny. Harriet Palmer received a gold ring with a lock of Fanny's fair hair set in gold and black enamel. The engraved inscription inside reads: "F. F. Austen ob. 6 Sept 1814 aet. 24." In later years Cassandra Austen always wore a gold ring that incorporated Fanny's hair together with that of Mary Austen, Frank's first wife, who died in 1823 after the birth of her eleventh child. Cassandra bequeathed this ring to her namesake and niece, Fanny's daughter Cassy. Jane was sensitive to Charles's continuing grief. She sent him an early copy of *Emma* after its publication on 13 November 1815. Charles registered his thanks, telling Jane that "Emma arrived in time to a moment. I am delighted with her, more so I think than even with my favourite Pride & Prejudice, & have read it three times in the Passage."[18]

Jane and Cassandra made concerted efforts to keep in touch with their three nieces. Jane went to Keppel Street to visit the recently bereaved children in late November 1814. She found them sad and restrained and declared: "[T]hat puss Cassy, did not shew more pleasure in seeing me than her Sisters ... she does not shine in the tender feelings. She will never be a Miss O'neal; more in the Mrs Siddons line."[19] Jane's assessment of Cassy's demeanour suggests that her niece had a flair for the dramatic, in the style of the great tragedienne Sarah Siddons, who was known for the grandeur of her emotional expression.[20] During October and November 1815 Jane managed to see the little girls several times. She sounds quite determined on this matter. She wrote to Cassandra that "nothing I trust will keep us from Keppel Street." She gladly reported several days later that "we got to Keppel Street ... which was all I cared for."[21] Jane also invited Harriet Palmer to pay a call with the children when Jane was visiting at her brother Henry's current address, 23 Hans Place, London. On occasions when Cassy was staying at Chawton Cottage, her Aunt Cassandra sometimes arranged a concurrent visit from her cousin Caroline Austen or from Mary Jane Austen, who lived at nearby Alton.

During the bleak period in the years immediately after Fanny's death, Charles received welcome emotional support from naval friends first met on the North American Station. His pocketbook records several meetings with

Edward Hawker before Charles sailed from England on the *Phoenix*. On a later occasion, "Mrs Hawker took the [Austen] children out in the carriage and gave them heaps of toys."[22] Charles also spent time with captains James, Lord Townshend, and Frederick Hickey. He kept up a correspondence with Lady Warren, who retained an interest in the children and on one occasion gave Cassy some clothes.

Irrespective of the support from family and friends, Charles remained emotionally devastated. Fanny was so much the centre of his life that it was impossible to forget her. His journal entries over the year after her death mirror his intense anguish. He fantasized that he had met her again and he dreamed he was "again blessed with her society."[23] His loss was "irreparable" and "ever lamented."[24] When the *Phoenix* was in port at Brindisi, Charles noticed a painting of Bathsheba in a private home. He detected the "same cast of Countenance as my Beloved Fannys and the same luxuriant Fair hair," but he insisted that his Fanny was "far more attractive."[25] The traditional naval toast for Saturday nights honoured "sweethearts and wives." Now he had neither. When he read one of his "Beloved Wife's letters," he was "much struck and affected by the exquisite tenderness and simplicity of her stile."[26] Anniversaries associated with her death were particularly painful. On 31 August 1815, he wrote: "[H]ow happy I then felt at what I esteemed my Beloved Fannys safe deliverance."[27] On 6 September, the date of her death, Charles wrote only two words in his journal: "Fatal day."[28] His feelings were still raw years later when he wrote: "[T]his is the fifth anniversary of my dear Fanny's death. I find my loss greater than on the first."[29]

For many years thereafter Charles relived his grief, particularly on other anniversaries associated with Fanny. On 3 December 1815 he wrote in his pocketbook: "my dear departed angels birthday on which she would have compleated her 26th year Alas."[30] He regularly noted "my beloved wife's Birthday,"[31] doing so even twelve years after her death.[32] He sadly recalled "the anniversary of my marriage with my dearest departed Fanny" twenty years after the fact.[33] The year before Charles was greatly distressed when he "broke the glass of my dearest Fanny's miniature by endeavouring to take out and clean it."[34]

Charles's plan to manage his grief by remaining fully occupied in the sea service was eventually thwarted. His commission had begun and continued with some success. Charles sailed from England in early April 1815 for the Mediterranean Station, only weeks after peace with France was broken by Napoleon's escape from Elba and his subsequent return to lead the French into war again. Once on his station, Charles, acting as the commodore of the *Phoenix*, HMS *Undaunted* (38 guns) and HMS *Garland* (22 guns), blockaded the Neapolitan coast, an exercise that caused Naples to desert the French cause. Following this success, he went in search of a reported flotilla of French warships in the Aegean Sea, again in company with HMS *Garland* but also joined by HMS *Aquilon* (32 guns) and HMS *Reynard* (10 guns). Their target was never located, and peace was restored by Napoleon's lasting defeat at the Battle of Waterloo. For Charles, the new situation meant his duties changed into peacekeeping activities in the Aegean where he strove to obstruct and eradicate pirates operating in the Greek archipelago. Then catastrophe struck. On 20 February 1816, the *Phoenix*, apparently ill advised by a local pilot and while sailing in the grip of a fierce storm, was forced ashore and wrecked in the harbour of Chisme, fifty-three miles west of Smyrna on the coast of Asia Minor.[35] All hands were saved, as were the guns and naval stores. Charles inevitably had to face a court martial, held aboard ship in the Bay of Tunis on 22 April. Although he was honourably acquitted, he knew that a captain who had lost a vessel could expect a long wait for another commission. He was now on half pay and would receive only £47 14s. per quarter to live on.[36] Further bad news soon followed. His brother Henry's bank failed in mid-March and Charles lost all his savings, amounting to £536.[37]

By late June 1816 Charles was back in England and reunited with his three daughters, having taken up residence with them in the Palmer household on Keppel Street. Charles was committed to be with his children, now aged seven, six, and three but on half pay and his savings gone, it was obvious he could not afford a separate residence for the long term. By now the children were used to living in London, where their grandparents and especially their Aunt Harriet had been caring for them since Fanny's death. A joint household was the best plan Charles could hope for.

He was greatly concerned to discover that Jane was ill. She was able to finish the manuscript of *Persuasion* in early August, but exhaustion and pain increasingly limited her activity. There is no consensus on what ailed her. Contemporary doctors were puzzled; modern speculation about the cause of her death centres either on Addison's disease, a tuberculosis of the adrenal glands, or possibly non-Hodgkin's lymphoma.[38] In late September Charles took his daughters and Harriet Palmer to visit Jane at Chawton Cottage. As space there was limited, she proposed they should stay at Chawton Great House, as Edward Knight's last tenant had recently left.[39] When Charles returned alone in mid-December, Jane's strength was further reduced. Although she had begun a new novel, *Sanditon*, in late January 1817, she only managed to work on it for the next seven weeks.

Jane wrote Charles on Easter Sunday 1817. She thanked him for his affectionate letter, admitting that she had "really been too unwell this last fortnight to write anything that was not absolutely necessary."[40] This was Charles's "last letter from Dearest Jane,"[41] a memento he treasured for the rest of his life. On 24 May Jane and Cassandra moved to Winchester, where they hoped more effective medical treatment might be available. But by 12 June the family were told that Jane would not recover. Charles travelled immediately by mail coach to Winchester. He feared, quite correctly, that this was his farewell visit to a beloved sister. He received word from Henry on 20 July that his "Dear Sister Jane" had died two days earlier. This second death, which caused Charles more great sadness, occurred less than three years after he had lost Fanny.

Charles's disappointing and financially constrained period on half pay lasted until 1820 when he took a job as an inspecting commander in the Coastguard. He was first posted to the district of Padstow on the north coast of Cornwall, and then in 1822 he was transferred to the smaller Plymstock district, two miles from Plymouth, Devon. Charles's job was to help prevent smuggling in these areas. He was expected to make routine coastal patrols on horseback and, if anything suspicious was sighted, to send out boats and men to investigate, but he was not required to go with them. Such a life was not the ideal employment for the capabilities of an experienced frigate captain like Charles, who thrived on the variety of naval life at sea and the pay and other benefits that went with it. Nonetheless, it was a fresh start involving an active yet landlubber's life. In addition, this posting came with an important decision about his domestic arrangements.

In February 1820 Charles's journal enigmatically refers to some "interesting conversations"[42] he had with Harriet Palmer's parents and her sister

Esther, who was visiting in London. Presumably, he was considering marrying Harriet and wished to discuss this idea with her family before raising the matter with her. Harriet, now age thirty-four, had cared unstintingly for his three daughters since their mother's tragic death, and Charles, who was immensely grateful, felt indebted to her. Harriet accepted his offer of marriage. She was genuinely fond of her nieces and she esteemed Charles, who at thirty-nine was still handsome and possessed all the virtues of affection, kindness, and a sweet temper. From Harriet's perspective, having a husband and children would surely be more desirable than spinsterhood on Keppel Street with aging parents. The couple married in the Kentish Town Chapel on 7 August 1820. The new family moved to a rented cottage at Padstow, Cornwall, where Charles took up his recent appointment in the Coastguard.

Harriet was not universally liked by members of the Austen family. As early as 1814 Charles's mother had observed that Harriet "to be sure is not agreable, but she is very good and very useful, and suffers so much from ill health that one must pity her, tho' one cant much like her." In 1818 Anna Lefroy, née Austen, Charles's niece, told her brother James Edward that she "cannot like Miss Palmer do what I will, which I should not care about, if I could but find out why I don't like her." James Edward bluntly described Harriet as "plain & sour countenanced" and "intollerably vulgar," an opinion their father, James Austen, thought rather too severe, although he admitted that "to Elegance indeed she had no pretensions – but as a Gentlewoman may pass muster fairly enough."[43] At best, Harriet was dutiful and dependable, but plain in appearance and low on charm, so very different from the lovely and captivating Fanny. Whatever their personal opinions, Charles's family members valued his happiness above all. Harriet was his choice, and they made her welcome within the family as best they could. In the past, Harriet had received certain courtesies as Charles's sister-in-law. When Jane Austen died in 1817, Harriet was given a lock of her hair. She and her father, John Grove Palmer, were asked to verify the signature on Jane Austen's will, presumably because he was a barrister.

There was a decided awkwardness about Charles's second marriage despite Harriet's suitability as a stepmother for his three children. Although it was not illegal to marry a deceased wife's sister, such unions were prohibited by the Table of Kindred and Affinity of the Church of England. Charles's mother was aware that he and Harriet might be socially ostracized in some quarters. She expressed her concern to her granddaughter Anna, writing that she was "now very glad his residence is at such a distance, by and bye wonder and censure will subside and in a year or two he may be willing to change his station for one nearer his family and friends. I hope they will be happy."[44] One of the bride's cousins, L. Strangways,[45] greeted the match with greater enthusiasm, commenting that "a union the result of genuine friendship and perfect esteem cannot fail of permanent felicity and lasting regards." Although such words do not speak of love or passion, the writer stressed the benefits of the match, chiefly that "the beloved children who have so long experienced the kindness and advantages of Miss P's increasing tenderness and anxious solicitude for them will rejoice in the certain continuance of her maternal affection."[46] By the time of the marriage, Mrs George Austen also spoke favourably of Harriet's motherly activities. She wrote: "Charles has certainly secured a careful and attentive mother to his children for such she has proved herself during the almost six years she has had the charge of them."[47]

To support a growing family Charles needed a larger income. He had long wished for active service in the navy and was thus delighted when several commissions came his way. He was posted into HMS *Aurora* (46 guns) from 1826 to 1828 and into HMS *Winchester* (52 guns) from 1829 to 1830, which he was forced to leave when he "received considerable hurt in his Chest by a Fall from the Mast of his Ship in a Gale"[48] in December 1830. Why he was up a mast in a storm is not known. While the captain of HMS *Bellerophon* (80 guns) from 1838 to 1841, he took part in a British, Austrian, and Russian campaign to prevent Mehemet Ali, viceroy of Egypt, from expanding his realm into Syria.[49] In consequence of this campaign, he received an additional clasp for his Naval General Service Medal: "Acre 1840" marked his participation in the successful bombardment of the fortress of Jean d'Acre.

Charles's appointment to the *Aurora* had arisen in unusual circumstances. He was in Plymouth when he learned of her captain's sudden demise on 31 May 1826, and he immediately made his availability known to the Admiralty, stating his "readiness to start at a moments warning for any part of the World."[50] As the *Aurora* was poised to depart for the West Indies to engage in the suppression of the slave trade, a new captain was an immediate necessity. By return post Charles received notice of his appointment. He was on board by 4 June and sailed the next day for the West Indies,[51] leaving Harriet alone in their Plymstock home on very short notice with their five-year-old son Charles John, their six-week-old baby, Henry, as well as whichever of her stepdaughters – Cassy, Harriet Jane, and Fan – were not in Keppel Street with their grandparents.

Charles was concerned that "my poor wife suffered much from the suddenness of my leaving her though I know not that it would have been any better had we had more time to think of it," adding that "the separation from my Family was doubtless most painful." Yet he stoically observed that "Sailors are bound for all weathers."[52] When duty called, the navy served regardless of the circumstances. Charles had been stranded on shore for the past ten years. Irrespective of family ties, he needed to be at sea again, not only to earn money, but also for his own well-being.

By a strange coincidence Charles had already had business in the past with the *Aurora*. She was a recommissioned French vessel, originally known as the *Clorinde* (40 guns) before she was taken by the British in 1814. Eight years earlier, in company with the *Renommée*, *Loire*, and *Seine*, she had been in close pursuit of the much smaller *Indian*, which had mercifully just managed to escape.[53] Now their roles were reversed. He was in command of the vessel instead of her being in chase of him.

Charles particularly welcomed a return to regular naval pay. Four years earlier he had written to his sister-in-law Mary Austen, widow of his late brother James, about his diminished income, which he said was due to "his Salary being curtailed" and the "paying off of the 5 per cents in which my little all was placed."[54] The reduced salary refers to his earnings as a lowly Coastguard officer, and the reference to "the 5 per cents" is to the loss of his investments in his brother Henry's bank when it had failed in 1816.

Charles's marriage to Harriet was tolerably happy. They produced four children, two of whom died very young: George (1822–24) and Jane (1824–25). The remaining two sons, Charles John (1821–67) and Henry (1826–51), lived to adulthood and pursued military careers. Charles rejoiced in the birth of a son in 1821, his first boy in an expanding family, but there are hints in his pocketbook that his household with Harriet was not uniformly happy. An entry for 18 May 1825 records: "in the Eveng much discord – How different from this day 18 years since."⁵⁵ He was referring to his wedding day with Fanny. Inevitably Charles could not stop thinking about the joys of earlier life with Fanny. Nor did he want his daughters to forget her. Another pocketbook entry, eight days later, records his walking "with the 2 girls to Kentish Town & [visiting] the tomb of their Dear Mother."⁵⁶

Since Fanny's death, Charles had retained a close connection with James and Esther Esten. They appear to have shown their regard for Charles when in September 1817 they gave their third son the same first name, although, distressingly, the baby died five months later.⁵⁷ Their elder son Palmer, the nephew who, as a boy, had shown such a decided fondness for the navy, had not opted for that career but had chosen law instead, which he pratised in London and Exeter.⁵⁸ He moved to Toronto in 1836, where he became an expert in the law of equity and a judge in the Chancery Court. His father, James Esten, retired as chief justice of Bermuda in 1834, and two years later he and Esther joined Palmer and his family in Toronto.⁵⁹ Hamilton Esten, Cassy's exact contemporary, had also moved to Upper Canada and become a major in HM Rifle Brigade. He died in 1878 in his seventieth year. Charles must have regretted the great distance that separated him from the Estens in later years. They had shared many happy times together during his courtship and marriage to Fanny, occasions that, as the reminiscences in his journals show, Charles did not readily forget. James Esten died in 1838, aged sixty-six, followed by Esther in 1849, aged seventy-four.

Charles remained in close touch with Fanny's parents, who lived to see her children grow up. Mrs Palmer, still on Keppel Street, died on 28 June 1830 aged seventy-three. John Grove Palmer was with Charles and Harriet at Alverstoke near Portsmouth at the time of his death on 11 May 1832. He was eighty-two.⁶⁰ Of Charles's remaining siblings best known to Fanny, Cassandra died in 1845, aged seventy-two, and Edward in 1852, aged eighty-five. Charles's brother Frank would outlive all his Austen siblings. He became Admiral of the Fleet in 1863, an honorary position by dint of the length of his service in the officer rank, and died on 10 August 1865 at the age of ninety-one.

By the 1840s Charles's two sons and three daughters were well into adulthood and established patterns of life. From 1847 to 1848 Charles John was flag lieutenant on HMS *Vindictive* (50 guns) for his uncle Admiral Sir

Fig. 33   Portrait of Frances (Fan) Austen,
youngest daughter of Fanny and Charles,
as a young woman.

Francis (Frank) Austen, the commander-in-chief on the North American
and West Indies Station. Like his father before him, he wed a colonial girl,
except his bride, Sophia Emma DeBlois, was a Nova Scotian from Halifax
at the northern end of the station, as opposed to Bermuda, the southern
base where Charles had met Fanny. His brother Henry pursued a career in
the British army until his sudden death at age twenty-five, the result of a
fall at the Cape of Good Hope on 21 October 1851 while serving with the
73rd Regiment.

Of the girls, Fan, the charming baby from the days on the *Namur*,
became an attractive young woman (Fig. 33). It was she who inherited
her Aunt Cassandra's "topaze cross," the much appreciated necklace that
Charles had bought for his elder sister over four decades earlier with some
of his prize money. Some years earlier her cousin Henry, one of her Uncle
Frank Austen's sons, sought her attentions with a playful acrostic based on
her name. It begins:

> *F*anny since long I have expected
> *A*n answer due from you to my last letter
> *N*ow I proceed to make you more my debtor,
> *N*ot cross though grieved, not sullen, though dejected,
> *Y*et much annoyed at being thus neglected ...[61]

However, Fan preferred his older brother, naval officer Francis William Austen junior, and wed him instead in 1843. Cassy and Harriet Jane led less adventurous lives. They never married and remained in their parents' household.

Much later in life Cassy shared with the family an important item connected to Jane Austen. When her cousin James Edward Austen-Leigh was preparing to write his *Memoir of Jane Austen*, published in 1869, he needed an image of Jane to accompany the text. Cassy owned both of the sketches that Cassandra had made of Jane: the rear view of a figure in a bonnet and the full-face pencil drawing and watercolour in which she appears somewhat austere.[62] Cassy agreed with her first cousins Caroline Austen, James Austen-Leigh, and Anna Lefroy that a more attractive image of Jane should be created. James Andrews was employed to produce a portrait based on Cassandra's sketch. Claire Harman described the result as a "pastel-coloured image of a chubby, vacant looking young woman with huge eyes and pink cheeks."[63] This picture became the source for the stippled engraving used in the frontispiece of the *Memoir*. It has been endlessly reproduced ever since and is thought by many to be a generally acceptable representation of Jane.

Cassy's verdict on the Andrews painting was matter-of-fact: "It is a very pleasing, sweet face, – tho' I confess, to not thinking it *much* like the original; but that the public will not be able to detect."[64] Cassy was a guardian of the two authentic images of Jane drawn by Cassandra, but she willingly endorsed the new, prettified Andrews image intended for public appreciation. She was also satisfied that the uninformed readers of the *Memoir* would never know they were being duped. Cassy was, in effect, part of a conspiracy to represent Jane's physical appearance in what the family thought was a pleasing way given the style and taste of the period. She was part of an inner circle whose decision influenced the public's perception of how Jane actually looked for decades to follow.

There is more to the story. In 1813 Jane had been critical of Cassy's looks. She had said, "I wish she were not so very Palmery – ... I never knew a Wife's family features have such undue influence."[65] These remarks, for whatever reasons Jane had, suggest that Cassy was not a pretty or attractive child and might never be one, certainly not when compared to her other Austen cousins. However, Cassy became an attractive young woman, as a contemporary sketch of her shows (Fig. 34). How ironic it is that the aunt

Fig. 34   Portrait of Cassandra (Cassy)
Austen, eldest daughter of Fanny and
Charles, as a young woman, probably
contemporary with her sister's portrait.

who vigorously criticized the young Cassy's appearance was not herself quite
so badly served in the matter of looks by that same niece fifty-six years later.

After thirty-eight years as a post-captain, Charles was promoted to admiral.
In accordance with naval policy, admirals rose in rank from rear-admiral to
vice-admiral to full admiral; there were three grades in each of these ranks,
in the ascending order of blue, white, and red.[66] Charles was delighted to
be made a rear admiral of the blue in November 1846 (Fig. 35). His future
progress up the ranks would depend on the additional number of years he
served. Early in 1850 he was appointed commander-in-chief of the East
India and China Station, based in Ceylon (the present-day Sri Lanka).
A description of Charles at age seventy, courtesy of his niece Anna Lefroy,
draws attention to his "very remarkable sweetness of temper, & benevolence
of character." She notes his "tall, erect figure, his bright eye & animated
countenance [which] would have given the impression of a much younger
man; had it not been for the rather remarkable contrast with his hair, which,
originally dark had become of a snowy white."[67] Charles, it appeared, was
ready for the new challenges he was about to undertake.

This commission had major consequences for Charles's children and
other family members. In exercising his freedom to select his officers,

Fig. 35   Portrait of Charles Austen in the 1840s in
his post-captain's uniform. He was promoted to rear
admiral in 1848.

Charles requested that his nephew and son-in-law Francis William Austen
be appointed flag-captain of HMS *Hastings* (74 guns) and that three great-
nephews be employed in other capacities: Edward Rice became squadron
commander, George Purvis served as flag lieutenant, and George Rice served
as another officer.[68] Charles also took along a female retinue: his wife Harriet,
his daughters Cassy and Harriet Jane as well as Fan, who was also the
flag-captain's wife. Imagine the excitement and trepidation of these women
who, in leaving behind a routine and settled land-based existence in familiar
southern England, embarked on a prolonged and challenging journey to
an exotic but unsettled and unfamiliar destination. Together with Charles,
they travelled east in early 1850, first by P&O paddle steamer, the *Ripon*, to
Alexandria, then overland to Suez, by ship to India, and finally to Charles's
base at Trincomalee, Ceylon.[69]

Charles's journal describes happy times with his kin. He danced in the New Year of 1851 and spent weeks on shore where local administrators feted his entire entourage. According to his journal, there were balls, dinners, excursions by horseback, and drives in barouches and carriages to nearby places of beauty and interest. Harriet, who lived aboard the *Hastings* with Charles, was less amused by the social whirl and little inclined to join the others on the deck on moonlit nights. She preferred that Charles read aloud from the *Christian Monitor* or some other religious tract. She often retired early, complaining that she was feeling unwell.[70]

It was truly a twist of fate that Fanny, the wife who would have revelled in the glamorous and entertaining activities of this posting, was not the one to share these novel experiences with Charles. Imagine her sentiments had she been there. How proud Fanny would have been if she, who had supported Charles throughout the early years of his career, had still been at his side in his new prestigious position. What a thrill for Fanny it would have been to see her namesake, Fan, fulfilling the role of flag-captain's wife, as she herself had done forty years earlier in Halifax. Moreover, short of behaving like Mrs Bennet in *Pride and Prejudice*, the mother who was relentlessly in search of husbands for her unmarried daughters, Fanny might have encouraged Cassy and Harriet to look for marriageable men among the local military establishment. But Fanny was long dead and the Charles Austen family behaved in the current situation as suited their different temperaments, inclinations, and opportunities. Cassy and Harriet eventually returned to England without marital prospects.

By March 1852 the situation on the station called for a more aggressive military stance. Trouble arose among British business interests in Rangoon, Burma, and the Burmese authorities. With danger in the offing, the unhappy Harriet packed her trunks and travelled back to England with her step-daughters. Charles transferred to the steam sloop HMS *Rattler* (12 guns) and on 1 April arrived from Singapore via Penang to join the flotilla assembled offshore from Rangoon. Between 5 and 14 April he spearheaded the successful capture of both Martaban and Rangoon in what became known as the Second Anglo-Burmese War. But even in the glow of victory, ill health dulled his enjoyment of success. Much weakened by recent attacks of cholera, he withdrew to Calcutta to recuperate.[71] *The Times* of London,

19 June 1852, noted that "in consequence of bad health Admiral Austen is likely to come home immediately." But contrary to this report, Charles returned to service in early September in time to lead an offensive on the wooden paddle-steamer gunship *Pluto* to secure the Irrawaddy River as far as Prome, 200 miles upstream. Charles again succumbed to cholera and died on board the *Pluto* on 7 October. His body was taken back to Ceylon, and he was buried in Trincomalee in the naval cemetery on Sober Island. He was seventy-three. An officer on board at the time of Charles's death wrote: "[O]ur good Admiral won the hearts of all by his gentleness and kindness when he was struggling with disease, and endeavouring to do his duty as Commander-in-chief of the British naval forces in these waters. His death was a great grief to the whole fleet. I know that I cried bitterly when I found he was dead."[72]

Hours before his death Charles finished his reports, "wrote a letter to [his] wife and read the lessons for the day."[73] He died peacefully and unattended.[74] But was he alone in his thoughts just before death? Fanny had been his angel in life, his "departed angel" after her death.[75] Could he hope to meet his dear one again? In the words of Fanny's epitaph, at God's will she will "rise unchanged an angel still." Charles was a committed Christian and, as such, a firm believer in an afterlife. Given his passion for Fanny and his unwavering commitment to her memory, it is fitting to think that in death, Charles was confident that he would be reunited with her in heaven. She was his "angel still."

CHAPTER 9

Being a Naval Wife: Fanny Austen's Life and Jane Austen's Fiction

FANNY AUSTEN WAS PART OF JANE AUSTEN'S FAMILY LIFE just as Jane was part of Fanny's. Both of them were deeply attached to Charles, the one as loving wife, the other as affectionate sister. They also shared attachments to each other's "children." Fanny's little girls were periodically under Jane's and Cassandra's nurturing care and educating influence. Fanny was privy to the birth and gratifying reception of Jane's first three literary "children" – *Sense and Sensibility*, *Pride and Prejudice*, and *Mansfield Park*. Fanny's and Jane's affections and interests coincided in many ways during the unfortunately brief period of Fanny's married life.

The two women were in touch for eight years, first through letters and then in person. Jane had corresponded with Fanny since her engagement to Charles in 1806 while he was serving on the North American Station. After Fanny came to England in the summer of 1811, there were conversations on occasions when Fanny and Jane were together at Chawton Cottage, Chawton Great House, or Godmersham Park. Fanny's letters show her to be reflective, expressive, and willing to share her views. Jane was vitally concerned about all aspects of Charles's career at sea, and that attentiveness extended to include Fanny's opinions and experiences. Over a period of time, Jane became privy to Fanny's reflections about her unique and diverse involvement as an officer's wife in a naval world.

Mansfield Park (1814) was Jane's first book with naval characters and themes. Shortly after Fanny's death, she would write a second novel with naval themes, *Persuasion*. How useful, even catalytic, was the material Fanny had incidentally provided about naval life when Jane came to create the naval wives in *Persuasion?* In what sense does the linkage of fact to fiction serve to illustrate the impact of Fanny's life story on Jane Austen's writing?

Previously, Fanny has not been seriously considered in any detailed way as a source for Jane's fiction.[1] Perhaps this is because the full details of her naval life simply were not known and hence it was not obvious that any sort of interesting connection could be made. However, with Fanny's story now told, it is time to consider her importance as a source of personal as well as naval detail that provided not only information, but inspiration for Jane's literary invention.

In his *Memoir of Jane Austen* (1869), Jane's nephew James Austen-Leigh briefly explores the influence her family had on her fiction. He focuses exclusively on the men of the family, in particular the naval expertise and experiences of Frank and Charles Austen. In the opinion of Austen-Leigh, the fact that her sailor brothers had honourable naval careers "accounts for Jane Austen's partiality for the Navy as well [as] for the readiness and accuracy with which she wrote about it ... [W]ith ships and sailors she felt herself at home, or at least could always trust to a brotherly critic to keep her right."[2] More recently, Brian Southam, author of *Jane Austen and the Navy*, addressed a similar theme. He contends that "the sailor brothers were the members of the family who contributed most, directly or indirectly, to the novels. Their lives and experiences provided Jane Austen with the basis for her naval characters and the sailor brothers played an important part in the writing of *Mansfield Park* and *Persuasion*, the two naval novels."[3] This sentiment is consistent with Southam's observation that "the portrait [in *Mansfield Park*] of the young midshipman William Price – eager, enthusiastic, and open – owes much to Charles's own boyishness and charm,"[4] and "it is very likely that Jane Austen's description of Harville's 'small house' at Lyme ... owes something to the scenes of [Frank's] family life at Rose Cottage, in Alton."[5] Additionally, Southam suggests that "what connects [Frank] with Captain Harville, himself the epitome of *Persuasion*'s 'domestic virtues,' is his skill as a handyman."[6]

Interesting as these observations may be, they concern the origins of male characters exclusively. But *Persuasion* includes three women with close associations with the navy. They are the assertive, good-humoured, and practical Mrs Croft, wife of Admiral Croft; Anne Elliot, who bitterly regrets her first refusal to become the wife of naval captain Frederick Wentworth, and the efficient and cheerful Mrs Harville, wife of Captain Harville. Jane Austen's knowledge about her naval brothers' personalities and careers was of limited use when she came to develop these female characters, who viewed the navy from a very different point of view. It was, therefore, fortunate that Fanny Austen had shared her experiences of the naval world.

It is likely Jane Austen's sensitivities to Fanny's life as a naval wife influenced some aspects of all three of these female characters in *Persuasion*. The portrait of Mrs Croft reflects the greatest similarity to Fanny, although there are some key differences between the two women. Mrs Croft champions the view that life at sea could be fulfilling, even rewarding, for women; she has lived aboard her husband's vessels and found the domestic quarters "superior" and providing "comfort."[7] This study of Fanny's letters has revealed she initially held a favourable opinion of the captain's quarters aboard the *Namur* that she shared with Charles. But her appreciation of them changed over time and she came to view the practicalities of domestic life at sea without any of the great enthusiasm expressed by Mrs Croft. Fanny was often frustrated by the harshness of the weather and rough seas that precluded keeping her children on board with her, and she was also vexed by the persistent difficulty of attracting and retaining competent domestic staff. By 1814 her initial euphoria about their accommodation had disappeared and she was more likely to call their quarters "uncomfortable."[8] Many of the realities of Fanny's domestic life on the *Namur* simply did not match the experiences of Mrs Croft while at sea.

Other differences are detectable. Mrs Croft is a more mature, thirty-eight-year-old woman, with a weather-beaten complexion, who has "been almost as much at sea as her husband."[9] She is a self-confident woman, well experienced in her role as helpmate to Admiral Croft. In contrast, Fanny was young, beautiful, and relatively new to her role as naval wife. Unlike the childless Mrs Croft, Fanny had young daughters to nurture, love, and teach. Mrs Croft has only the admiral's well-being to consider, whereas Fanny had

Charles's interests at heart while still caught up with the demands of being a mother. She was also pregnant for half of the time she was aboard the *Namur*; Mrs Croft never had to cope with prospective motherhood, as far as we are told. Moreover, Mrs Croft thinks retrospectively about her past experiences. She "looks back on her domestic life at sea and from a now secure position – her husband is an Admiral with wealth to enable them to live at Kellynch Hall."[10] In contrast, Fanny's assessment of her life style on the *Namur* was immediate and fresh, and was made in the context of professional and financial uncertainty for Charles in mid-career.

Yet there are striking similarities between Fanny and Mrs Croft in terms of attitudes, behaviour, and practical good sense. There are resemblances in their patterns of travel, in the actual experience of living on board a naval vessel, and in their ability to handle seasickness. Moreover, both women are strongly attached to their husbands and duly anxious when separated from them. As well, the speech patterns of both Fanny and Mrs Croft demonstrate their familiarity with naval expressions and vocabulary. More fundamentally, Fanny and Mrs Croft share emergent elements of what has come to be acknowledged as feminist traits in the conduct of their lives. Detecting and understanding these parallels adds substantial support to the claim that Jane Austen's close association with Fanny was catalytic to her creation of Mrs Croft.

On the point of travel patterns, both wives made voyages with their husbands. Fanny sailed with Charles a number of times between Bermuda and Halifax, and she travelled to England with him on the *Cleopatra*. Mrs Croft has sailed the Atlantic four times and accompanied Admiral Croft on many other voyages as well. In ascribing these particular transatlantic crossings to Mrs Croft, Jane Austen appears to include a reference to the North American Station. Mrs Croft tells Mrs Musgrove that she "never was in the West Indies," adding that "we do not call Bermuda ... the West Indies."[11] Her familiarity with Bermuda and her exclusion of the West Indies as a place she has lived imply that the Crofts have probably been based at Halifax and Bermuda just as Charles and Fanny Austen had been. Mrs Croft made her home on five of Admiral Croft's ships; Fanny periodically lived on four of Charles's – the *Indian*, the *Swiftsure*, the *Cleopatra*, and the *Namur*. Both Fanny and Mrs Croft staved off periods of seasickness when under sail. Mrs Croft admits that she is "a little disordered always the first twenty-four hours of going to sea, but never knew what sickness was afterwards."[12] Fanny, in describing her voyage to Halifax from Bermuda in May 1810, is pleased that "neither Lady Warren or myself were thoroughly sick, tho' we felt uncomfortable, the first day."[13] Fanny never mentions being seasick when she was living aboard the *Namur*.

Both Fanny and Mrs Croft were most content when sharing their husband's life.[14] Fanny's Halifax letters speak of her great pleasure in being with Charles. In them, she conveys the image of a popular pair who thoroughly enjoy each other's company. In a later letter from the *Namur* she wryly admits that she is like her sister Esther, who is "never happy but when she is with her husband."[15] Likewise, Austen depicts Admiral and Mrs Croft as a "particularly attached and happy"[16] couple, be they driving their gig near the ancestral Elliot home, Kellynch, out walking, or enjoying the company of naval friends in Bath. Jane's appreciation of Fanny's strong desire to support Charles, to find a commonality of friends, and to be his constant and affectionate companion, may have influenced her ascription of these traits to Mrs Croft.

During their husband's absence at sea, both wives became greatly worried. A noticeable undertone of anxiety runs through Fanny's letters from Halifax and on occasion breaks out expressly. When Charles was transporting troops to Portugal in the summer of 1810, a frightened Fanny wrote Esther in Bermuda about "Captain Austen's sudden departure, & the uncertainty, about his returning." She had reason to be alarmed, as the delivery of troops would bring him into waters patrolled by enemy vessels. She agonized that "if he is not here by the middle of Sepr. I shall give him up."[17] Similarly, Mrs Croft, in conversation with Mrs Musgrove about a winter when she had been left on shore, reminisces that it was the only time that she "really suffered in body or mind … [and] lived in perpetual fright at that time, and had all manner of imaginary complaints not knowing what to do with myself, or when I should hear from him next."[18] According to Mrs Croft, "the happiest part of my life has been spent on board a ship. While we were together … there was nothing to be feared. Thank God!"[19] Like Fanny, Mrs Croft is anxious when she does not know what dangers her husband is facing; she is most content in his company.

In his biography of Jane Austen, Park Honan suggests that she "drew on some aspects of [Fanny] for Mrs Croft" and that she admired Fanny's "unfussiness and gallant good sense."[20] Fanny's letters reveal evidence for Honan's contention. Essentially, Fanny was disposed to making the most of her circumstances. Although she was periodically frustrated in her domestic endeavours, there are also instances where she gives the impression of a young naval wife determined to put aside the inconveniences of her situation and ensure her family's comfort to the best of her abilities under difficult conditions at sea. Her letters from the *Namur* together with her pocket diary show her methodically juggling the timetable of her domestic arrangements, organizing lists of necessities to buy for her family, planning how to acquire fresh food at good prices, and deliberating how best to begin her daughter Cassy's formal education. In a similar vein, within the scope of her domestic activities, Mrs Croft is direct and sensible when addressing household matters. When she and Admiral Croft are negotiating the tenancy of Kellynch, she asks the right questions in matters of "the house, and terms, and taxes." Moreover, she is "conversant with business."[21] In practical matters of daily life, Mrs Croft is organized and efficient, qualities that Fanny also displayed.

Jane Austen always created characters whose expressions and speech patterns are appropriate to their positions and roles in the novels in which they appear. In Mrs Croft's case, her use of naval vocabulary contributes to the authenticity of her persona as a naval wife. She sounds like an insider when she tells Mrs Musgrove that "we do not call Bermuda or Bahama, you know, the West Indies."[22] Given her extensive record of travel on Admiral Croft's various vessels, she is scrupulously correct in her geographic references. Elsewhere, Mrs Croft knowingly refers to "the accommodations of a man of war ... of the higher rates."[23] In speaking this way, she shows an understanding of the Royal Navy's system of classifying vessels on a descending scale of 1 to 5, depending on the number of guns they were pierced to carry.[24]

Fanny's letters often include naval expressions and references. When referring to Charles's mission to Portugal, she wrote that Captain Jane "spoke" an American ship, meaning he communicated directly with the officers on board. This foreign vessel had seen six of the vessels that Fanny possessively calls "our Lisbon fleet." Fanny refers to the coordinates of latitude and longitude when describing the positioning of the "four ships and two brigs" that were sailing "in company."[25] On the topic of Charles's job opportunities, she noted that "Coquette is paid off … [and] the only two commands that were vacant have just been disposed of, viz. the River and Cork."[26] She is observing that the sloop *Coquette* had completed its commission and the wages of its officers and crew have been paid. She was concerned that several areas of sea command had been recently filled. Fanny seemingly had Admiral Williams's next appointment in mind. Had he been given either Cork (the home station of the Irish squadron) or the River (the Thames), he might have asked Charles to serve as his flag-captain again.

Fanny did not confine her use of naval speech strictly to military activities. She observed that a London party included "as many Bermudians as the old gentleman [Mr Leonard] cou'd Muster."[27] Here is a nice variation in the use of the military term "muster," which typically refers to assembling a ship's company. Fanny is a good example of how a naval wife would use naval terminology when apt, but her use of language was not so technical as to puzzle others. Jane may have thought of Fanny's ready and effective use of naval vocabulary within the context of everyday speech when she came to write Mrs Croft's dialogue.

Fanny also displays traits associated in more recent times with feminism, and Jane echoes these in her portrait of Mrs Croft. Such traits include being capable, being assertive, and valuing independence. In Fanny's case, such attitudes underpin her continuing search for self-identity. Fanny shows her capabilities through adeptly dealing with whatever situation she encounters; she resourcefully manages a complicated domestic life under unusual and difficult conditions. She is interested in self-realization. She seeks to be assertive about her needs and wishes as a naval wife. Yet, as her letters show, she sometimes finds it difficult to behave in accordance with her ideals. For instance, she hesitates to tell Charles exactly what she thinks about their arrangements while visiting the Williams, although she willingly confides in writing to Harriet her feelings concerning that situation. Fanny appears to seek greater empowerment, but at the same time she does not want to jeopardize her happy, sharing relationship with Charles. Sadly, Fanny died before she was able to realize the autonomy she was developing within what was, from all available evidence, a very successful marriage with Charles.

Some of Fanny's evolving character traits have found a much fuller expression in Mrs Croft. She is a woman who has energy and intelligence, who is clearly confident about expressing her views. She argues against Frederick Wentworth's apparent attitude that all women should be treated as "fine ladies instead of rational creatures." Mrs Croft shows her confidence in women's abilities to cope with life's challenges, and she rests her case with the sentiment that "we none of us expect to be in smooth water all our days."[28] In nautical experience, smooth waters often occur prior to periods of unsettled seas. A sailor understands the significance of calm before turbulence and sails his ship accordingly. With this distinction in mind, Mrs Croft implies that a rational woman will be confident in her powers of judgment; she will be capable of meeting and dealing decisively with the problems that occur between the periods of peace and calm in everyday life.[29]

The parallels between the naval elements of Fanny Austen's conduct and speech and the manner and characteristics of Mrs Croft directly relate to their respective real and imagined lives around warships and in association with their husbands as naval officers. These similarities are centred on the activities of individuals in the navy and involve very little of its social culture and relationships. Jane Austen was equally aware of Fanny's experiences within the wider world of the navy, and she may have used this knowledge to develop the character of Anne Elliot, the heroine of *Persuasion*.

In the novel, there are several references to Frederick Wentworth's warm and supportive relations with his fellow officers. Wentworth speaks in Anne's presence of his unswerving commitment to "assist any brother officer's wife that I could."[30] In Lyme, Anne is confronted with impressive examples of naval collegiality. She enjoys the warm-hearted hospitality of Captain and Mrs Harville; she hears of Wentworth's kindness to the grieving Captain Benwick. Austen writes: "Anne felt her spirits not likely to be benefited by an increasing acquaintance among [Wentworth's] brother officers. 'These would have been all my friends' was her thought; and she had to struggle against a great tendency to lowness."[31]

These references to brotherly behaviour are reminiscent of the personal support Fanny received from the naval communities in England and North America. Fanny spoke of the "warmth of manner"[32] of Admiral Sir Thomas Williams, Charles's superior on the station at the Nore. On the North American Station, she experienced the supportive friendships of Charles's colleagues: captains Edward Hawker (Cassy's godfather), Frederick Hickey, Samuel Pechell, and others. She enjoyed the affable company provided by

Admiral and Lady Warren, first when Fanny was their guest in Halifax in the summer of 1810 and then later when she met them in social circles in London in 1813–14.

The community of support among naval officers was also enriched by the care and encouragement that could be offered by their wives. These qualities are exhibited in Fanny's own interactions with the young trainee officers on Charles's vessels. She was kind to ten-year-old Volunteer First Class Douglas Jerrold; she mentioned Lieutenant McNamara (formerly of the *Namur*) in a letter to her sister Esther so that she might introduce him to good company when he arrived in Bermuda. She took an affectionate interest in the well-being of Tom Fowle, who had progressed through the ranks from midshipman (on the *Indian)* to lieutenant (on the *Namur*). When he left the *Namur* for HMS *Elephant* (74 guns), she kept in close correspondence. Austen had ample opportunity to learn how Fanny contributed to the welfare of the naval community. She appreciated the significance that support among naval families provided in real life, and she memorialized its important role in *Persuasion*.

At the end of *Persuasion*, when Anne finally marries Captain Wentworth, she expects to be welcomed into his network of naval friends, which she could previously only admire from afar. But this is not all. She will undoubtedly also have opportunities to contribute to his, and now also her, naval community. Consider also the example Jane Austen provides of Mrs Harville, who insists on caring for the gravely injured Louisa Musgrove even though her tiny premises are ill-equipped for the task and her own family obligations are many. Her spontaneous generosity is due in part to her husband's firm friendship with Captain Wentworth and the assumption (which is false) that there is a close bond between Frederick Wentworth and Louisa, but an impression is also left that Mrs Harville is a compassionate and helpful individual.

There is another feature of Fanny's behaviour – suggestive of what will subsequently be identified as a feminist value – that has a possible resonance in Austen's portrait of Anne Elliot. Fanny appreciates the bonds of friendship and support of other women. While on the *Namur*, she misses her coterie from earlier days in Bermuda but happily anticipates a reunion with one of them, her friend Betsy Holliday, whose husband was about to become the naval chaplain at Sheerness. Fanny also feels a link with other naval wives of her acquaintance. She empathizes with Lady Warren, who is unable to join Sir John in North America, and with Mrs Sawyer, who is too ill to join the Admiral Sawyer at Cork. Of most significance is the bond with her sister Esther, her confidante and supporter. Jane Austen would have known about their closeness, and perhaps she learned about Fanny's other female relationships too. She certainly observed Fanny at Austen gatherings over the years where Fanny's sympathetic interactions with the women present would be evident.

Anne Elliot, too, values her relations with other women. As Austen reveals, Anne has a particular closeness with her godmother and mentor, Lady Russell. Although she has no sisterly support from the self-centred and vain Elizabeth and the hypochondriacal Mary, Lady Russell provides strong affection similar to that which Fanny received from her eldest sister, Esther. In rekindling relations in Bath with her long-lost school friend, Mrs Smith, Anne is compassionate in regard to Mrs Smith's diminished circumstances, which she helps to resolve through the agency of Captain Wentworth. Anne also immensely likes and admires Mrs Croft and will be delighted to become her sister when she marries Frederick. Though Anne's female relationships were few in number, they were strong and lasting, and definitely significant in her life.

There are additional ways in which Austen's characterization of Anne is reminiscent of Fanny. By the end of the novel, Anne's fortunes have changed. She and Captain Wentworth reunite and marry. Nonetheless their lives will be affected by political and military contingencies in the future. *Persuasion* is set in the contemporary context of the closing of the Napoleonic Wars in the summer of 1814, when many of the naval officers who had fought for years would be living on shore again.[33] Yet the experience of the war taught that the peace might not hold. The British navy would go on roaming the seas and the separation for naval families would continue. In this context, Jane Austen concludes *Persuasion* with a prophecy about her heroine's prospects: "The dread of a future war [was] all that could dim [Anne's] sunshine; She gloried in being a sailor's wife, but she must pay the tax of quick alarm for belonging to that profession."[34] In these final lines of *Persuasion*, Austen has identified the delights and the fears facing a naval wife who loves her husband dearly. There were to be times of great happiness and pride in his occupation, in which Anne "gloried"; there would also be times of "quick alarm," of uncertainty, of sudden separation, and of the danger of naval action. These would "tax" even the most stalwart of naval wives.

In marrying Charles and agreeing to share his professional life in a very direct way, Fanny Austen exposed herself to the alarms and risks of her husband's naval world. Her feelings oscillated between keen satisfaction and deep anxiety. Fanny experienced periods of a happy, intimate family life within the naval community, but there were darker times. For example, in 1813 she empathized with Charles's unhappiness with his commission on the *Namur*, and she suffered anxious spells of worry about their financial stability whenever Charles was without a vessel to command. In addition, as long as Charles was working in the active sea service in the context of warfare, there were particular hazards on the job over which she had no control. *Persuasion* ends before Anne is faced with the sorts of challenges and anxieties Fanny encountered. However, Jane's understanding of the highs and lows of Fanny's life as a naval wife may have inspired her to capture Anne's prospects with the phrase "the tax of quick alarm," words that so succinctly characterize the vicissitudes a naval wife may face.

Jane Austen had a significant message about naval life to convey in *Persuasion*. As Deborah Kaplan puts it, Austen was interested in the "advocacy of particular values which [she] assigned to Naval officers and their families. The novel sometimes simplifies and idealizes, but it does so to construct a profound, ideological vision of cultural change. It champions a spirited professional and entrepreneurial social group, showing it to be morally superior to the traditionally dominant landowning gentry and aristocracy, and to offer women as well as men happier and more vital social roles."[35] The direct and capable Mrs Croft is well qualified to be a significant actor in the new moral and social culture that Austen envisages. It is intriguing that some of her admirable traits can be found in Fanny as well.

There is also a way in which Fanny's colonial knowledge and experiences may have been of significance to Jane. Jane was concerned with the abolition of slavery, obliquely raising it in her novel *Persuasion*, and Fanny was the only member of the immediate Austen family who had been part of a slaveholding household. The evidence of Jane's interest and views may be found in one of her letters and in a reported conversation with her brother

Frank. Jane wrote very favourably about abolitionist Thomas Clarkson in a letter to Cassandra.[36] Her enthusiastic description suggests that she had been greatly impressed by his books, one of which was *The History of the Abolition of the African Slave-Trade*.[37] Moreover, her naval brother Francis was "implacably opposed to the [slavery] system." In 1808, after involvement in the Battle of San Domingo in the West Indies, he decried the "harshness and despotism" of the treatment of slaves by "the landholders or their managers." In commenting on Francis's views, Frank Gibbon expressed "no doubt that he and his sister discussed [West Indian slavery] fully."[38] Given Jane's interest and Fanny's experience, it is likely that the two women also talked about slavery together.

In *Persuasion* there are two passing references to the West Indies in relation to two female characters, first Mrs Croft and then Mrs Smith. Speaking about her travels with the Admiral, Mrs Croft tells Mrs Musgrove that she "never was in the West Indies." She explains that "we do not call Bermuda or Bahama … the West Indies."[39] Consistent with Fanny's experience of slavery in Bermuda, Jane Austen appears to be drawing a distinction between the conditions of slavery there and in the West Indies. As discussed in chapter 1, Fanny grew up in a society that treated slaves in a more humane manner than as described by Francis Austen in relation to the West Indies. Jane Austen is presumably drawing the attention of her contemporary readers to the contrasting conditions of slavery in the two different colonial contexts and also, implicitly, to the moral problems inherent in the slavery system itself.

Jane reinforces these purposes when she reverts to the plight of Mrs Smith at the end of *Persuasion*. The impoverished Mrs Smith has lost the right to her late husband's sequestered property in the West Indies, which is likely a plantation operated by forced slave labour. Frederick Wentworth's assistance to the helpless Mrs Smith in recovering her property is besmirched by the implicit moral questions about its administration. Unlike Mrs Croft, whom Jane Austen places in the Bermuda of Fanny's experience, Mrs Smith's associations are with the far more brutal and despicable West Indies that Francis Austen had described. The contrast is striking.[40] In sum, a consequence of Jane talking to Fanny, who had a background in a slave-owning culture, could be Jane's increased awareness of the nuanced complexities of the slavery system, which finds reflection in her fiction.

There are several other places in *Persuasion* where details relating to Fanny's life appear to inform the narrative. For example, Captain Benwick, Wentworth's lieutenant on the *Laconia*, had been engaged to the beautiful young Fanny Harville. He is made desolate by her death while he is away at sea and is in deep mourning when the reader first meets him. A similar catastrophic event shattered Fanny and Charles's relationship when Fanny died suddenly in childbirth. This unexpected death of a sister-in-law, who was only twenty-four, occurred less than a year before Jane began to write *Persuasion*. She was saddened by Fanny Austen's demise and by the deep effect it had on the grieving Charles. Her closeness to this event may explain her characterization of the emotionally devastated Captain Benwick when he first appears in the novel. In describing the intensity of his friend's grief at that time, Wentworth asserts that he"believed it impossible for man to be more attached to woman than poor Benwick had been to Fanny Harville, or to be more deeply afflicted under the dreadful change [that her death has caused]."[41] To some extent this description mirrors the depths of Charles's love for Fanny and intensity of his response to his loss of her.[42]

Additionally, Jane Austen chose to name Captain Benwick's ill-fated betrothed "Fanny." Was this a mere coincidence? The naming of Fanny Harville in *Persuasion* does invite speculation. Was this Jane's private acknowledgment of Fanny Austen's untimely death? There may have been a personal significance for Jane in this particular choice of name.

Jane Austen knew or knew of other naval wives. Should they too be considered as possible sources of inspiration for her naval fiction? Brian Southam has suggested that "Jane Austen may have modelled her portrait ... [of] Mrs. Croft ... [on] Lady Warren,"[43] who was Fanny's vigorous hostess in Halifax in 1810 and friend in England from 1812 onwards. Southam apparently assumes that Jane would have heard about Lady Warren's personality from Fanny, if not Charles. Southam posits a link between Mrs Croft and Lady Warren on the grounds of the latter's assertiveness. In particular, he sees a parallel between Mrs Croft's gentle guiding of the Admiral's hand as he drives their gig about the Kellynch estate and contemporary gossip in the American newspapers in 1814 that "upon good authority *Lady Warren* is expected out to supersede him [Admiral Warren] in command."[44] As far as taking control is concerned, Lady Warren's overt organizational skills find, at best, a much gentler, subtler manifestation in *Persuasion*. Whereas Mrs Croft is discreet, insightful, considerate, and well-mannered in the matter of influencing and giving directions, Lady Warren had the reputation of saying exactly what she thought; moreover, she was fond of issuing orders based on her perceived rank in society and her husband's professional standing. Compared to the assertiveness of Lady Warren, Mrs Croft's behaviour bears greater likeness to Fanny's more discreet manner in both naval and family company.

The other naval wife of the family, Mary, was married to Jane's brother Frank. From late 1806 to 1808, Jane, Cassandra, Mrs Austen, and Martha Lloyd made their home in the seaport of Southampton with Mary and Frank, although he was away at sea from April 1807 to June 1808. Unfortunately, not much is known about Mary. In 1865, after Frank Austen's death, their daughter Fanny Sophia burned the letters Mary had received from Jane, and Jane's own extant letters provide no illuminating picture of Mary's personality, let alone insights on her views about the navy. In October 1808 Jane refers to the Frank Austen family's favourable seaside location at Yarmouth, where "with fish almost for nothing, & plenty of Engagements & plenty of each other, [they] must be very happy."[45] This description suggests a devoted sociable couple but reveals nothing more about Mary's character. Thus, it is tricky to locate features in Mary's life that might have inspired Jane Austen in her creation of a fictional naval wife.

Although Jane Austen did make one remark about the lifestyle of naval wives, it has dubious applicability to Mary Austen's experiences. In 1801, at the point when her family are moving away from Steventon, Jane was contemplating the pleasures of "future summers by the Sea." She wrote: "[F]or a time we shall now possess many of the advantages which I have often thought of with Envy in the wives of Sailors."[46] But, for a grass widow like Mary, additionally burdened by responsibility for many children, the seaside would scarcely be the place of relaxation and pleasure that Jane envisaged.

There are, however, some small points of similarity between Mary and Mrs Croft. Mary Austen must have worried greatly about the safety of a husband off at sea in wartime, just as Fanny and the fictional Mrs Croft did. Jane would have observed that anxiety first-hand when she was sharing a house with Mary in Southampton. An additional link between Mary and

Mrs Croft involves the places where both women lived. Mrs Croft speaks of "the winter that I passed by myself at Deal, when the Admiral (*Captain Croft*, then) was in the North Seas."[47] Mary occupied seaside lodgings with her children at Deal during 1811 and 1812, when Frank was captain of HMS *Elephant* and serving on the North Sea and the Baltic. Mary also once lodged at Yarmouth as did Mrs Croft.

Additionally, Mary's way of life bears a likeness to another character in *Persuasion*. Mary kept her household functioning and cared for her ever-increasing number of children, sometimes in small quarters and certainly not in homes she could call their own. Her efficiency in these tasks, like Fanny Austen's, is reminiscent of *Persuasion*'s Mrs Harville, who is the lynchpin that keeps the members of the Harville family content in their small rented house at Lyme.

When compared to Mary, Fanny provided a much richer template of a woman's life aboard sailing ships and on naval stations. Mary's involvement was, by dint of circumstance, limited to her experiences as a shore-based naval wife. Over the years she received letters from Frank telling her about his life at sea. However, she was a stranger to the seagoing life that Fanny understood from personal observation. Mary did not travel within a foreign station or cross the North Atlantic Ocean, all of which shaped Fanny's perception of what it was to be the helpmate of an officer in the sea service. Mary never lived on a working naval vessel as Fanny did for two and a half years on the *Namur*. Fanny most likely had a broader, more nuanced naval vocabulary, even though Mary could recognize nautical expressions encountered in Frank's letters and had heard naval language spoken in her Southampton social circles. On balance, aspects of Fanny's attitudes and behaviour have the greater claim for influencing Jane Austen's choice of defining characteristics for Mrs Croft and, to a lesser degree, for Anne Elliot and Mrs Harville.

In sum, there is intriguing evidence that Jane Austen's naval wives, their characters and their way of life, resonate with Fanny Austen's experiences on both sides of the Atlantic Ocean. The positing of biographical origins for a character or an episode in a work of fiction, such as *Persuasion*, is bound to be conjectural, but even so, suggesting such links adds interest and pleasure to the reading of it. We do not and cannot know exactly how

Jane Austen came to construct the wonderful characters in her novels. But we can enjoy speculating how Jane's knowledge of Fanny, both as a person and as a naval wife, influenced her creative genius. Her connections to Fanny gave Jane a great wealth of events, feelings, attitudes, and points of view about naval life from a woman's perspective. From this great store of actions, opinions, and emotions associated with Fanny, Jane could select features and imaginatively mould them for her own purposes. She had both materials and means to round out the portrayal of her female characters whose lives were conditioned by naval influences.

Fanny had the good fortune to become part of Jane Austen's close-knit family. She was a dedicated naval wife to Charles and an engaging trans-atlantic sister to Jane. If Fanny's experiences on the North American shores of the Atlantic and her years at sea on board the *Namur* in British waters served, as argued here, to inspire Jane to incorporate aspects of Fanny's life into her fiction, then it is our good fortune that Jane Austen had such an interesting and articulate sister as Fanny.

Description of Fanny's
Letters and Pocket Diary

(1) APPEARANCE OF THE LETTERS, THEIR
PROVENANCE, AND EDITORIAL ADJUSTMENTS

Fanny's letters are written in a clear hand on watermarked paper of rag quality. In most of the letters all available space is filled and thus the text appears as a continuous whole. Fanny's punctuation is variable. She sometimes uses a dash to indicate a period. There are instances where punctuation appears to be missing, although it may be that, given the condition of the original letters, it is no longer detectable. Fanny's use of underlining has been preserved, a device she employs either for emphasis or to highlight an ironic comment. Fanny regularly used red sealing wax on her letters, although the area where the imprint of the seal occurs has been damaged in most cases. The exceptions are two of the letters written to James Christie Eaten in Bermuda. Oval wax impressions show the name "Fanny" on her letter of 4 October 1813 and the image of a pair of scissors on her letter of 30 June 1814. On Fanny's letter to Esther, 8 March 1814, the imprint of the "Fanny" seal is still evident.

Fanny's letters were passed down within the Charles Austen family. In the 1930s R.W. Chapman, the editor of Austen's novels for Oxford University Press, made his own transcription of Fanny's letters while they were still in the possession of a granddaughter of Charles and Harriet, Jane Austen. He described them as "interesting in their own way." Fanny's letters remained in the family until they were sold at auction in 1970, when they were bought by scholar and collector Gordon N. Ray. He bequeathed them to the Pierpont Morgan Library in 1987 (now known as Morgan Library and Museum – MLM), where they are catalogued as the Gordon N. Ray Collection MA 4500.

In the 1980s Deirdre Le Faye consulted the Chapman typescript and made some corrections after studying photocopies of Fanny's letters provided by the Pierpont Morgan Library. The amended text printed in this book is based on my study of the original letters at the Pierpont Morgan Library during October 2012 as well as on an examination of Chapman's transcription of them together with Le Faye's emendations.

In the interests of revealing the flow of Fanny's narrative, some paragraphing has been introduced.[1] Her misspellings have been preserved, and when a word is obscured due to damage to the original document or is simply missing, one of appropriate sense has been inserted and enclosed in a square bracket.

Catalogue of Fanny's Letters

Fanny Austen's twelve extant letters reprinted in this book are each addressed to one of her sisters, either Esther or Harriet Palmer, or to her brother-in-law, James Christie Esten, chief justice of Bermuda. Some of the letters are of considerable length, as they include instalments written over several days or weeks while Fanny waited for a means to send them to their destination.

The twelve letters are as follows:[2]

1. Fanny Palmer Austen at Halifax, Nova Scotia, to Mrs J.C. [Esther] Esten at Bermuda, includes 1, 12, and 17 June 1810.
    Addressed: Mrs. J: C: Esten/at the Chief Justice's/
    St George's/Bermuda.
    No postmark.
    MLM: MA 7293

2. Fanny at Halifax to Esther in Bermuda, includes 4, 12, 14, 15, 17, and 18 August 1810.
   Addressed: Mrs. J: C: Esten/St George's/Bermuda.
   No postmark or endorsement.
   MLM: MA 7294

3. Fanny at Halifax to Esther in Bermuda, includes 23 and 24 September 1810.
   Addressed: Mrs. J: C: Esten/St George's/Bermuda/Honored by Lieut Innis/H.M. Sch: Chub.
   MLM: MA 7295

4. Fanny on HMS *Namur* at the Nore to James Christie Esten in Bermuda, 21 January 1812.
   Addressed: The Honble. The Chief Justice/St George's/Bermuda.
   Endorsements: pr. Elizabeth and Margaret, Merchant Ship. 21 Jany. recd. 28 Augt. 1812.
   MLM: MA 7299

5. Fanny on the *Namur* to Esther in London, 5 March 1812.
   Addressed: Mrs. J: C: Esten/22 Keppel Street/Russell Square/London.
   Postmarks: Sheerness 51. A/6 MA 6/1812.
   MLM: MA 7296.

6. Fanny on the *Namur* to Esther in London, 6 March 1812.
   Addressed: Mrs. J: C: Esten/22 Keppel Street/Russell Square/London.
   Postmark: 10 o'clock/ MR.7/1812/F. Nn, and another illegible postmark.
   MLM: MA 7297

7. Fanny on the *Namur* to James Christie Esten in Bermuda,
    4 October 1813.
    Addressed: The Honble. The Chief Justice/St George's Bermuda.
    Per Packet.
    Endorsed: PostPaid Oct 5th. 1813 C.J.A. A large endorsement over
    the address in red ink: P 2/3.
    Postmark: A/PAID/6 OC 6/ 1813. Seal impression, the name Fanny, in
    red sealing wax.
    MLM: MA 7300

8. Fanny on the *Namur* to Harriet Palmer in London,
    22nd November, 1813.
    Addressed: Miss Palmer/22 Keppel Street/Russell Square/London.
    Endorsed: post-paid Novr. 22nd 1813 C.J.A.
    Postmarks: A/PAID, SHEERNESS 51.
    MLM: MA 7302

9. Fanny at Sheerness to Harriet in London, 5 and 6 February 1814.
    Addressed: Miss Palmer/22 Keppel Street/Russell Square/London.
    Postmarks: SHEERNESS 51; C/PAID/7 FE 7/1814.
    MLM: MA 7303

10. Fanny at the Commissioners, Dock Yard, Sheerness to Harriet
    in London, 16 February 1814.
    Addressed: Miss Palmer/22 Keppel Street/Russell Square/London.
    Endorsed: Post paid Feby. 16th 1814 C.J.A.
    Postmark: A/PAID 17 FE 17.
    MLM: MA 7304

11. Fanny on the *Namur* to Esther in Bermuda, 8, 11, and 17 March 1814.
    Addressed: Mrs. J: C: Esten/St George's/Bermuda.
    Endorsed: Honor'd by Lieut. Tattnall, HM Ship Tonnant.
    MLM: MA 7298

12. Fanny on *Namur* to James Christie Esten in Bermuda, 30 June;
    Keppel Street, 8 July 1814.
    Addressed: The Honble. The Chief Justice Esten/St George's/
    Bermuda/Per Halifax/pr. Packet/8 July 1814/R.J.P.
    Endorsed: Rec'd 8th Sept. answered 23 Sept.
    Postmark: 2/2 J.B.4.
    MLM : MA 7301

(2)   FANNY AUSTEN'S POCKET DIARY 1814

Made of red morocco, with a tuck-in flap and showing signs of wear, the
pocketbook measures 10 cm by 7 cm. Title page: "*Pocket Magnet, or elegant
Picturesque Diary, for 1814*. It was sold by the granddaughters of Charles
Austen to R.W. Chapman. His son Michael Chapman resold it to David
Gilson, who gave it to King's College, Cambridge, 2013.

Letters about Fanny

1. Esther S. Esten to Captain Charles Austen, at Halifax, Nova Scotia, 26 July 1808.[1]

Bermuda July 26th 1808

I have been endeavouring my dear Brother, ever since you left us, to perform my promise, which I certainly shou'd have done before this had I not been prevented by many unexpected occurrences – Among the first I shall mention my own Accident, which had nearly proved a serious one, to my dear Palmer[2] – He was standing with me at the very moment that a Mug of boiling Water slipped from my hands, and nothing but my getting between him and the Mug, saved him from it – you will agree with me that it was a most fortunate thing – I got all the contents on my foot, which has confined me to the House for these last ten days, and deprived me the pleasure of accompanying my dear Fan[3] in her usual evening walks – She has not however suffered at all, as our friend Mrs. Dickinson[4] is always ready to supply my place upon all occasions –

It is with great delight that I say she is doing very well, and wants nothing but your presence to make her quite comfortable – Her Appetite (by the assistance of bitters) is pretty good – A very good one you cannot expect her to have just now. Indeed Capt. Hickey[5] told her yesterday, that she had grown quite plump in the face, which I was not a little proud to hear –

We are anxiously looking out and hoping that an arrival from Halifax, will bring us early accounts of you – I hope you have had pleasing accounts from your friends in England. We have not been so fortunate, altho' Mrs. Grant and others have had good news by the Packet –

Mr. Esten[6] has been taking a course of Medicine, which I think will be of great service to him – He unites with me in our sincere wishes for your return – Palmer often talks of you and I think will be glad to see you –

The Prize Vessell and Cargo[7] are to be sold to morrow, and are likely to fetch a good price – I have been a little nervous for you this last week, lest an Arrival of Provision shou'd lower the sale of yours – You will allow that that I am a little selfish, (because you know that a supply of every kind of Provision wou'd be so beneficial to the Island) but the best of us are given to that failing and I must not expect to be exempted –

Present my best regards to Tom Fowle,[8] and all enquiring friends on board the Indian – Shou'd you see our worthy friend Sir Robert Laurie,[9] say every thing kind for us – And present our united Compts.[10] to the Admiral's family,[11] who I am glad to hear, do not like Halifax as well as our little Spot[.] Mrs Dickinson begs to be kindly remembered to you –

I forgot in my list of articles for Fan, to mention flannel. You will remember to send her twenty or thirty yards, of fine white flannel, as there is none to be got here fit for her use –

I must now bid you Adieu. That health and happiness may attend you is the fervent wish of your

> *very affectionate*
>> *Esther S. Esten*

Captain Charles John Austen
H. M. Ship Indian
Halifax

2. Captain Charles Austen to Cassandra Austen, in Southampton, Hampshire[12]

> *Bermuda December 25th, 1808*

My Dear Cassandra[13]

I am sure you will be delighted to hear that my beloved Fanny was safely deliver'd a fine girl on the 22nd of December and that they are both doing remarkibley well. The Baby besides being the finest that ever was seen is really a good looking healthy young Lady of very large dimensions and as fat as butter I mean to call her Cassandra Esten and beg the favour of you to be a Sponsor your Coadjutress will be Mrs. Esten and Captain Hawker[14] of HMS Melampus your other partner. I esteem myself very fortunate in having been allowed to be in port at this criticale moment to support my Fanny who has been prevented from enjoying her Sisters society owing to her having been employed in the same way. She was safely delivered of a little Boy just a week[15] before his Cousin Cassandra made her entre into this world contrary to all rule she is by far the largest but he is a healthy little fellow and as well as his mother doing very well which I am sure will give you pleasure tho you are not personally acquainted with the party's.

I wrote to Jane[16] about a Fortnight ago acquainting her with my arrival at this place and of my having captured a little Frenchman which I am truely sorry to add has never reached this port and unless she has run to the West Indies I have lost her and what is a real misfortune the lives of twelve of my people two of them mids, I confess I have but little hopes of ever hearing of her the weather has been so very severe since we captured her.[17]

The Admiral[18] and his family arrived here just a Fortnight ago and are fixed for the winter. I find them as friendly as ever. I wish you a merry and happy Xmas in which Fan joins me as well as in bespeaking the Love of her Dear Grandmother and Aunts &c for our little Cassandra.

The October and November mails have not yet reached us so that I know nothing about you of late; I hope you have been more fortunate in hearing of me. I expect to sail on Tuesday with a small convoy for the Island of St. Domingo and after seeing them in safety open sealed orders which I conclude will direct me to cruize as long as my provisions &c will allow which is generally a couple of months. My companion the Vesta[19] is to be with me again, which I like very much. I dont know of any opportunity of sending this but shall leave it to take its chance. When I get to sea I shall write to my other correspondants and will thank you to say so to any of them you communicate with. Tom Fowle is very well and is growing quite manly.

I am interrupted by Mr. De Passau[20] who is going to Baptize the Children but as they are not quite made up he has consented to eat Cake & drink some wine whilst I conclude this by assuring you how truely I am your affect Friend and attached Brother Charles Jno. Austen

I sent Mary²¹ the arrowroot she wrote for [to]the Vessel I mentioned [,] having written to Jane. I suppose her request portends as usual a probability of increase. I am very anxious to hear how Dear Elizabeth²² has got thro her late confinement.
Miss Austen
Castle square
Southampton
Hants

Fanny Palmer Austen's Kindred

A mid-eighteenth-century description of the structure of English society identified five classes in descending order: "the Nobility, the Gentry, the Genteel Trades, the common Trades and the Peasantry."[1] Implicit in this classification was the notion of rank, with its emphasis on lineage, as if social status was a function of birth and descent. In contrast, class, which was measured to some extent by income and socio-economic status, was a function of productivity and material wealth. In the England of 1803, about 300 families constituted the peerage – comprised of dukes, marquesses, earls, viscounts, and barons – while the gentry society consisted of roughly 540 baronets, 350 knights, 6,000 landed squires, and 20,000 gentlemen.[2] This grouping in total amounted to just 1.4 per cent of the population.[3] Jane Austen's novels are set in the world of the gentry society, where ownership of land over time was a mark of rank, and wealth, titles, and inherited property were determinants of status. Military achievement and honours, as well as money acquired through trade or professional success, such as in the law, provided an acceptable entrée into society. In addition, linking one's family by marriage to another of higher class – "marrying up" – was a strategy that offered immediate social and, usually, economic benefits.

The Austen family belonged to the gentry class. Though they were "relatively disadvantaged in financial terms, [they] could boast aristocratic descent and ongoing connections ... The family treasured a surviving letter to Jane's great-grandmother Mary Brydges, sister to the first Duke of Chandos, as a mark of inherited distinction."[4] Charles brought his family's status to Fanny when they married, but her family's origins and connections also counted as she and Charles established their place together in social circles.

One way of signifying descent, as well as familial affection, was to transfer significant names from generation to generation. Fanny's parents were familiar with the practice of passing on well-known family names to their children. By bestowing mutual forenames, and sometimes surnames, upon successive generations, they were recording blood relationships and commemorating them. Although the source of Fanny's first and second names, Frances and FitzWilliams, is mystifying, her three siblings were all given names associated with the Palmer, Strangways, Ball, and Hutchinson families from whom they were descended. These were the families who defined Fanny's origins. Her membership in gentry society depended on their claims to accomplishments, wealth, and aristocratic connections.

THE PALMER FAMILY OF ENGLAND AND IRELAND

By tradition, the surname Palmer originates from the medieval name for pilgrims who, returning from their travels to the Holy Land, brought palm fronds that they showed as proof. According to his obituary, Fanny's father, John Grove Palmer, belonged to "a branch of the Palmers of Howletts in Kent";[5] yet this group of Palmers in east Kent had even earlier roots further west in the county. Edward Hasted, the eighteenth-century Kent historian, identified a baronet, Sir Thomas Palmer, who died in the early years of the fifteenth century, as the common ancestor of both the original Palmers of "Tottington, near Alysford," close to Maidstone in west Kent, and the later branch of the family, to which Fanny's father claimed a link, known as the Palmers "of Howletts and Bekesbourne," near Canterbury in east Kent.[6]

The first Sir Thomas was buried in Snodland, Kent, in 1407. His epitaph reads as follows:

Palmers al our faders were
I, a Palmer, livyd here
And travylled till worne wythe age
I endyd this worlds pylgramage
On the blyst Assenton day
In the cherful month of May
A thowsand wyth fowre hundryd seven
And took my jorney hense to Heven.[7]

One of Sir Thomas's descendants married strategically. Sometime before 1446, a grandson, the third Sir Thomas, of Court Lodge, Snodland, received the manor of Tottington[8] from his father-in-law, Robert de Poynings. This property passed to his son, Sir John, and on to his son, the fifth Sir Thomas, who died while still in possession of it in 1507. His heir, the sixth Sir Thomas, sold the manor during the reign of Henry VIII to Richard Warup.[9] These Palmers were sufficiently important to be granted a coat of arms. It consists of a silver chevron between three black palmers' purses tasselled and buckled in gold.[10]

As Fanny was descended through her father from the Palmers of Howletts, she was distantly connected to Sir Henry Palmer (1550–1611), who had a naval career of distinction. After serving under the Earl of Leicester in the Netherlands, he was knighted by him in 1586 and was granted his own coat of arms. Two years later he was captain of the *Antelope* in an action against the Spanish Armada. In recognition of his record of distinguished service,[11] he was made controller of the navy in 1599, a post he held for the next twelve years until his death in 1611.[12] Military success gave Sir Henry the means to acquire more property – Howletts at Bekesbourne in 1590 and nearby Cobham Court, Well Court Lodge, and Hode. His richly ornamented memorial, placed high in the nave of St Peter's Church, Bekesbourne, pays tribute to his earthly success. It incorporates a kneeling figure of Sir Henry in full armour. His heraldic coat of arms, appearing on the decorated surround above, includes the silver chevron between three black palmers' purses, which are found in the coat of arms assigned to the Palmers of west Kent.

A branch of the Palmers of Howletts left England during the reign of Charles II and settled in Ireland.[13] Fanny's Anglo-Irish great-grandfather,

Robert Palmer, lived at Clonmacken, near Limerick, where the family prospered. Clonmacken House, built by Rev. Edmund Palmer in 1700, was an early Georgian mansion, designed with five bays, a simple pedimented doorway, and a walled garden to the east and northeast.[14] His property gave the impression of being a comfortable and stylish gentleman's house with a "magnificent curved staircase leading from the hall,"[15] a carriage sweep in front, and a ha-ha[16] to keep grazing livestock out of the garden while still preserving the view.

Fanny's grandfather John Palmer was born about 1716 in Clonmacken.[17] As the third son of Robert Palmer, he was not in line to inherit family property, so he needed to provide his own livelihood, which probably explains why he chose to become a barrister and was admitted to study at the Middle Temple in London on 17 July 1740.[18] John Palmer subsequently enjoyed a successful law practice in London and established connections with Kentish Town, then a rural village south of Hampstead, where he took up residence. He acquired freehold and copyhold[19] properties in the English counties of Essex and Hertford and an estate near Listowel in County Kerry, Ireland, which included a residence, Banemore House,[20] built in 1770. When he died in 1801, aged eighty-four, Fanny's father, John Grove Palmer, was his heir. Evidently both John Palmers valued their Irish roots. The senior John Palmer's will mentions his affiliation with Baunmore, County Kerry.[21] His son, John Grove Palmer, was buried in the parish churchyard at Alverstoke, near Gosport in Hampshire. His headstone records that he was "of Baunmore, Co Kerry" and had been the attorney general of Bermuda.

There is reason to think that the Kentish Town Palmers and the Clonmacken Palmers kept in touch. In 1792 John Palmer's brother, the Reverend Edmund Palmer,[22] of Clonmacken House was rudely awakened in the early morning of 6 January by a gang of robbers who bludgeoned open the front door. Fortunately, the intruders were repelled by the swift action of Reverend Palmer and two servants. One of them was a black man named Robert St George, who "gallantly defended [his master's house and] shot dead, with others, the principal of the party" of sixteen ruffians.[23]

Assuming they heard about this attack, the John Palmers would be appalled to think how dire the consequences might have been for Edmund and his family, but perhaps they were gratified to learn of Robert St George's quick and decisive action. There was a reason why Robert's heroism would be of interest. In the eighteenth century it was considered an important status symbol among wealthy English families in Ireland to have a black man as a servant, although it was extremely rare to find one at this time. It is at least possible that Reverend Palmer's nephew, John Grove Palmer, already attorney general of Bermuda by 1783, had arranged for a young black slave to be taken into his uncle's service. Slaves and servants sometimes bore a surname that identified their place of origin. If John Grove Palmer was the agent in this case, he may have acquired Robert in St George's, Bermuda, thereby explaining how the young man came to be known as Robert St George.

Fanny's only brother, Robert John, was named to show his connections to the male line of his family. He bore the names of his father (John Grove Palmer), grandfather (John Palmer), and great-grandfather (Robert Palmer). By the terms of the entail in his grandfather's will, he inherited the Irish property in County Kerry, including Banemore House, at the death of his father in 1832. It is not known when he and his wife, Isabella née Studdard, and their three children first began to live there.[24] The name "Banemore" derives from the Irish Gaelic, "An Ban Mor," meaning the big tract of open ground or grassland.

John Palmer's life in Ireland is difficult to trace. Census records for 1821 through 1851 have not survived, although information from Griffith's Evaluation, the first comprehensive assessment of individual property in Ireland, gives a good idea of the scope and nature of his estate in 1852. It was comprised of 170 acres, of which 19 were rented in separate parcels to seven tenants. The rest he kept for himself: a plantation (woodland, 34 acres), land (40 acres), the house, out buildings, and grounds (39 acres). A mountain (71 acres)[25] completed his personal domain.[26]

Palmer's property sounds attractive, with its variety of cultivated land, woodlands, and a prominent hill. In 1837 Samuel Lewis, in his *Topographical Dictionary*, identified Banemore House as "the seat of Robert John Palmer" and described it as "romantically situated on the brow of a mountain which is extensively planted."[27] But in the years to follow, agricultural Ireland was ravaged by a potato blight that destroyed the crop and led to the Great Famine, a disaster that lasted from 1845 to 1852. Among the Irish poor, thousands died of starvation; more emigrated. By the time of Griffith's

Evaluation in 1852, agricultural land had fallen drastically in value. John Palmer's woodlands, land, Banemore House, and mountain were valued at £5 5s.; his tenants land and cottages at £20 11s. Sometime during the Great Famine the house was the site of a soup kitchen. It is not known when the Palmer family relinquished Banemore House; it is now a ruin.

THE STRANGWAYS FAMILY
OF YORKSHIRE AND DORSET

The Strangways,[28] who had been resident in Yorkshire since medieval times, were Fanny's most aristocratic ancestral connection. According to genealogist John Burke, the Strangways family, "which boasts of high antiquity, is allied, through females, to the noble houses of Percy, Kyme, Umfreville, Talboys, Berners etc."[29] Fanny traced her descent from Sir James Strangwish, a judge and son of Henry Strangwish of Strangwich Hall near Manchester. From this Sir James descended five male heirs of the same name, several of whom married heiresses. The second James, who occupied Harsley Castle, North Yorkshire, in 1432, married Elizabeth, co-heir of Philip, Lord Darcy; his son, the third James, of Whorlton Castle, married Anne, co-heir of Sir Richard Conyers of Ormsby and Hornby. From this line descends Fanny's great-grandfather, John Strangewayes of Well, Yorkshire, who married Gratiana Preston. Fanny's grandmother, Dorothy Strangways, who was their fifth and youngest child, married Fanny's grandfather, John Palmer. The link with Fanny's family was made explicit when Esther Palmer, Fanny's oldest sister, was given the second name "Strangways." Her name not only recognized family ties, but also marked Esther's connection to a family of note, something that could be of considerable advantage to her in later years. In the next generation, Esther bestowed it on her short-lived son, Charles Strangways Esten, who, sadly, died aged five months.

The Yorkshire Strangways were related some generations back by a common ancestor to the wealthy landed Dorset Strangways. Through this connection, Fanny can be linked, albeit very distantly, with the gentleman pirate Henry Strangwich (Strangways) and an army wife, Lady Harriet Ackland. As far as can be determined, Henry Strangwich (1527–1562) was probably Fanny's third cousin eight times removed.[30] From the early 1550s, Henry was "a highly successful pirate captain operating on both sides of the Irish Sea ... he was imprisoned for piracy on more than one occasion" but always managed to be pardoned. A portrait of him, painted by German artist Gerlach Flicke in 1554[31] while both men were imprisoned, probably in the Tower of London, shows him to be "elegantly dressed in black, with a penetrating, direct stare." He holds a lute. Known for his fiery red hair, Strangwish was popularly called "The Red Rover of the Channel."[32] It is a mere coincidence that Fanny was known for her red-gold hair, yet it is tempting to speculate that it was possibly an inheritance through the Strangways line.

Another of Fanny's distant relatives from the Dorset branch of the family was her tenth cousin three times removed, Lady Harriet Acland.[33] She was the third surviving daughter of Stephen Fox and Elizabeth Strangways-Horner. Her father, who became 1st Earl of Ilchester, had taken the additional name and arms of the Strangways on his marriage in 1736. Lady Harriet's family were part of the eighteenth-century Whig aristocracy and her second cousin was the politician Charles James Fox.

Lady Harriet, like Fanny, became a military wife. In January 1771, she married Sir John Acland, the eldest son of Sir Thomas Acland, seventh baronet, a Dorset landowner and politician. Sir John was an enthusiastic supporter of the British efforts to defeat the American Revolution. Seeking action in that conflict, Acland bought a major's commission in the 20th Foot, just before the regiment was sent with General Burgoyne's army to North America. Lady Harriet accompanied her husband on his deployment across the North Atlantic in April 1776, leaving her daughter Elizabeth, aged three, behind in Dorset.

Things did not go well for Sir John. He was wounded and captured behind enemy lines, but was fortunate in having Lady Harriet to act vigorously for his release.[34] On learning of his plight, she determined to rescue him. She secured an open boat, and flying a white flag of truce, she crossed the Hudson River together with the chaplain, Mr Brudenell, her maid, and her husband's valet. On 10 October 1776 the party reached an American outpost at night, where they were challenged and forbidden to land until daybreak, some eight hours later. Lady Harriet's journal records that "half dead with anxiety and terror, [she] persuaded the sentinel to deliver her laissez-passez to General Gates, the senior American officer."[35]

What might have easily turned out badly did not. Lady Harriet charmed her adversaries, including General Gates, who described her as "the most amiable, delicate little piece of Quality you ever beheld."[36] The Fox-Strangways family motto is "faire sans dire," which translates as "deeds without words." Lady Harriet lived it to the hilt. She was reunited with Sir John at Still Water, nursed him back to health, and accompanied him to Albany, New York. Their troubles were not yet over because the Continental Congress did not honour the return of prisoners. Luckily for them, General Burgoyne was determined to negotiate their release and General Gates was interested in an exchange of prisoners. Perhaps Lady Harriet's pregnancy was a contributing factor, as she was due to give birth in approximately three months. Lady Harriet and Sir John were released and sailed for England early in 1778, where their second child, a son John, was born and later baptised on 21 March.

Lady Harriet's exploits in America were very well known in England, partly because the artist Robert Pollard painted and subsequently published an engraving in 1784 depicting her dramatic crossing of the Hudson River. Fanny may have known about this very distant cousin's pluck and bravery, since her story had all the makings of a family legend. Fanny's father, who was of a similar age and generation as Lady Harriet, chose her name for his second daughter, who was born two years after the popular print became available. Harriet's middle name, Ebel, was likely bestowed in recognition of a cousin, Deborah Ebel, who was listed as a beneficiary in her grandfather John Palmer's will.

THE BALL AND HUTCHINSON
FAMILIES OF BERMUDA

Fanny's North American colonial connections were with Bermuda families of English origin. She was the great-granddaughter of the first Ball ancestor of note, a mariner named Captain George Ball. His son, also named George, married Esther Hutchinson on 27 July 1756[37] at St George's. Esther was the daughter of Robert Hutchinson and Dorothy Smith; her maternal grandparents were Thomas and Esther Smith. On 15 June 1764 Esther Smith gave her granddaughter Esther Ball, née Hutchinson, a property in St George's, standing on a hill, facing Water Street and located close to the State House. It was built between 1713 and 1715 and was known as Casino.[38] The house has survived relatively unaltered and is considered to be "typical of an 18th century merchant's house, with living quarters above, and storage space in the high cellars below."[39]

From the time of the gift, Casino likely became the home of George and Esther Ball and their family, including their six-year-old daughter, Dorothy, who would become Fanny's mother. After Dorothy Ball married John Grove Palmer and began to have children, she did not forget how her family came to have Casino, for she named their first daughter Esther, presumably after the child's maternal grandmother (Esther Ball) and great-great-grandmother (Esther Smith).

The practice of giving real estate to female members of the family continued. In 1782 Fanny's grandfather, George Ball, gave his daughter Dorothy and her two children at the time, Esther Strangways and Robert John, Smith Island and part of Hen Island, properties located in the approach to St George's Harbour.[40] At the time of Fanny's birth in 1789, Casino was described as the "house of John Grove Palmer, Esq."[41] This reference might suggest that Fanny's family was living in Casino, but this is less likely given the size of the house and the number of children and servants to be accommodated. Casino later became the home of Alexander Forbes Ball, Fanny's uncle, who sold it in 1824.[42]

The story of Fanny's forebears shows that the Palmers, the Strangways, and the Balls were people of some accomplishment, wealth, and standing within their own societal circles. Fanny could be proud of her ancestral roots.

Notes

ABBREVIATIONS

AGNS   Art Gallery of Nova Scotia
BA   Bermuda Archives
BM   Bermuda Masterworks
LAC   Library and Archives Canada
MLM   Morgan Library and Museum, New York
NMA   National Museum of Art, Washington
NMM   National Maritime Museum, Greenwich, UK
NPG   National Portrait Gallery, UK
NSA   Nova Scotia Archives
NSARM   Nova Scotia Archives and Records Management
SL   Southend Library, UK
TNA   The National Archives, UK

INTRODUCTION

1 Cassandra Austen to Phylly Walter, in Austen-Leigh, *Austen Papers*, 249.
2 They are published here for the first time.
3 For the influence of Fanny Austen's life on Jane Austen's fiction, see chapter 9.

CHAPTER ONE

1 Although Fanny's middle name is given as Fitzwilliam in some writings
about the Austen family (Le Faye, *Family Record*, 375), it is spelled
FitzWilliams in two baptismal registers. Alexander Richardson's Register
of the parish of St George's, Bermuda, records her baptism on 21 February
1790 with the spelling FitzWilliams for her middle name. See Hallet, *Early
Bermuda Records*, 157. The Baptismal Book for Robert Stanser, St Paul's
Church, Halifax, Nova Scotia, which records Cassy Austen's baptism on
6 October 1809, refers to her mother as "Frances FitzWilliams Austen." The
FitzWilliams spelling appears in the notice of her marriage in the *Bermuda
Gazette* (see Hallet, *Bermuda Index*, vol. 2, 1013). It also occurs on Fanny's
memorial tablet, which was in the Kentish Town Chapel and then in its suc-
cessor church, St John the Baptist church, Kentish Town. The latter building
is now Christ Apostolic Church.

2 He was attorney general in 1781 and again from 1783 to 1801.

3 Mary died aged four months, 1792; William died at birth 1795; and
Georgina died aged two and one-half years, 1796. Another brother, Thomas
Hutchinson Palmer was baptised 19 February 1797 in St George's but did not
survive infancy. See Hallet, *Early Bermuda Records*, 157, 158, 188. Yet another
sibling, listed only as "Child" in the parish baptismal records was baptised
on 13 January 1782. John Grove Palmer is listed as the father but there is
no one named as the mother. As Fanny's parents had married in 1775, it is
most likely a clerical error that Dorothy Palmer's name does not appear. This
"child" presumably died almost immediately after birth. See Hallet, *Early
Bermuda Records*, 157.

4 Captain Philip Broke to his wife Louisa, 11 December 1811, Sir James
Saumarez papers, HA 93/9/78, LAC.

5 Description of the house from the *Bermuda Gazette*, 31 October 1812.

6 The house no longer exits. The property is now referred to as Welch's
Grant in recognition of the first grantee of the land, John Welch Jr on
28 February 1707.

7 St George's Parish Assessments, BA ANG/SG/PAS I.

8 Bernhard, *Slaves and Slaveholders in Bermuda*, 275.

9 See Packwood, *Chained on the Rock*, 98. As Bermuda never enacted laws
prohibiting teaching slaves to read and write, a number of adult slaves

attained some degree of literacy and slave children in some areas had access to education. Significantly, although laws intended to control and punish slaves were passed, Bernhard contends that "both blacks and whites found ways to ignore or circumvent them" (Bernhard, *Slaves and Slaveholders in Bermuda*, 275).

10 Census records for the whole population of Bermuda are sketchy. The Black Census for 1799 records that there were 4,846 negro slaves and slaves of colour. The Bermuda *Blue Book* for 1824 records a population of 4,648 whites, 722 free blacks and 5,242 slaves. At Emancipation, 1 August 1834, of a population of 8,818, there were 4,259 whites and 4,559 blacks. See Packwood, *Chained on the Rock*, 80–2.

11 Wilkinson, *Bermuda Sail to Steam*, vol. 1, 229.

12 Fanny's father may also have been instrumental in acquiring a black slave for her father's uncle in Ireland in the 1780s. See Appendix 3, n. 23.

13 Esther, who was twenty-seven, had been married to thirty-year-old James since 16 November 1799. See Hallet, *Early Bermuda Records*, 153.

14 James Christie Esten was recognized for his relatively liberal views, for the time, about the treatment of Bermuda's slaves and the importance of providing them with educational opportunities. His point of view would be known and respected in the household where Fanny was growing up.

15 Honan, *Jane Austen: A Life*, 331. In May 1800 the Bermuda Assembly and Council passed an act to exclude persons not invested in holy orders according to the Church of England from propagating the gospel or keeping a school. The act was designed to restrict the preaching of John Stephenson, a Methodist missionary sent to Bermuda from Ireland by the Methodist Society. He was convicted, jailed, and fined. See Hallet, *Early Bermuda Records*, 341.

16 John Palmer's will, PROB 11/1358/10, 3, TNA.

17 Hubback and Hubback, *Jane Austen's Sailor Brothers*, 54.

18 Jane Austen, *Jane Austen's Letters*, no. 18, 22 January 1799, 39. Hereafter Austen, *Letters*.

19 Sutherland, *Jane Austen's Textual Lives*, 238. For the texts of these very short stories, see Jane Austen, *Catherine and Other Writings*, ed. Doody and Murray, 38–9, 40–1.

20 Commander was a rank between lieutenant and post-captain. Sea officers were ranked from lieutenant through commander, post-captain, commodore

(a temporary status given when in command of a particular squadron), and the three levels of admiral: rear, vice, and full admiral. See Lavery, *Nelson's Navy*, 1994, 94–9.

21　Britain and Spain subsequently became allies against France in July 1808.

22　See Caplan, "The Ships of Charles Austen," 147. It is extremely difficult to establish a modern equivalence for the economic power of money in Jane Austen's time. In "Money in Jane Austen," Robert Hume explains why "the 'basket of goods and services' dear to twenty-first century economists is so different in 1810 and 2012 as to be almost entirely incommensurable, 302." For example, paper, clothes, and food were very expensive in 1810, less so in proportion to income in 2012. Services provided by people were very cheap in 1810 compared to their relatively high cost in 2012. "Having compared prices and incomes then and now for a wide assortment of purchases and occupations," Hume suggests that "a figure in the range of 100 to 150 times the 1810 sum often yields a rough equivalency in early twenty-first century terms," 303. For an alternative economists' approach to the scaling of monetary values between the nineteenth and twenty-first centuries, see https://measuringworth.com. This study will use Hume's multiple of 100 to 150 to calculate a crude modern equivalency of the purchasing power of the sums of money mentioned throughout the text.

23　A naval vessel's tonnage was the builder's measurement, a formula used in calculating the carrying capacity of the hull. See Winfield, *British Warships in the Age of Sail*, xi. The *Indian*'s dimensions were length 107 feet, breadth 29 feet 11 inches, and 14 feet 8 inches deep in the hold. Her tonnage was 399 bm. See Winfield, *British Warships*, 270.

24　ADM 101/50, MG 2582, file 7, NSARM.

25　The doubloon was a gold Spanish/Spanish American coin worth about $4. During this period, they were used extensively as currency in both Nova Scotia and Bermuda. "Doubloons" and "Dollars" refer to the prize money Charles hoped they would acquire.

26　The wording of Charles's recruitment notice offered a reasonable set of inducements that he hoped would tempt seamen to sign up. In a similar document, the captain of HMS *Leander* (50 guns) promised to provide seamen with "a lower deck like a barn where you may play leap frog when the hammocks are hung up" and described his vessel as a "whacking double banked frigate [which] is fitting for the fine full-bellied Halifax station where you may get a bushel of potatoes for a schilling, codfish for a biscuit and a glass of boatswain's grog for two pence." Recruitment notice for HMS *Leander*, MG 13, vol. 4, NSARM. This recruitment notice probably dates to 1801 or 1802 when the *Leander* was being refitted in England before going out to the Halifax end of the North American Station.

27 Wilkinson, *Bermuda from Sail to Steam*, vol. 1, 240.

28 A caulker was an artificer who made watertight a seam between two planks either on the ship's bottom or deck planking. A shipwright was a ship's carpenter. See Gwyn, *Ashore and Afloat*, 322, 325.

29 Hawker's early connection to the navy was not unique. Provo Featherstone Wallis, a clerk to the master shipwright in the Halifax Naval Yard, put his son Provo's name on the books of several vessels from the age of four. Provo William Parry Wallis became Admiral of the Fleet in 1877 by dint of seniority at the age of eighty-six.

30 Journal of Winckworth Norwood, 3 July 1805, MG 13, vol. 4, NSARM.

31 Fanny Austen to Esther Esten, 14 August 1810, MA 7294, MLM (Morgan Library and Museum, formerly the Pierpont Morgan Library).

32 Esther Esten to Charles Austen, 26 July 1808, MA 4500, MLM. See Appendix 2.

33 Charles was to rescue Captain William Henry Byam and his crew when HMS *Bermuda* (18 guns), another of *Indian*'s sister ships, was wrecked and abandoned on the Little Bahama Reef, 3 June 1808. Byam had been a fellow student with Charles at the Naval Academy, Portsmouth. Gustavus Stupart of HMS *Emulous* (18) was another regular colleague of Charles's. He served on the station between 1807 and 1810. Widowed in 1802, he married Zephyretta Hyndman in 1812.

34 Gwyn, *Ashore and Afloat*, 325. Privateers also sought to capture prizes. A privateer was a "privately-owned vessel, heavily-armed and crewed, with a government commission to sail against enemy shipping." Gwyn, 188.

35 The distribution of the shares of the remaining three-eighths of prize money was as follows: one-eighth to the sailing master, lieutenants and physicians; another eighth to the warrant officers, master's mates and chaplain; and another eighth to the inferior warrant officers and midshipmen. See Southam, *Jane Austen and the Navy*, 129.

36 An agent took care of such details as monitoring the court proceedings, arranging for the storage and auction of condemned goods, paying court fees and other costs, and the paying out of prize money in accordance with the established formula. According to Richard Hill, an "agent would in effect be acting as solicitor, accountant and banker in addition to his principal and specialized function in matters of prize." Hill, *The Prizes of War*, 149. In addition to reviewing accounts with his agents, Charles may have periodically discussed with them the principles of prize law and the effects of recent judgments of the Vice Admiralty Courts.

37 Andrew Belcher, a prominent businessman in Halifax, was appointed to the Legislative Council in 1801 and thus was entitled to be addressed as "Honourable."

38 The Austen was Henry Austen, Charles's brother, who was in a banking partnership in London with Henry Maunde. See HCA 49/99, 1806, TNA.

39 See O'Byrne, *Naval Bibliographical Dictionary*, 26–7.

40 This sum is roughly equivalent to between £24,600 and £36,900 in modern currency. See note 22.

41 Sweden had owned the island of Saint-Barthelemy (St Barts) in the Caribbean since purchasing it from France in 1784. Perhaps the *Dygden* was carrying contraband cargo and thus liable to arrest as a prize.

42 The wine was particularly valuable. Hon. Andrew Belcher, in his capacity as merchant, spent £1,888 for Catalonia wine when *Dygden*'s cargo was auctioned. See Vice Admiralty Court of Nova Scotia fonds, RG8/IV/142, 180, LAC.

43 Ibid., RG8/IV/62, LAC.

44 *Nuestra Senora del Carmen* was taken on 25 July 1806; *La Lustorina* was captured on 25 May 1806.

45 Vice Admiralty Court of Nova Scotia fonds, RG8/IV/64, file 2, LAC.

46 See High Court of Admiralty records, HCA 46/48, TNA.

47 It would be roughly equivalent to between £54,100 to £81,150 in modern terms. See note 22.

48 See George Hulbert's Cash Book, 1808–1812, HUL/23, 5, NMM.

49 Esther Esten to Charles Austen, 26 July 1810, MA 4500, MLM. See Appendix 2.

50 Austen, *Letters*, no. 54, 26 June 1808, 138.

51 Charles Austen's journal, 31 July 1826, AUS/118, NMM.

52 Austen, *Persuasion*, vol. 1, chap. 8, 65.

53 Robert Simpson's prize money would be roughly equivalent today to £3,000,000–4,500,000. See note 22.

54 Austen, *Persuasion*, vol. 1, chap. 8, 66–7.

55 The vessels concerned were all American: the ship *Sally*, the brig *Joseph*, the ship *Eliza*. Charles probably also lost the cases pertaining to the brig *Friends Adventure*, taken on 1 June 1806, and the ship *Baltic*, taken on 10 January 1807.

56 The *Indian*'s logbook, Master's log, 6 May 1806, ADM 52/3631, TNA.

57 Information from Clive Caplan, May 2012.

58 At latitude 30° north and longitude 55° west.

59 Charles Austen to Admiral Sir George Cranfield Berkeley, 23 October 1807, ADM 1/ 497, TNA.

60 Admiral Sir George Cranfield Berkeley to Hon. William Pole, Secretary to the Admiralty, 23 October 1807, ADM 1/497, TNA.

61 See Hallet, *Bermuda Index, 1784–1914*, vol. 2, L–Z, 1013.

62 See Hallet, *Early Bermuda Records*, 157.

63 For details about Fanny's ancestry, see Appendix 3.

64 According to Austen biographer George Tucker, "Mrs Austen herself attributed her cleverness to 'my own Sprack wit,' a brisk Old English country phrase denoting a lively perception of the characters and foibles of others." Tucker, *Jane Austen's Family*, 66.

65 Fanny Knight's pocketbook, 13 August 1807, quoted in Le Faye, *Chronology*, 341.

66 Fanny Knight's pocketbook, 15 September 1807, quoted in Le Faye, *Chronology*, 344.

67 Austen, *Letters*, no. 63, 27 December 1808, 167; no. 65, 17 January 1809, 173; no. 66, 24 January 1809, 176.

68 Bitters refers to a mixture commonly made of herbs and bark in alcohol that was taken to stimulate the appetite.

69 Frederick Hickey of HMS *Atalante*.

70 Esther Esten to Charles Austen, 26 July 1808, MA 4500, MLM. See Appendix 2.

71 See Selwyn, *Jane Austen and Children*, 2.

72 Charles Austen to Cassandra Austen, 25 December 1808, MA 7280, MLM.

73 Jane Austen described this incident as "a small prize [taken] in his late cruize [21 November 1808]; a French schooner laden with Sugar, but Bad weather parted them, & she had not yet been heard of." Austen, *Letters*, no. 66, 24 January 1809, 176.

74 Charles Austen to Cassandra Austen, 25 December 1808, MA 7280, MLM. See Appendix 2. This child grew up to be the "little Cassy" whom Jane Austen mentions many times in her letters. In 1813 alone: no. 84, 20 May, 219; no. 86, 3 July, 225; no. 89, 23 September, 234; no 92, 14–15 October, 248–50; no. 93, 21 October, 252; no. 94, 26 October, 254; no. 95, 3 November, 259; and no. 99, 9 March 1814, 273.

75 Austen, *Letters*, no. 65, 17 January 1809, 173.

76 John Claus de Passau was the rector of St Peter's Church, St George's, from December 1806 to February 1812.

77 Sometimes referred to as the Halifax and Bermuda Station.

78 Andrew Belcher to the Halifax Vice Admiralty Court, 31 August 1808, Vice Admiralty Court of Nova Scotia fonds, RG8 IV/52, 23448, LAC.

79 "My dearest Frank," in Austen, *Letters*, 26 July 1809, no. 69, 186. "Over-right us" means "directly opposite us."

CHAPTER TWO

1 Chebucto derives from the local Mi'kmaq word "Chebookt," meaning "chief harbour" or "great long harbour."

2 He was made Duke of Kent in 1799.

3 Captain James Cook described the harbour in the early 1760s as "without a doubt one of the best in America sufficiently large to hold all the Navy of England with safety." "Captain James Cook's Description of the Sea Coast of Nova Scotia, Cape Breton Island and Newfoundland," in *Report of the Trustees of the Public Archives*, 23.

4 Philip Broke to Louisa Broke, 3 October 1811, Sir James Saumarez Papers, HA 93/9/78, LAC.

5 A crimping house was "a low lodging house into which men were decoyed and plied with drink, to induce them to ship or enlist as soldiers or sailors." See *Webster's New International Dictionary*, revised ed. (Springfield, MA: G & C Merriam, 1913).

6 In October 1805 Sir Andrew Mitchell, commander-in-chief of the Station, "allowed press gangs from HMS *Cleopatra* to storm the streets of Halifax. Marines reportedly pushed all before them with bayonets. [Mitchell's] warrant [to press] had expired and with no authorization from [Governor] Wentworth, the Council or other civil authorities a major riot ensued in which one man was killed and several others injured. Mitchell paid heavy fines in civil court because a press gang broke open the store of Forsyth and Company looking for deserters." Mercer, "Sailors and Citizens," 103.

7 See Warren to Pole, 29 April 1809, ADMI/499, TNA.

8 The Admiralty's response to the petition is not known.

9 Edward Hawker captured the French Corvette *La Colibre* (16 guns) on 16 January 1809. James, Lord Townshend, captured the French schooner *La Caroline* on 2 March 1809. Both vessels were commissioned into the navy, as HMS *Colibri* and as HMS *Caroline*.

10 The petitioners included their friends Sir Robert Laurie of HMS *Milan*, John Shortland of HMS *Squirrel* and HMS *Junon*, and Gustavus Stupart of HMS *Emulous*.

11 At this time the Bermuda Naval Yard was in the very early stages of development and could only offer a fraction of the services available at the Halifax Yard.

12 Although the facility was formally known as a naval yard, it was often referred to as the "Dock Yard."

13 Sir John Wentworth was lieutenant-governor of Nova Scotia from 1792 to 1808.

14 Hallam, *When You Are in Halifax*, 66.

15 Quoted in Fingard, Guildford, and Sutherland, *Halifax: The First 250 Years*, 25.

16 Vincent, "The Inquisition: Alexander Croke's Satire on Halifax Society during the Wentworth Years": Canto 4th, ll. 57–8; ll. 61–2; ll. 65–6; ll. 69–72: 426–7.

17 Admiral Cochrane was commander-in-chief of the Leeward Islands squadron of the Royal Navy.

18 Marianne Belcher, Andrew's wife, was the aunt of Captain Frederick Marryat, who became famous for the naval novels *Peter Simple* (1834) and *Mr Midshipman Easy* (1836).

19 Samuel Hood George to Lady George, 18 October 1809, George Family Papers, MGI, vol. 2160, no. 244, NSARM.

20 When Charles had been in port on earlier visits, he may have attended a comedy, such as *The Wheel of Fortune* or *The Foundling of the Forest*; a farce, such as *Neck or Nothing*; or a tragedy, such as *Douglas*.

21 Quoted in Joan Paysant, *Halifax: Cornerstone of Canada*, 85.

22 See Charles Austen to Cassandra Austen, 25 December 1808, MA 7280, MLM. See Appendix 2.

23 Stanser's abbreviation for daughter.

24 Register of Baptisms of the Parish of St Paul, Halifax, Nova Scotia. Robert Stanser, Rector, St Paul's Church Archive, Halifax, Nova Scotia.

25 A court martial for twenty-three men had been held in Halifax Harbour. Apart from the six condemned to death (the boatswain, three seamen, and two marines), some were flogged as punishment, others were classified as convicts and deported.

26 Samuel Hood George to Sir Rupert George, 29 September 1809, George Family Papers, MG1, vol. 2160, NSARM. Georges Island was closer to the townsite of Halifax than McNab's Island.

27 The *Indian*'s log, 29 November 1809, ADM 51/1991, TNA.

28 It is not known why the *Indian* sent the signal. HMS *Thistle* (10 guns) did survive the voyage to Bermuda but was wrecked off Sandy Hook near New York on 6 March 1811.

29 The *Indian*'s log, 6 and 7 December 1809, ADM 51/1991, TNA.

30 Ibid., 10 December 1809, ADM 51/ 1991, TNA.

31 Frances Boscawen, née Evelyn-Glanville (1719–1805), was a letter writer and member of the British Blue Stockings Society, a gathering of intellectual women who met to discuss literature. As literary hostess she welcomed to her London home guests that included Elizabeth Montagu (founder of the society), Elizabeth Carter, Dr Johnson, James Boswell, Joshua Reynolds, Frances Reynolds, and later Hannah Moore. She was married to Admiral Edward Boscawen (1711–1761).

32 Aspinall-Oglander, *The Admiral's Wife*, 126.

33 First-rate vessels carried 100 or more guns; second rates 90 to 98 guns; third rates 64, 74, or 80 guns; fourth rates 50 or 60 guns; fifth rates were frigates carrying 30 to 40 guns; and sixth rates carried 20 to 30 guns. Sloops of war like the *Indian* were not rated. See Lavery, *Life in Nelson's Navy*, 1994, 40.

34 According to the *Bermuda Gazette*, Captain Conn "fell overboard, while the ship was in chase, going at a rate of 8 knots." However, as Clive Caplan notes, "this account was erroneous, for the log records that the ship was not in chase at the time and its speed was only 3 knots, as a sail having split." The cause of Conn's death was never made apparent. See Caplan, "The Ships of Charles Austen," 149.

35 See Admiralty pay ledger, ADM 24/5, 257.

36 Half pay was the portion of pay an officer received by statutory right. It could amount to as little as 10s. 6d. per day.

37 Charles Austen's journal, 10 May 1815, AUS/102, NMM.

38 *Naval Chronicle*, vol. 3 (1800): 358.

39 Vernon is quoted in N.A.M. Rodger, *The Wooden World*, 261. Admiral Edward Vernon (1684–1757) was himself highly accomplished in languages, mathematics, navigation, and gunnery.

40 The boy, George John Sedley, born in 1803, later became the 5th Lord Vernon.

41 Charles Austen to Cassandra Austen, 25 December 1808, MLM. See Appendix 2.

42 Anson, *The Life of Admiral Sir John Borlase Warren*, 21.

43 Sir John remarked that "this was the first time I have been fighting with a pen instead of a sword." Anson, *The Life of Admiral Sir John Borlase Warren*, 151.

44 Ibid., 145.

45 Ibid., 148.

46 Wilkinson, *Bermuda from Sail to Steam*, vol. 1, 293.

47 "Yards" are cross spars on the masts of a square-rigged ship from which its sails are set.

48 Rear-Admiral Herbert Sawyer to the Admiralty, 6 August 1811, ADM 1/50.

49 Masting sheers, a type of two-legged crane used to install or remove a ship's masts, were operational in the yard at the Sheer Wharf.

50 Samuel Hood George to Lady George, 24 May 1810, George Family Papers, MGI, vol. 2160, no. 302, NSARM.

CHAPTER THREE

1 Austen, *Letters*, no. 96, 6–7 November 1813, 263.

2 Austen, *Emma*, vol. 2, chap. 1, 157.

3 Fanny Austen to Esther Esten, 17 June 1810. See Appendix 1 for more details about the identification of Fanny's letters.

4 Fanny's daughter, Cassandra.

5 Mrs Sedley, later Lady Vernon, was born Frances Maria Warren. Subsequently, her inheritance included the estates of her distant relative, Elizabeth Harriet Warren, a ninth cousin twice removed. Frances's husband, George, eventually became the 4th Baron Vernon of Sunbury Hall.

6 Mrs Territt, née Anne Catherine Parkyns, married Judge William Territt of the Bermuda Vice Admiralty Court in 1810. She was a daughter of Admiral Warren's sister, Frances.

7 Lieut. William Bowen Mends of HMS *Vesta* (10 guns).

8 Lady Prevost, née Catherine Phipps, wife of Sir George Prevost, lieutenant-governor of Nova Scotia, 1808–1811.

9 Sir George Prevost, lieutenant-governor of Nova Scotia.

10 James Christie Esten, by now chief justice of Bermuda.

11 Austen, *Letters*, no. 57, 7 October 1808, 149.

12 Esther's young sons.

13 Captain George William Blamey of HMS *Harpy* (18 guns).

14 St George's Anglican Church, built in 1800, was near the Halifax Naval Yard. Its common name, used by Fanny, describes its unusual shape.

15 An exclusive men's dining club on the shore of Bedford Basin, which is an extension of Halifax Harbour.

16 Probably Mrs Edward Brabazon Brenton, née Catherine Taylor, whose husband was a Halifax lawyer and surrogate to the judge of the Vice Admiralty Court.

17 Arrowroot was a nutritious food used as a thickener in cooking and a good source of starch; the quality of Bermuda arrowroot was greatly esteemed.

18 Alexander Forbes Ball, brother to Fanny's mother.

19 Her later Halifax letters mention Richard (4 August), Jones (14 August), and Molly and Toddings (23 September).

20 Quoted in Ingalls and Ingalls, *Sweet Suburb*, 68.

21 Naftel, *Prince Edward's Legacy*, 67.

22 See also the useful comments in Susanne Notman, "Fanny Austen's Letters."

23 Haliburton, *A Colonial Portrait*, 121.

24 Charles Yorke to Admiral Sir John Warren, 20 July 1810, Yorke Papers, MS 9334, 39, NMM.

25 Tudor Hinson, a member of the Bermuda Council, was the father of Fanny's friend Mary Hinson.

26 Brig. Gen. John Hodgson, Governor of Bermuda, 1806–1810.

27 HMS *Emulous* was an 18-gun brig-sloop under the command of Captain Gustavus Stupart.

28 HMS *Penelope* (36 guns).

29 Major Mark Anthony Bozon was the brigade-major under General Hodgson, 25 June to 1 September 1810. He was paid £3 15s. 6d. for his services, as recorded in *Journals of the House of Commons*, Sess. 1814–15, vol. 70.

30 Dennis Victor Lagourque was the father of Fanny's friend Elizabeth (Betsy) Matilda Lagourque.

31 Straw plaits were used to make bonnets. While onshore in Bermuda naval captain Philip Broke acquired "pieces of plait straw for my Lou's bonnet, they tell me there is enough for three hats." Philip Broke to Louisa Broke, January 1812, Sir James Saumarez Papers, HA 93/9/85, LAC.

32 Fanny's nursery maid who came with them from Bermuda.

33 Wilkinson, *Bermuda from Sail to Steam*, vol. 1, 261. He refers to her as the "fascinating little" Mrs Hodgson.

34 During the Napoleonic Wars, "death from shipwreck or fire amounted to more than 13,000, twice as many as died in battle … [Additionally] 72,000 men (out of a fleet that never numbered more that 142,000) … died of disease or from small accidents such as a fall from the rigging." Lavery, *Life in Nelson's Navy*, 2007, 33.

35 Charles Austen's Journal, 28 April 1815, AUS/102, NMM.

36 Lieut. Henry Jane, who became commander of the *Indian*.

37 Here Fanny has crossed out the words "which account agrees exactly with."

38 The Azores.

39 Frank Austen, currently the captain of HMS *St Albans* (64 guns), was Charles's next older brother, who had been in active naval service since 1788. He was to have a long career in the navy, rising to the rank of Admiral of the Red in 1848.

40 Captain James Bradshaw of HMS *Eurydice* (24 guns). He was on the North American Station in 1809–1810.

41 Admiral Sir Richard Strachan, 4th Baronet (1760–1828), had served in the navy with considerable success until he was appointed naval commander of the Walcheren Campaign, an offensive to attack the island of Walcheren, at the mouth of the Scheldt estuary in Holland, and to destroy the French arsenals in the Scheldt. It lasted from July to December 1809. When this huge offensive, which involved 264 warships, 352 transports, and 44,000 troops, was abandoned, Strachan was blamed for the poor performance of the navy. Even though there must have been talk in naval circles that he might succeed Warren as commander-in-chief of the North American Station, he received no further commissions. When Strachan inherited his uncle's baronetcy in 1777, he too became a baronet of Nova Scotia (Strachan of Thornton, later of Inchtuhill), a Scottish title dating from 1625. Had he replaced Warren, he would probably have been the only holder of that title to live and work in Nova Scotia by that time. See "Sir Richard Strachan, *Oxford Dictionary of National Biography*, www.oxforddnb.com/view/article/26620.

42 Captain Edward Hawker of HMS *Melampus* (36 guns).

43 James, Lord Townshend of HMS *Aeolus* (32 guns).

44 The *Swiftsure*'s log, 11 July 1810, ADM 52/4627, TNA.

45 See Brian Southam, *Jane Austen and the Navy*, 103.

46 This is roughly equivalent to £150,000 to £225,000 in today's currency. See chap. 1, note 22.

47 See "Captain's Shortland's Dog," in Tracy, ed., *The Naval Chronicle*, vol. 5, 10.

48 Ibid., 10, 12.

49 James Orde, until recently commander of the 99th Regiment.

50 Dr William Territt, judge of the Bermuda Vice Admiralty Court from 1802 to 1815.

51 A spencer is a short jacket.

52 John Howe was the postmaster in Halifax in 1801–18. In 1803 and 1809 he undertook spying missions to the United States at the request of the Nova Scotia government. His son, Joseph (Joe), 1804–1873, became a prominent Nova Scotia journalist, politician, and public servant.

53 An ornamental frill for a dress front.

54 Esther Esten to Charles Austen, 26 July 1808. See Appendix 2.

55 *Royal Military Calendar*, 362.

56 Austen, *Letters*, no. 73, 29 May 1811, 196.

57 John Jervis, Earl St Vincent, served in the navy from 1747 to 1807, led the victory at Cape St Vincent in 1797, and became Admiral of the Fleet in 1799.

58 Quoted in Gwyn, *Ashore and Afloat*, St Vincent to Spencer, 68.

59 For the reference in Croke's poem to Inglefield and the *Centaur* disaster, see Vincent, "The Inquisition," 426, ll.51–4.

60 A light-weight yellow cloth.

61 Captain William Byam of HMS *Opossum* (10 guns).

62 Fanny's sister in London.

63 Jaconet.

64 Jane Austen described one of these arrangements: "Mr Fowle [begs] the Charts &c may be consigned to the care of the Palmers. – Mrs Fowle has also written to Miss Palmer to beg she will send for them." *Letters*, no. 59, 16 October 1808, 155.

65 See ADM 24/5, TNA.

66 In the *Cleopatra*'s case her tonnage was 689 bm. See Winfield, *British Warships*, xi.

67 Lavery, *Life in Nelson's Navy*, 2007, 17–18.

68 *Royal Nova Scotia Gazette*, 16 May 1805.

69 This was the one major battle during the invasion of Portugal in 1810. Of the Anglo-Portuguese army of 50,000 (half British, half Portuguese), there were 1,250 dead or wounded. The French force of 65,000 men suffered 4,500 dead or wounded. See www.peninsularwar.org/Bussaco.

70 Sandra Paikowsky, "Robert Field," *Dictionary of Canadian Bibliography*, www.biographi.ca/bio/field_robert_5E.

71 Some of Field's work has greatly increased in value. A miniature of George Washington sold for $303,000 in 2008. See O'Neill, Catalogue for "In the Artist's Footsteps," an exhibit at the Art Gallery of Nova Scotia, Halifax, March-October 2016.

72 See Piers, *Robert Field*, 99.

CHAPTER FOUR

1 The *Cleopatra*'s log, 19 December 1810, ADM 51/261, TNA.

2 See HCA 49/9, Stephen, TNA.

3 ADM 49/98, TNA.

4 The *Cleopatra*'s logbook, 10 December 1810, ADM 51/261, TNA.

5 See HUL/23, 33–4; 66–7, NMM.

6 Rodger, *Command of the Ocean*, 559.

7 See "Glimpses of Nova Scotia 1807–24," *Bulletin of the Public Archives of Nova Scotia*, no. 12: 46.

8 Lambert, *The Challenge*, 213.

9 Austen, *Letters*, no. 70, 20 April 1811, 188–9; no. 71, 25 April 1811, 191–2.

10 Horatio Nelson to Sir John Warren, from the *Victory*, 14 February 1804, quoted in Anson, *The Life of Admiral Sir John Borlase Warren*, 205.

11 *Gentleman's Magazine*, 1811, quoted in the endnotes to Austen, *Mansfield Park*, ed. Wiltshire, 726.

12 See Rodger, *Command of the Ocean*, 520–1.

13 No letters survive from their transatlantic correspondence in the years before Fanny arrived in England.

14 Austen, *Persuasion*, vol. 1, chap. 1, 7.

15 Fanny Austen to James Esten, 8 July 1814.

16 Some of the children born on Keppel Street became famous in later years. They included Augustus Pugin (1812), who made a career in Gothic church architecture, and Anthony Trollope (1814), the future novelist.

17 Pope-Hennessy, *Anthony Trollope*, 34.

18 Her fine flower paintings were widely admired and would be exhibited at the Royal Academy in 1814. See "Robert Abraham," *Oxford Dictionary of National Biography*, www.oxforddnb.com/view/article/54.

19 Batey, *Jane Austen and the English Landscape*, 20.

20 Ibid., 110.

21 Her mother, Philadelphia, was sister to Charles's father, Rev. George Austen.

22 Eliza was pleased that Henry Austen's brother officers of the Oxford Militia were "acquainted with my having been a <u>Comtesse</u> and politely give me precedence which Courtesy grants to that title in England." Le Faye, *Jane Austen's 'Outlandish Cousin,'* 154.

23 Eliza was writing to her cousin Philadelphia (Phylly), née Walter, in 1792. For the letter, see Le Faye, *Jane Austen's 'Outlandish Cousin,'* 116. Maggie Lane also observes that "as Jane grew up, the sisters-in-law [Jane and Eliza] seem to have become good friends." See Lane, "The Real Lady Susan," 48.

24 Cassandra Austen to Phylly Walter, now Mrs George Whitaker, Austen-Leigh, ed., *Austen Papers*, 249.

25 Southam, "Jane Austen and North America," 26.

26 Austen, *Persuasion*, vol. 1, chap. 8, 63.

27 Born in 1761, Phylly (Philadelphia) was the daughter of Rev. George Austen's half-brother William Hampson Walter. A serious, rather shy woman, Phylly gives the impression of a dutiful daughter who had long cared for her aging parents. By the summer of 1811, at the age of fifty, she had married George Whitaker and was living at Pembury, near Tonbridge, Kent.

28 Cassandra Austen to Mrs George Whitaker, quoted in *Austen Papers*, 249.

29 Admiralty files, ADM 24/8, Ledger 7, 260, TNA. On Charles's next vessel, the delay in receiving his final instalment of pay ranged from three months (1812) to five months (1813) and to two and a half months (1814).

30 Popular investments included government bonds, known as consols, which returned an estimated 4 to 5 per cent during the time Jane Austen was publishing her novels. Alternatively, there were bonds known as Navy 5% s. See Hume, "Money in Jane Austen," 301.

31 Fanny Knight's pocketbook, 1–4 October, quoted in Le Faye, *Chronology*, 412.

32 Anna was James Austen's daughter by his first marriage to Anne Mathew, who died in 1795 when Anna was two. She was very close to Jane and Cassandra and spent considerable time with them at Chawton Cottage. James Edward later took the surname Austen-Leigh, when he became heir to the estate of his childless great-aunt, Mrs Leigh Perrot. She was the former Jane Cholmeley, who had married James Leigh, brother of Mrs George Austen in 1764. James Leigh took the additional name Perrot so that he might inherit the estate of his great-uncle Thomas Perrot.

33 Le Faye, *Country Life*, 18.

34 Caroline Austen, *Reminiscences of Caroline Austen*, 26.

35 See Selwyn, ed., *Jane Austen: Collected Poems and Verse of the Austen Family*, 50.

36 These two volumes are now in the Houghton Library, Harvard University. For their description, see Gilson, *A Bibliography of Jane Austen*, 436.

37 See Le Faye, *Chronology*, 414.

38 An entry for Charles in O'Byrne's *Naval Bibliographical Dictionary*, 27, states that "from 20 November 1811 we find him in the *Namur*." He did not actually begin his commission until 16 December 1811.

39 She was the daughter of Mrs George Austen's older sister Jane, the wife of Reverend Dr Edward Cooper. Charles's other two first cousins were Edward, son of Reverend and Mrs Cooper, and Eliza Austen, née Hancock, Henry's wife.

40 Fanny Austen to Esther Esten, 8 March 1814.

41 Lavery, *Life in Nelson's Navy*, 1994, 231.

42 This was known as razeeing a vessel.

43 Information from Andrew Choong, May 2016, NMM.

44 See Winfield, *British Warships*, 15.

45 See "Command of the Oceans," The Historic Chatham Naval Yard, www.thedockyard.co.uk.

46 See Copeland, "Money," 323.

47 Austen, *Letters*, no. 49, 8 January 1807, 121.

48 Admiralty Pay ledger for the *Namur*, 1812, ADM 24/8, 260.

49 See chap. 1, note 22. At the time, "the top 5% of family incomes [amounted] to £250 per annum or more." Hume, "Money in Jane Austen," 298.

50 See ADM 6/203 for the record of his official leaves.

51 Slater, *Douglas Jerrold*, 14.

52 Keverne, *Tales of Old Inns*, 70.

53 See the insightful article by Kaplan, "Domesticity at Sea," 113.

54 Hickman, "The Jane Austen Family in Silhouette," xv.

55 Cassandra Austen to Mrs George Whitaker, quoted in *Austen Papers*, 251.

CHAPTER FIVE

1 Douglas Jerrold came aboard the *Namur* as a trainee officer in December 1812. His description of arriving at the *Namur* is quoted in Southam, *Jane Austen and the Navy*, 278.

2 Responding to a query about the dimensions of the captain's cabin on the *Namur* in 1812, Jeremy Mitchell, historic photographs and ship plans manager, NMM, replied: "Unfortunately, as there are no surviving deck

plans for *Namur* (1756), we cannot supply the dimensions of the [captain's] cabin in question. To complicate things a little more, she was an altered 1745 Establishment design and cut down (razeed), so the cabin arrangement is not really known."

3 A spencer was worn regularly by women and sometimes by children, as Fanny's letter of 14 August 1810 has reported. For an adult it was a "short jacket ending just below the bust." A pelisse was a "long sleeved coat cut on the same lines as [a] dress, trimmed or lined with furs … for extra warmth." Blank, "Dress," 240.

4 If the Navy Board was to pay for the job, no expensive colours could be used – no lilacs, pinks, bright greens, or dead whites. See Gwyn, *Ashore and Afloat*, 160.

5 See Gilson, "Cassandra Austen's pictures," 299–301.

6 Amanda Vickery presenter and author, "At Home with the Georgians," BBC 2, 2010, director Neil Crombie, B-F-S Entertainment and Multi Media, Ltd (Canada), 2010, DVD, running time 180 min.

7 Kaplan, "Domesticity at Sea," 113.

8 Lavery, *Life in Nelson's Navy*, 1994, 140.

9 The officers' quarters were in the stern of the ship directly below the captain's cabin. The wardroom was usually between the rows of officers' cabins on each side of the ship. See Lavery, *Nelson's Navy*, 1994, 109–10.

10 Admiralty pay ledger, *Namur*, ADM 24/8, 260, TNA.

11 Ibid.

12 Fanny Austen to James Esten, 30 June 1814.

13 "John Manning to his brother, 3 August," 1812, *Current Archeology*, no. 275 (February 2013): 4–5.

14 Clarkson Stanfield, alias Roderick Bland, to Mary Stanfield, 29 August 1813, Ms 79/159, NMM.

15 Clarkson Stanfield to his father, James Stanfield, 22 October 1816, quoted in van der Merwe and Took, *The Spectacular Career of Clarkson Stanfield*, 14. He was elected a member of the Royal Academy of Art in 1835.

16 *Namur*'s log, ADM 51/2619, vol. 7, TNA.

17 For Charles's abhorrence of flogging, see Southam, *Jane Austen and the Navy*, 290.

18 Charles Austen's journal, 25 December 1826, AUS/120, NMM.

19 Lavery, *Life in Nelson's Navy*, 1994, 217.

20 The *Namur's* log, 5 March, 1813, ADM 51/2619, TNA.

21 Quoted in Southam, *Jane Austen and the Navy*, 285.

22 Edward Hawker, *Statement Respecting the Prevalence of Certain Immoral Practices in His Majesty's Navy* (London: Ellerton and Henderson, 1821), 34–5, quoted in Stark, *Female Tars*, 43.

23 Byrne, *The Real Jane Austen*, 139.

24 Slater, *Douglas Jerrold*, 25.

25 Fanny Austen to Esther Esten, 5 March 1812.

26 Vickery, *The Gentleman's Daughter*, 11.

27 Ibid., 31.

28 Cassandra Austen to Mrs George Whitacker, Austen-Leigh, *Austen Papers*, 251–2.

29 Deal is a town on the east coast of Kent near Dover. The river referred to is the Thames. The "Downs" is an anchorage also on the east coast of Kent, situated between the North and South Forelands (roughly off shore from Ramsgate), and is protected by the shifting Goodwin Sands.

30 A family name for Esther.

31 Captain John Erskine Douglas of HMS *Bellona* (74 guns) was known to Fanny as he had served on the North American Station in 1806–8.

32 Polly is Esther's maid.

33 Fanny's maid.

34 A nearby seaside resort.

35 Possibly Charles Strangways R.N. (1789–1835), a member of the Dorset branch of the Strangways family and a very distant cousin.

36 John Grove Palmer, Fanny's father.

37 He became King George IV in 1820.

38 It was renamed the Royal Terrace after Princess Caroline's visit.

39 *Chelmsford Chronicle*, 21 July 1813.

40 Ibid., 1813.

41 Advertisement for the Royal Hotel, 1813.

42 Pollitt, *Southend, 1760–1860*, 26.

43 Burrows, *Southend-on-Sea*, 182. Its estimated cost was £500.

44 Pollitt, *Southend, 1760–1860*, 30. Jane Austen saw Kean play Shylock at the Drury Lane Theatre, London, on 4 March 1814. She declares: "I cannot imagine better acting." *Letters*, no. 98, 5 March 1814, 268.

45 Slater, *Douglas Jerrold, 1803–1857*, 22.

46 Unfortunately, the theatre did not thrive in the long run. By 1817 it still bore the label Theatre Royal but was described as looking like a "very small chapel or meeting house." See Pollitt, *Southend, 1760–1860*, 30.

47 See Byrne, *The Real Jane Austen*, 311–12.

48 See Payne, *Southend-on-Sea: A Pictorial History*, plate 26.

49 "A letter from Mrs. George Austen to Anna LeFroy, [5 July 1815]," *Jane Austen Society Report for 2003*, 228.

50 The Molly, mentioned by Jane Austen in her letter of 14 September 1804, was likely her dipper. See Byrne, *The Real Jane Austen*, 315; and Austen, *Letters*, no. 39, 14 September 1804, 99.

51 PoemHunter.com, http://www.poemhunter.com/poem/retirement-23.

52 Fanny Knight's pocketbook, 4 July 1812, quoted in Le Faye, *Chronology*, 426.

53 Austen, *Letters*, no. 77, 29 November 1812, 205.

54 It was agreed that Mrs Knight would receive an income of £2,000 a year from the property for life. See Le Faye, *Family Record*, 108.

55 There was a tradition in the Knight family of adopting an heir in the absence of a natural one and of having him take on the family name. Thus the name Knight was taken successively by the Martins and Brodnaxes when they come into the possession of the Chawton estate. Thomas Brodnax of Godmersham changed his name to May (1727) to inherit family property and then to Knight (1738) when he acquired the Chawton property. It was his son, Thomas Knight II, who adopted Edward Austen.

56 Hussey, "Godmersham Park, Kent: II," 333.

57 Ibid., 332.

58 Fanny Knight's pocketbook, 11 October 1804, quoted in Le Faye, *Chronology*, 303.

59 Austen, *Letters*, no. 55, 1 July 1808, 144.

60 See Selwyn, ed., *Jane Austen: Collected Poems*, 56. The dates of the poem and of George Knight's parody of it are unknown.

61 Ibid. "'Pincher' was a popular name to call a hunting dog, from its diligence in 'pinching' or harrying the quarry." See Selwyn, *Jane Austen: Collected Poems*, 102.

62 See Hillan, *May, Lou & Cass*, 39.

63 Austen, *Letters*, no. 48(C), ?24 July 1806, 118.

64 Fanny Knight's pocketbook, quoted in Le Faye, *Chronology*, 427.

65 Le Faye, *Jane Austen's Country Life*, 237–8.

66 Ibid., 238.

67 Batey, *Jane Austen and the English Landscape*, 102.

68 See Lavery, *Life in Nelson's Navy*, 1994, 264.

69 See Captains Letters, Charles Austen to the Admiralty, 5 September 1812, ADM 1/1453, no. 22, TNA.

70 See Sir Thomas Williams to the Admiralty, September 1812, ADM 1/748, 7, no. 1272, TNA.

71 See the *Bermuda Gazette*, 31 October 1812.

72 Vickery, *The Gentleman's Daughter*, 104.

CHAPTER SIX

1 See Lambert, *The Challenge*, chap. 3," Looking for a Way Out," 83–116.

2 Austen, *Letters*, no. 78, 24 January 1813, 209.

3 Ibid., no. 79, 29 January 1813, 210.

4 Le Faye, *A Family Record*, 196.

5 Wilkinson, *Bermuda from Sail to Steam*, vol. 1, 282.

6 Born 18 June 1805, Caroline was three and a half years older than Cassy.

7 Caroline Austen, *My Aunt Jane Austen*, 6.

8 Cassandra Austen's memorandum about the periods when Jane Austen was working on each novel suggests that *Mansfield Park* was "finished soon after June 1813." Quoted in Le Faye, *Family Record*, 197.

9 A surviving copy is inscribed with the names of both Frank and Jane Austen. For its description, see Gilson, *A Bibliography of Jane Austen*, 442.

10 Caroline Austen, *Reminiscences of Caroline Austen*, 25.

11 See Doody, Introduction, in *Catherine and Other Writings*, xix. Doody traces this observation to Deirdre Le Faye's *Family Record* (1989), 164.

12 See Doody, Introduction, in *Catherine and Other Writings*, xix, xx.

13 Cassandra Austen, who inherited Jane's manuscript notebooks, bequeathed *Volume the First* to Charles, presumably because it contained the stories originally written for him. See Le Faye, *Family Record*, 271.

14 Caroline Austen, *My Aunt Jane Austen*, 10.

15 Born 27 April 1807, Mary Jane was about one and a half years older than Cassy.

16 The misspelling is Caroline's.

17 Caroline Austen, *My Aunt Jane Austen*, 10.

18 Austen, *Letters*, no. 60, 24 October 1808, 156.

19 Fanny Austen to James Esten, 4 October 1813.

20 The *Namur's* log, 22 February 1813, ADM 51/2618, TNA.

21 Jane Austen identifies these flowers and fruits as growing in the Chawton Cottage garden in May. See Austen, *Letters*, no. 73, 29 May 1811, 196.

22 See Willoughby, *Chawton*, 9–10.

23 The Lewknor tapestry, woven in wool and silk and of Flemish creation, measures sixteen feet three inches by seven feet two inches. It had hung at Chawton Great House from the time Thomas Brodnax Knight inherited it in 1737 from the Martin family, who in turn had inherited it from the Lewknor family. The tapestry was sold by the Knight family to the museum in 1958. See The Met, "The Lewknor Armorial Table Carpet," www.metmuseum.org/art/collection/search/228752.

24 Fanny Knight, letter to Miss Chapman, her former governess, 26 August 1807, quoted in Le Faye, *Fanny Knight's Diary*, 12.

25 Selwyn, *Jane Austen: Collected Poems and Verses of the Austen Family*, 55.

26 Jane reported playing "jeu de violon" three years later at her brother Frank's home in Alton. See Austen, *Letters*, no. 144, 4 September 1816, 333.

27 See Fanny Knight's pocketbook, quoted in Le Faye, *Chronology*, 445.

28 Austen, *Letters*, no. 86, 3 July 1813, 225.

29 Selwyn, *Jane Austen and Children*, 101.

30 Austen, *Letters*, no. 92, 15 October 1813, 248.

31 Ibid., no. 149, 23 January 1817, 340.

32 Ibid., no. 86, 6 July 1813, 225.

33 Ibid., no. 114, 30 November 1814, 299.

34 Ibid., no. 97, 2 March 1814, 267.

35 Ibid., no. 99, 9 March 1814, 273.

36 The letter now belongs to the Morgan Library and Museum.

37 Austen, *Letters*, no. 148, 8 January 1817, 338–9.

38 Ibid., no. 92, 15 October 1813, 250.

39 Austen, *Mansfield Park*, vol. 3, chap. 9, 398.

40 The existence of only two letters in 1813 may be explained by the fact that Fanny did not write so much to her family members in England, as they

were closer at hand and more readily available to speak to in person, compared to her brother-in-law James Esten, to whom she composed a very long letter in October. By comparison, the other existing letter to Harriet at Keppel Street was of a practical nature, dealing with arrangements for Fanny's children and household. Alternatively, there may have been additional letters that have not survived.

41 Betsy, her maid.

42 Sir Thomas Williams.

43 Here crossing begins in red ink over the first three pages of the letter.

44 Probably a reference to both Esther and Fanny.

45 Fanny's friend Betsy Holliday, née Lagourque, wife of the Reverend Evan Holliday.

46 Once again Fanny mentions Bermuda servants in her letters.

47 Winfield, *British Warships in the Age of Sail*, 1263.

48 As Deborah Kaplan observes, "Fanny was unlikely to have [expressed her discontent] to her husband, for well-bred women, schooled in domestic ideology, hid their dissatisfaction and anger from their male kin." Kaplan, "Domesticity at Sea," 119.

49 Fanny apparently liked Admiral Sawyer, and she may have reminded him of another young attractive woman whose presence had also contributed to the happiness of the social life of the North American Station. That was his late sister Sophia Elizabeth, "a very handsome woman of eighteen years," who had died suddenly in Halifax, 31 January 1788, after an operation to remove a swelling in her arm; at the time, his father, another Herbert Sawyer (1730–1798), was commodore on the station. Sophia had recently danced at a ball with Lieutenant Dyott of the 4th Regiment; days later, Halifax, both military and civilian, mourned her passing. See Harris, *The Church of St Paul in Halifax*, 294.

50 Broke later remembered Charles as "such a good temper'd sociable little fellow in our *evening tea party* at the Academy – that I always recollect you with pleasure." Philip Broke to Charles Austen, 11 December 1824, MA 4500, MLM.

51 In this epic and important sea battle, Broke was severely wounded but survived. Since his first lieutenant was killed, his second lieutenant, Provo Wallis, brought the prize back to Halifax to a tumultuous reception.

52 See Robert Hume's method of calculating equivalences, chap. 1, note 22.

53 Wilkinson, *Bermuda from Sail to Steam*, vol. 1, 342. According to Kert, there had been 334 adjudications before the Halifax court alone from 1812 to 1813. See Kert, *Prize and Prejudice*, 131.

54 Philip Broke to Louisa Broke, 3 October 1811, Sir James Saumarez Papers, HA 93/9/78, LAC.

55 Lambert, *The Challenge*, 84.

56 Admiral Warren anticipated that Lady Warren would eventually be arriving in North America. In early January 1813, he wrote privately to Sir John Sherbrooke, lieutenant-governor of Nova Scotia, at Halifax mentioning that he did "not expect Lady Warren to join him till the Spring." Haliburton, ed., *A Colonial Portrait*, 86.

57 See Placement of Vessels on the North American Station December 1813, ADM 8/100.

58 Austen, *Letters*, no. 92, 14 October 1813, 248.

59 Ibid., no. 92, 15 October 1813, 249–50.

60 Ibid., no. 81, 9 February 1813, 215.

61 Ibid., no. 92, 15 October 1813, 249.

62 Austen, *Northanger Abbey*, vol. 1, chap. 12, 91.

63 Austen, *Mansfield Park*, vol. 2, chap. 5, 222.

64 Le Faye, *Chronology*, 464. Fanny visited "Kennington, Mrs. Sherers, Spring Grove & the two Scudamores."

65 Lizzy Knight to Cassandra Austen, 18 October 1813, quoted in Austen, *Letters*, no. 93, 18 October 1813, 252.

66 Austen, *Letters*, no. 91, 12 October 1813, 245. Old Michaelmas Day was traditionally celebrated on 11 October.

67 Caroline Austen, *My Aunt Jane Austen*, 7.

68 The fashionable pursuit of netting involved knotting and crocheting.

69 Austen, *Letters*, no. 88, 16 September, 1813, 231.

70 Le Faye, *Chronology*, 464.

71 Austen, *Letters*, no. 92, 15 October 1813, 248, 250, 251, 250; no. 94, 26 October 1813, 254.

72 Ibid., no. 54, 26 June 1808, 140. In Jane's view, Mary sometimes created tension within the family. For example, she persisted in telling Mrs Austen, who was recovering from an illness, about the impolite behaviour of her

granddaughter Anna's fiancé, Ben Lefroy. This caused Jane to exclaim: "How can Mrs. J. Austen be so provokingly ill-judging? … Now my Mother will be unwell again … every dinner-invitation he refuses will give her an Indigestion." Austen, *Letters*, no. 89, 23 September 1813, 234.

73   Ibid., no. 90, 25 September 1813, 241.

74   Quoted in Le Faye, *Family Record*, 201.

75   Austen, *Letters*, no. 38, 27 May 1801, 95. "We shall be unbearably fine," wrote Jane.

76   See Austen, *Mansfield Park*, vol. 3, chap. 7, 380.

77   Austen, *Letters*, no. 92, 15 October 1813, 251.

78   Notably, Charles's interest in Young Kendall may have had an echo in *Persuasion*, where Captain Wentworth concerns himself with improving Dick Musgrove's conduct, although in the novel Musgrove is seen as very recalcitrant, whereas there is no reason to think Young Kendall was similarly behaved.

79   A. Walton dates the composition of *Emma* from January 1814 to March 1815. See Litz, "Chronology of Composition," 48.

80   Austen, *Emma*, vol. 1, chap. 12, 101.

81   Austen, *Letters*, no. 92, 15 October 1813, 249.

82   The misspelling is Jane's.

83   Austen, *Letters*, no. 92, 15 October 1813, 250–1.

84   Ibid., no. 93, 21 October 1813, 253.

85   Ibid., no. 94, 26 October 1813, 254–5.

86   Ibid., no. 93, 21 October 1813, 253.

87   Other authors have interpreted Jane's remark differently. For example, in *Becoming Jane*, Jon Spence describes Charles as "over-attached to his wife and children" and says he exercises "a hovering concern for his wife and children." See 119–200. Spence's opinion does not reflect an appreciation of Charles's and Fanny's dual roles as parents. The Hubbacks in *Jane Austen's Sailor Brothers* understand Jane's reference to her "good deed" not as a condemnation of Charles's behaviour but, in their view, "a hint" that "his domesticity [is] somewhat overdone." See Hubbacks, 254.

88   Austen, *Letters*, no. 92, 15 October 1815, 249.

89   Either an apothecary in Sheerness or the *Namur*'s surgeon, who would have trained as an apothecary during his period of study.

90 Mr Joseph Fearon was the *Namur's* chaplain.

91 The reference is to a small square-shaped cake made from flour, butter, milk, eggs, yeast, and rather less sugar than a tea cake. "These are cut in half – hence the name tops and bottoms – and baked and dried." Pavy, *A Treatise on Food and Dietetics Physiologically and Therapeutically Considered*, 241.

92 Jane wrote Cassandra in early November: "I am glad to hear our being likely to have a peep at Charles & Fanny at Christmas." See Austen, *Letters*, no. 95, 3 November 1813, 259.

CHAPTER SEVEN

1   Previous Frost Fairs were held in 1683–84, 1716, 1739–40, and 1789.

2   See Tom de Castella, "Frost fair: When an elephant walked on the frozen river Thames," online BBC News: www.bbc.co.uk/news/magazine-25862141 and Mark Duell, "Thrills of the frost fair: Fascinating paintings and memorabilia show how Londoners celebrated when the River Thames froze over," online MailOnline: dailymail.co.uk/news/article-2524252.

3   Charles Austen to the Admiralty, 20 January 1814, ADM 1/1455, no. 26, TNA.

4   Charles corresponded with Broke in later years and received a reply saying he would be happy to see Charles at Broke Hall. See Philip Broke to Charles Austen, 11 December 1824, MA 4500, MLM.

5   A fine, soft silk material.

6   Austen, *Letters*, no. 98, 6 March 1814, 269.

7   There were 20 shillings (s.) in a pound (£) and 12 pence (d.) in a shilling. Sometimes goods were priced in guineas. A guinea was worth £1 1s.

8   As coach travel ordinarily cost 3d per mile, Fanny must have travelled 22 miles. For fares per mile, see Hume, 304.

9   See Hume, "Money in Jane Austen," 291.

10 The rectified totals should be £9 13s. 8½d. (January) and £4 3s. 11½d. (first part of February). Deirdre Le Faye first noted these corrections.

11 See "Knitted and Netted Purses," online CandiceHern.com: http://candicehern.com/regencyworld/knitted-and-netted-purses.

12 He thinks all young ladies are accomplished, for "they all paint tables, cover skreens and net purses." See Austen, *Pride and Prejudice*, vol. 1, chap. 8, 39.

13 Fanny Austen to Esther Esten, 10 June 1810.

14　Fanny Austen to James Esten, 4 October 1813.

15　In Fanny's words, Cassy "composed a very nice little letter to her Papa the other day (in answer to one he wrote her) which her Aunt Cassandra committed to paper." Fanny Austen to Esther Esten, 8 March 1814.

16　These would be *A Description of a Set of Prints of Ancient History: Contained in a Set of Easy Lessons. In Two Parts* (1786); *A Description of a Set of Prints of Roman History: Contained in a Set of Easy Lessons* (1789); and *A Description of a Set of Prints of English History: Contained in a Set of Easy Lessons* (1792).

17　Trimmer, *A Geographical Companion to Mrs. Trimmer's Scripture*, xiii.

18　This was the text chosen to match a location on Geographical Companion Map Number 60.

19　Southam, *Jane Austen and the Navy*, 34.

20　The book in question was likely *A New Grammar of the French Language*, 1790.

21　Charles Austen's pocketbook, 3 January 1817, AUS/109, quoted in Le Faye, *Chronology*, 552.

22　Vickery, *The Gentleman's Daughter*, 8.

23　Ibid.

24　Cassandra Austen.

25　Mrs Lobb was the wife of Captain Lobb, commissioner of the Dock Yard, Sheerness.

26　Probably Captain James Wallace, who served in the navy from 1794 to 1815. See O'Byrne, *Naval Bibliographical Dictionary*, 1242.

27　This is Fanny's first reference to her brother John in her letters.

28　The letter is crossed from this point on.

29　Harriet was born on 19 February 1810.

30　She closes her letter with the word "adieu" by which she simply means "goodbye."

31　The current Lady Yorke had interesting connections to the nobility. Had she been present she would have added flair to the party. Her father, George Paulet, 12th Marquis of Winchester, had been a courtier who served both Frederick, Prince of Wales and later Augusta, the Dowager Princess of Wales as Extra Gentleman Usher Daily Waiter. Her first husband, Henry de Burgh (1743–1797), 12th Earl and later Marquis of Clanricarde, was an Irish MP and member of the Privy Council of Ireland. In 1814 she was the mother of a seven-year-old son, Peter, whose father was her second husband, Col. Peter

Kington. On all the available evidence, the former Lady de Burgh had little in common with one of Jane Austen's most famous minor characters, Lady Catherine de Bourgh in *Pride and Prejudice*.

32 Clarkson Stanfield of the *Namur* had decorated Sir Thomas's ballroom in late spring 1814.

33 See Jensen, ed., *The Medical World*, 219.

34 Fanny's pocket diary for 1814 records that "Miss Palmer [Harriet] has settled for the Ham and Butter."

35 HMS *Dolphin* (44 guns).

36 Plumpness.

37 HMS *Diadem* (64 guns).

38 Elizabeth (Betsy) Holliday, née Lagourque. See *Bermuda Index*, vol. 1, 401. Evan Holliday was the rector of St Peter's Church, St George's, from August 1813 to June 1814.

39 Eliza Tudor Pigot married Edward Moore in St George's, 12 September 1812. He was the town major of the garrison. See Hallet, *Early Bermuda Records*, 402.

40 Mary Hinson, a daughter of Tudor Hinson, married Henry Folger, 5 October 1822. His first wife, Catherine, had died in March of the same year. See Hallet, *Bermuda Index*, vol. 1, 416.

41 Probably Jane Hinson married Joseph Stewart Hunter of the 98th Battalion, 14 November 1813. See Hallet, *Early Bermuda Records*, vol. 1, 401.

42 Louisa Goodrich married Ensign Eneas McGoldrick, 62nd Regiment, 22 July 1816. See Hallet, *Bermuda Index*, vol. 1, 502.

43 John Palmer's second wife, Mary.

44 The last full page of the letter in crossed in red ink from this point on.

45 HMS *Tonnant* (80 guns). By sending her letter on a naval vessel Fanny would not have had to pay postage.

46 Georgiana and Kate are most likely servants Fanny knew in Bermuda.

47 Fanny has signed her name with a fine flourish, including a nice curl on the final "n" in Austen. This contrasts with the stylized unadorned "Austen" in her letters to Harriet. Her seal with the name "Fanny" is clearly imprinted in the red wax.

48 Probably Hon. N.T. Butterfield (1788–1868), member of H.M. Bermuda Council, judge of the Court of General Assizes, and merchant. See *Bermuda Index*, vol. 1, 173.

49 In adult life Frances Mary Territt was considered a great beauty. As Viscountess Forbes she served as a lady of the bedchamber to Queen Victoria.

50 John Palmer's will of 12 December 1796, probated 4 May 1801, PROB11/1358, 1, TNA.

51 See Hallet, *Early Bermuda Records*, 401.

52 Austen, *Letters*, no. 145, 8 September 1816, 334.

53 Uden and Cooper, *A Dictionary of British Ships and Seamen*, 287.

54 Muster Book for the *Namur*, ADM 37/4056, TNA.

55 Lavery, *Life in Nelson's Navy*, 1994, 88.

56 *Life in Nelson's Navy*, 2007, 3.

57 Slater, *Douglas Jerrold*, 25.

58 Ibid.

59 Among other roles, he played a Norman page boy in his father's production of *Adelgitha* in September 1810 at Southend.

60 Edward Augustus Kendall (1776–1842) was known for his book *Keeper's Travels in Search of His Master* (1798) and other children's books with a moral message, such as *The Canary Bird: A Moral Fiction, Interspersed with Poetry* (1797). Instead of treating animals in a fantastical or allegorical way, Kendall portrayed them naturally and empathetically. They became characters with voices in his stories. See Wikipedia, https://en.wikipedia.org/wiki/Edward_Augustus_Kendall.

61 Austen, *Letters*, no. 92, 15 October 1813, 251.

62 Assuming Young Kendall was the son of Edward Augustus Kendall, this relationship might explain why Jane Austen, who probably knew of the father as a writer, was taking an interest in the progress of the son as he began naval training aboard the *Namur*.

63 Charles Austen's journal, AUS/118, 17 August 1826, NMM.

64 Tracy, *Britannia's Palette*, 333.

65 See van der Merwe and Took, *The Spectacular Career of Clarkson Stanfield 1793–1867*, 180–1.

66 Tracy, *Britannia's Palette*, 331.

67 See "Clarkson Frederick Stanfield," online Wikipedia, https://en.wikipedia.org/wiki/Clarkson_Frederick_Stanfield.

68 Some detainees preferred personal projects to occupy their time. Lieutenant Tuckey, of HMS *Calcutta*, while living in Verdun from 1805 to 1814, wrote

a "bulky three-volume work on maritime geography, which he published in England on the restoration of peace. A Captain Molyneux exercised his inventive faculties in constructing a carriage 'propelled by sails, which could run at seven or eight miles an hour.'" Unfortunately, it frightened horses on the road and upset a cart, after which "the peasants took to stoning the inventor when they met him out on his runs." The governor of Verdun ordered his experiment stopped. This did not prevent Molyneux from inventing an iceboat with sails in which he happily took spins on the frozen Meuse River in the winter. See Fraser, *Napoleon the Gaoler*, 45.

69 Ibid.

70 As she refers to him in her letter to Harriet, 5 February 1814, and to Esther, 8 March 1814.

71 At the time of writing this letter, she would not have known that 1,100 detainees at Verdun were being released and left to make a long and arduous journey back to England by whatever means they could arrange.

72 Jane Austen later observed in a letter to Charles that "it is impossible to be surprised at Miss Palmer's being ill." *Letters*, no. 157, 6 April 1817, 354.

73 All three pages of this letter are crossed in red ink; so too is the flap adjacent to the address panel.

74 Probably a reference to Esther.

75 Hon. Robert Kennedy, colonial secretary of Bermuda, 1808–1859.

76 Probably Sophia Byng (1788–1855), wife of George John Byng.

77 Mary, formerly Molly, was Cassy's nurse maid in Bermuda and in Halifax in 1810.

78 Anne Richardson, a teacher of young children, died in St George's 19 October 1821 aged sixty. See Hallet, *Early Bermuda Records*, 414.

79 Fanny's brother, John Palmer.

80 Hon. Daniel Leonard, former chief justice of Bermuda, 1782–1806, who died in London in 1829, aged 89, when he accidentally killed himself while cleaning a gun. At the time, he lived on Judd Street, close to Keppel Street.

81 Robert Richardson, a St George's merchant who promoted the production and marketing of Bermuda arrowroot. "In 1809 [arrowroot] was packaged and offered [in London] with a handsome little steel engraving to show its tropical origins and Richardson's insistence on genuineness." See Wilkinson, *Bermuda from Sail to Steam*, vol. 1, 28.

82 Betsy Holliday, née Lagourque.

83 Bernhard, *Slaves and Slaveholders in Bermuda*, 275.

84 Austen, *Letters*, no. 101, 14 June 1814, 275.

CHAPTER EIGHT

1   Nokes, *Jane Austen: A Life*, 450.

2   Austen, *Letters*, no. 106, 2 September 1814, 286.

3   Quoted in Le Faye, *Chronology*, 488.

4   The Kentish Town Chapel was designed by well-known architect James Wyatt and built in 1784. It was succeeded by another structure on the same site, the Church of St John the Baptist, Kentish Town. Decommissioned as an Anglican church in 1993, the building is now Christ Apostolic Church.

5   Lane, *Growing Older with Jane Austen*, 215.

6   Charles remained in contact with Reverend Fearon, writing him on 14 January 1817 with the enclosure of a pound note. See Charles Austen's pocketbook, AUS/109, NMM.

7   Notebook recording burials at Kentish Town Chapel, P90/PANI/180 (m/f x.30156), 167, no. 1335.

8   The palm is also a symbol of the resurrection.

9   Passerby is the original meaning of "passenger."

10 Quoted in Le Faye, *Chronology*, 489.

11 See Austen, *Letters*, no. 107, 18 September 1814, 288.

12 Ibid., no. 79, 29 January 1813, 210.

13 Ibid., no. 71, 25 April 1811, 190.

14 Charles Austen's journal, 29 April 1815, AUS/ 102, NMM.

15 Ibid., 23 June 1815, AUS/103, NMM.

16 Ibid., 29 May, 1815, AUS/103, NMM. Quoted in Le Faye, *Chronology*, 508.

17 For information about the Irish branch of the Palmer family, see Appendix 3.

18 Austen, *Later Manuscripts*, 239.

19 Austen, *Letters*, no. 114, 30 November 1814, 299.

20 Mrs Siddons (1755–1831), who starred on the London stage from 1774 to 1812, was famous for her interpretation of Shakespeare's Lady Macbeth. A woman of great sensitivities, she is said to have fainted at the sight of the Elgin Marbles. To her great regret, Jane just missed seeing her play the role of Constance in *King John* at Covent Garden in April 1811. See Austen,

Letters, no. 71, 25 April 1811, 192. Eliza O'Neal (1791–1872), whose highly successful career on the London stage spanned the five years just after Mrs Siddons's retirement, was known for her ability to engage the audience with her tears and her displays of tenderness and passion.

21 Austen, *Letters*, no. 127, 24 November 1815, 312; and no. 128, 28 November 1815, 313.

22 Charles Austen's pocketbook, 18 May 1817, AUS/101. Edward Hawker married Mary Joanna, née Poore, in 1817. She bore him nine children before her death in 1833, aged thirty-three. For meetings between Charles and Edward, see entries on 6 and 13 January and 30 April 1815, AUS/101, NMM.

23 Charles Austen's journal, 24 May 1815, AUS/102, NMM.

24 Ibid., 16 April 1815, AUS/102, NMM; 19 February 1816, AUS/105, NMM.

25 Ibid., 29 May 1815, AUS/103, NMM.

26 Ibid., 25 April 1815, AUS/102, NMM.

27 Ibid., 31 August 1815, AUS/104, NMM.

28 Ibid., 6 September 1815, AUS/104, NMM.

29 Ibid., 6 September 1819, AUS/110, NMM.

30 Charles Austen's pocketbook, 3 December 1815, AUS/101, NMM.

31 Charles Austen's journal, 3 December 1817, AUS/109; also "my dear … Fanny's birthday," 3 December 1827, AUS/125, NMM.

32 Charles Austen's journal, 3 December 1826: "the anniversary of the birthday of my dearest departed Fanny," AUS/120, NMM.

33 Ibid., 19 May 1827, AUS/122, NMM. The date was actually 18 May. Charles got it right in a journal entry the year before.

34 Ibid., 29 June 1826, AUS/118, NMM.

35 Chisme is now known as Çeşme.

36 Charles Austen's pocketbook, 11 February 1817, AUS/109. Quoted in Le Faye, *Chronology*, 556.

37 See Corley, "Jane Austen and Her Brother Henry's Bank Failure 1815–1816," 147. Charles's loss would be roughly equivalent to between £53,600 and £80,400. See chap. 1, note 17.

38 See Lane, *Growing Older with Jane Austen*, 186.

39 Austen, *Letters*, no. 145, 8 September 1816, 334.

40 Ibid., no. 157, 6 April 1817, 354.

41 Le Faye, *Chronology*, 564.

42 Charles Austen's journal, 20 and 23 February 1820, AUS/ III, NMM.

43 Quoted in Le Faye, *Family Record*, 264.

44 Mrs George Austen to Anna Leroy, 30 August 1820, quoted in Le Faye, *Family Record*, 264.

45 See Appendix 3 for information about the Palmer family's links to the aristocratic Strangways family.

46 L. Strangways to John Grove Palmer, August 1820, MA 4500, MLM.

47 Quoted in Le Faye, *Family Record*, 264.

48 Le Faye, *Family Record*, 264.

49 See Caplan, "Ships of Charles Austen," 154–6.

50 Caplan, "A Bogus Tale: Ellman, Charles Austen and HMS Aurora," 13.

51 Charles's personal conduct in the West Indies has been questioned in an article in *Modern Philology*, vol. 112, no. 3 (February 2015), 554–68, "Jane Austen's Afterlife, West Indian Madams, and the Literary Porter Family," by Ruth Knezevich and Devoney Looser. The authors speculate about the relationship Charles might have had in early 1828 with two mixed-race freewomen who kept hotels (brothels) in Georgetown, Barbados. The evidence adduced is suggestive but not proof of a significant issue about Charles's life while he was on shore in Georgetown.

52 Charles Austen to Sir Robert Liston, 4 July 1816. Quoted in Le Faye, *Chronology*, 631.

53 See chap. 1, 27.

54 Charles Austen to Mary Austen, 5 May 1822, quoted in Austen-Leigh, ed., *Austen Papers*, 272.

55 Charles Austen's pocketbook, 18 May 1825, quoted in Le Faye, *Chronology*, 628.

56 Le Faye, *Chronology*, 628.

57 See Hallet, *Early Bermuda Records*, 407.

58 Under the Slave Abolition Act of 1833, the British government agreed to pay £20,000,000 to slave owners. Surprisingly, Palmer Esten applied and was awarded £47 1s.1d. in compensation for three enslaved individuals. See Bermuda claim 1041, dated 29 February 1836. Why he had retained ownership of three slaves is not known. Perhaps he had inherited them through his Bermuda family, or perhaps there was still family property in

Bermuda for which he had some responsibility. Neither of his parents nor his brother Hamilton made claims for compensation. For details about the Slave Compensation Commission, see "Legacies of British Slave-Ownership, a project at University College, London," url: www.ucl.ac.uk/lbs.

59 James Esten had continued to support projects of the Wesleyan Methodists directed towards the literacy of slaves. He made possible the release of the land in Bermuda where slaves built their own church, Cobb Hill Methodist, in 1825. In 1837 he published a pamphlet titled *A Plan for the Instruction etc. of the Emancipated People of Colour.*

60 See Hallet, *Bermuda Index*, vol. 2, 1013.

61 Hopkinson, "Frivolities and Affections," 92.

62 This sketch can be seen at the National Portrait Gallery, London, England. See http://www.npg.org.uk/collections/search/portrait/mw00230/Jane-Auste n?LinkID=mp00179&search=sas&sText=Jane+Austen&role=sit&rNo=1.

63 Harman, *Jane's Fame*, 115. This watercolour was sold at Sotheby's in December 2013 for £164,500. The catalogue note includes the mistaken claim that Cassy had never known Jane Austen herself. See www.sothebys. com>lot.283.html.

64 Harman, *Jane's Fame*, 116.

65 Austen, *Letters*, no. 92, 15 October 1813, 250.

66 See Southam, *Jane Austen and the Navy*, xv.

67 Quoted in Le Faye, *Family Record*, 265.

68 Edward Bridges Rice and George William Rice were sons of Charles's niece Elizabeth Rice (Edward Knight's daughter). George Thomas Maitland Purvis junior was the eldest son of his niece Mary Jane Purvis (Frank Austen's oldest daughter).

69 Caplan, "The Ships of Charles Austen," 156–7.

70 Charles Austen's journal, 1851, AUS/161, AUS/162, NMM.

71 For details of his campaign, see Caplan, "The Ships of Charles Austen," 156–7.

72 Quoted in Tucker, *A History of Jane Austen's Family*, 190.

73 Ibid. Tucker is quoting from Charles's logbook entry, 6 October 1852.

74 See Hammond, "The Naval Connection," 178.

75 Charles Austen's pocketbook, 3 December 1815, AUS/101, NMM.

CHAPTER NINE

1　See the brief comments in Kindred, "The Influences of Naval Captain Charles Austen's North American Experiences on *Persuasion* and *Mansfield Park*," 119–21.

2　Austen-Leigh, *A Memoir of Jane Austen*, 18.

3　Southam, "Jane Austen's Sailor Brothers," 34. On a similar theme, Southam has speculated that "Charles's return to England [in 1811,] and the interest of his account [about service on the North American station], may well have suggested to Jane the idea of introducing naval characters to her current work *Mansfield Park*." Southam, "Jane Austen and North America," 26.

4　Southam, "Jane Austen and North America," 27.

5　Southam, *Jane Austen and the Navy*, 292.

6　Ibid., 70.

7　Austen, *Persuasion*, vol. 1, chap. 8, 69. Admiral Croft is a rear-admiral of the white, the second rung of seniority within the lowest rank of admiral. At this rank he could expect to be commissioned into a second- or third-rate vessel, the sort of ship Mrs Croft would enjoy for its reasonably spacious accommodation. She has, however, also lived in much smaller quarters on fifth-rate vessels, such as smaller frigates, when Admiral Croft would have held the rank of post-captain, probably about the time of the Battle of Trafalgar.

8　Fanny Austen to Harriet Palmer, 5 February 1814.

9　Austen, *Persuasion*, vol. 1, chap. 6, 48.

10　Kaplan, "Domesticity at Sea," 119.

11　Austen, *Persuasion*, vol. 1, chap. 8, 70.

12　Ibid., 71.

13　Fanny Austen to Esther Esten, 1 June 1810.

14　Kaplan notes that Mrs Croft thinks "comfort is to be found on board in the intimacy preserved by keeping husbands and wives together." Kaplan, "Domesticity at Sea," 115.

15　Fanny Austen to James Christie Esten, 4 October 1813.

16　Austen, *Persuasion*, vol. 1, chap. 8, 63.

17　Fanny Austen to Esther Esten, 4 August 1810.

18　Austen, *Persuasion*, vol. 1, chap. 8, 71.

19　Ibid., 70.

20 Honan, *Jane Austen: Her Life*, 331.

21 Austen, *Persuasion*, vol. 1, chap. 3, 22.

22 Ibid., vol. 1, chap. 8, 70.

23 Ibid.

24 See chap. 2, n. 33 for an explanation of the rating of naval vessels.

25 Fanny Austen to Esther Esten, 12 August 1810.

26 Fanny Austen to James Esten, 4 October 1813.

27 Ibid., 8 July 1814.

28 Austen, *Persuasion*, vol. 1, chap. 8, 70.

29 For discussion of Jane Austen and feminism with reference to Mrs Croft, see Kirkham, *Jane Austen, Feminism and Fiction*, 153–4; Johnson, *Jane Austen: Women, Politics and the Novel*, 151–3.

30 Austen, *Persuasion*, vol. 1, chap. 8, 69.

31 Ibid., vol. 1, chap. 11, 98.

32 Fanny Austen to Esther Esten, 8 March 1814.

33 According to R.W. Chapman, *Persuasion* ends on 1 February 1815.

34 Austen, *Persuasion*, vol. 2, chap. 12, 252.

35 Kaplan, "Domesticity at Sea," 120.

36 See Austen, *Letters*, no. 78, 24 January 1813, 207.

37 Gibbon, "The Antiguan Connection," 303.

38 Ibid.

39 Austen, *Persuasion*, vol. 1, chap. 8, 70.

40 In *Jane Austen in the Context of Abolition*, Gabrielle White argues that "there appears to be authorial intention [on Jane Austen's part] to keep issues that could be associated with abolition before the reader's eye." The saga of Mrs Smith's sequestered property calls up questions about property and money and, by implication, the morality of slave labour. White thinks that Austen may have introduced Mrs Smith's West Indian property to "involve a contemporary reader in abolition-specific thinking. Topical questions would abound amongst some of the readers and their acquaintances." White, *Jane Austen*, 78–9. Edward Said takes a very different view. In *Culture and Imperialism*, he mounts an attack on Jane Austen, alleging that in several novels she is upholding both colonialism and slavery. For critical discussion about Said's thesis, see the publications of Melissa Burns, Susan Fraiman, Susan Morgan, and Gabrielle White, cited in the bibliography.

41 Austen, *Persuasion*, vol. 1, chap. 11, 96–7.

42 Charles's grief for Fanny was authentic and long-lasting. In that dimension, it differs from Benwick's grief over the death of Fanny Harville, which, even if he sustained some state of mourning, did not keep him from falling in love with Louisa Musgrove about seven months later. The possible parallel between Charles and Benwick in their grieving is therefore only partial. The key point of comparison is the gut-wrenching intensity of the grief both felt; for Charles, this was long-lasting, for Benwick, apparently, of much shorter intensity.

43 Southam, "Jane Austen and North America," 32.

44 Quoted in Julian Gwyn, *Frigates and Foremasts*, 142. At the time, Sir John Warren was back in North America and in command of the combined North American and West Indies squadrons.

45 Austen, *Letters*, no. 56, 2 October 1808, 147.

46 Ibid., no. 29, 3–5 January 1801, 71.

47 Austen, *Persuasion*, vol. 1, chap. 8, 71.

APPENDIX ONE

1 Page breaks are not indicated.

2 These descriptions are courtesy of Deidre Le Faye.

APPENDIX TWO

1 MA 4500, MLM.

2 Palmer Esten, aged three.

3 Fanny Austen.

4 Martha Dickinson, née Esten, Esther's sister-in-law.

5 Capt. Frederick Hickey of HMS *Atalante* (18 guns).

6 Esther's husband, James Christie Esten, attorney general of Bermuda and later chief justice of Bermuda.

7 A reference to the auction in Bermuda of Charles's prize, the French privateer *La Jeune Estelle* (4 guns) and her cargo, which he had captured on 19 June 1808.

8   Tom was a younger son of Rev. Fulwar Craven Fowle of Kintbury. He was serving on the *Indian* as a midshipman.

9   Captain Sir Robert Laurie of HMS *Milan* (44 guns).

10 Compliments.

11 Admiral Sir John Borlase Warren and Lady Warren. Sir John was the commander-in-chief of the North American Station.

12 MA 7280, MLM.

13 Charles's sister Cassandra.

14 Capt. Edward Hawker was a very successful prize taker on the North American Station. He was a close friend of Charles and Fanny Austen.

15 Esther gave birth to a son, John Hamilton, to be known as Hamilton, on 15 December.

16 This letter to Jane Austen was written 7 December 1808; she received it 23 January 1809.

17 Charles's fears were confirmed. The prize vessel, including its prize crew of men belonging to the *Indian*, was lost.

18 Admiral Sir John Borlase Warren.

19 The *Vesta* (10 guns) captained by Lieut. George Mends.

20 Rev. J.C. de Passau was the vicar of St Peter's Church, St George's.

21 Probably Frank Austen's wife, Mary.

22 Elizabeth Knight, wife of Charles's brother Edward, who died after the birth of her eleventh child on 10 October 1808.

APPENDIX THREE

1   Quoted in Keymer, "Rank," 387.

2   Keymer, "Rank," 390.

3   They received 15.75 per cent of the national income.

4   Keymer, "Rank," 388.

5   *Gentleman's Magazine*, vol. 102, pt 1, 1832, 569.

6   Hasted, *The History and Topographical Survey*, vol. 4, 431.

7   Ibid., vol. 7, 467.

8   It was located half a mile north of the priory at Aylesford.

9   See Hasted, *The History and Topographical Survey*, vol. 4, 431–2.

10   In heraldic language the Palmer shield is described as "Argent, a chevron
      between three palmers' scripts, sable, tasselled and buckled, or." Hasted, *The
      History and Topographical Survey*, vol. 7, 467.

11   He served as third in command under Lord Seymour and played a major
      part in the battle of Gravelines against the Spanish Armada in 1588. He also
      commanded in the English Channel in 1589 and took part in the blockade
      of Calais in 1596. David Loades, "Palmer, Sir Henry," *Oxford Dictionary of
      National Biography*, oxforddnb.com/view/article/21186.

12   Ibid.

13   Obituary of John Grove Palmer. See note 5 above.

14   See www.buildingsofireland.ie, Clonmacken House.

15   See Clonmacken House, Limerick, in "Some Georgian Houses of Limerick
      and Clare" by S. Stewart and R. Herbert. See www.limerickcity.ie/
      LocalStudiesFiles.

16   A ha-ha is a wall set in a trench such that the view of the landscape is not
      interrupted even as it creates a vertical barrier against straying farm animals.

17   See the entry for John Palmer in Ronald Dunning, "Jane Austen's Family
      Tree," www.janeaustensfamily.co.uk/recent-research/recent-research.index.
      html.

18   See H.A.C. Sturgis, *Register of Admissions to the Hon. Society of the Middle
      Temple from the 15th century to 1944*, vol. 1, 326. The relevant entry
      reads: "Admitted 17 July 1740 John Palmer 3rd son of Robert Palmer of
      Clonmackon, Limerick, gent."

19   Copyhold was an early form of land tenure in England evidenced by its
      inscription or copy in manorial court records. Originally held at the pleasure
      of the lord of the manor, over time copyhold attracted a right of occupation
      akin to freehold.

20   Banemore House (known in some sources as Baunmore House) was in the
      parish of Kilfeighny, Barony of Clanmaurice. According to Valerie Bary,
      Banemore House was in the possession of the Palmer family from the
      eighteenth to the early twentieth century. Bary, *Historical and Genealogical
      notes of some Houses of Kerry*; and NUI Galway, "Banemore House," http://
      landedestates.nuigalway.ie:8080/LandedEstates/jsp/property-show.
      jsp?id=2083.

21   John Palmer's will, PROB 11/1358/10, TNA.

22 John Palmer's will mentions Mrs Mary Palmer, the widow of his late brother Rev. Edmund Palmer. Presumably this was the Edmund Palmer who was awarded an MA from the University of Dublin in 1752. His relation to the Edmund Palmer who built Clonmacken House in 1700 has not been determined.

23 John Curtin, "A Brave Slave, Robert St George," *The Old Limerick Journal*, www.limerickcity.ie/media/brave%20slave.pdf.

24 Sons John and Thomas were said to be born in 1825 and 1828. There was also apparently a daughter Arabella.

25 The evaluator who visited Banemore used the term "mountain" in his report on the property. It was presumably something like a distinctively high hill.

26 See Ask about Ireland, www.askaboutireland.ie/griffith-valuation. For the original record about Banemore, see the entry under Palmer, Robt. John at www.askaboutireland.ie/griffith-valuation/index.xml?action=doNameSearch&Submit.x=22&Submit.y=15&familyname=Palmer&firstname=robt.john&baronyname=&countyname=KERRY&unionname=&parishname=.

27 Lewis, *Topographical Dictionary of Ireland*, LibraryIreland, www.libraryireland.com/topog.

28 Sometimes spelled as Strangwich, Strangewayes, or Strangeways.

29 Burke, *A Genealogical and Heraldic History of the Commoners of Great Britain and Ireland*, vol. 3, 136.

30 He was probably a third cousin to Fanny's sixth great-grandfather, James Strangways of Ormsby.

31 The painting can be viewed on the webpage of the National Portrait Gallery: http://www.npg.org.uk/collections/search/portrait-list.php?search=sp&sText=NPG%206353&firstRun=true.

32 Jowitt, *The Culture of Piracy, 1580–1630*, 199.

33 Her full name was Lady Christian Henrietta Caroline (Harriet) née Fox Strangways.

34 See Acland and another, *The Acland Journal*, xxii. The journal (which covers events from 1 March 1776 to 2 January 1778) was jointly written by Lady Harriet and an unknown author, possibly Sir John's valet.

35 Ibid., xxvii.

36 Ibid., xxvi, xxx.

37 Hallet, *Early Bermuda Records*, 162.

38 Jarvis, *Bermuda's Architectural Heritage*, 79.

39 Ibid., 81.

40 Bermuda Book of Deeds, vol. 1, 150.

41 Ibid., vol. 2, 10.

42 When Fanny's uncle Alexander Ball advertised Casino for sale in 1824, it was described as having "five rooms upstairs with closets, an excellent kitchen, tank and outhouses, enclosed with a substantial wall and a large cellar." See *Bermuda Gazette*, 14 February 1824.

Bibliography

PUBLISHED SOURCES

Acland, Lady Harriet, and another. *The Acland Journal: Lady Harriet Acland and the American War.* Winchester: Hampshire County Council 1993

Adkins, Roy, and Leslie Adkins. *Jane Austen's England.* New York: Viking 2013

Anson, Walter. *The Life of Admiral Sir John Borlase Warren.* London: Simpson, Marshall, Hamilton, Kent, and Co. 1914

Aspinall-Oglander, Cecil. *The Admiral's Wife.* London: Longmans 1940

Austen, Caroline. *My Aunt Jane Austen: A Memoir.* London and Colchester: Jane Austen Society 1991

– *Reminiscences of Caroline Austen.* Introduced and edited by Deirdre Le Faye. Chawton, Hampshire: Jane Austen Society 2011

Austen, Jane. *Catherine and Other Writings.* Edited by Margaret Doody and Douglas Murray. Oxford: Oxford University Press 1993

– *Jane Austen's Letters.* Edited by Deirdre Le Faye. 4th ed. Oxford: Oxford University Press 2011

– *Juvenilia.* Edited by Peter Sabor. Cambridge: Cambridge University Press 2006

– *Later Manuscripts.* Edited by Janet Todd and Linda Bree. Cambridge: Cambridge University Press 2008

– *Mansfield Park*. Edited by R.W. Chapman. 3rd ed. Oxford: Oxford University
  Press 1934
– *Mansfield Park*. Edited by John Wiltshire. Cambridge: Cambridge University
  Press 2005
– *Northanger Abbey*. Edited by R.W. Chapman. 3rd ed. Oxford: Oxford
  University Press 1933
– *Persuasion*. Edited by R.W. Chapman. 3rd ed. Oxford: Oxford University
  Press 1933
– *Pride and Prejudice*. Edited by R.W. Chapman. 3rd ed. Oxford: Oxford
  University Press 1932
Austen-Leigh, James. *A Memoir of Jane Austen and Other Family Recollections*.
  Edited by Kathryn Sutherland. Oxford: Oxford University Press 2002
Austen-Leigh, Richard A. *Austen Papers 1704–1856*. Printed privately, London 1942
Bary, Valery. *Historical and Genealogical Notes of Some Houses of Kerry*.
  Whitegate, County Clare: Ballinaken Press 1994
Batchelor, Jennie. "The Austens and Their Pocket Books." *Austentations*, Spring
  (2011): 7–15
Batey, Mavis. *Jane Austen and the English Landscape*. London: Barn Elms
  Publishing 1996
Bermuda Gazette, 1805–1824
Bernhard, Virginia. *Slaves and Slaveholders in Bermuda*, 1616–1782. Columbia,
  MS: University of Missouri Press 1999
Blank, Antje. "Dress." In *Jane Austen in Context*, edited by Janet Todd, 234–51.
  Cambridge: Cambridge University Press 2005
Bulletin of the Public Archives of Nova Scotia, no. 12. Halifax, NS: PANS, 1957:
  33–46
Burke, John. *A Genealogical and Heraldic History of the Commoners of Great
  Britain and Ireland enjoying territorial possession or high official rank but
  uninvested with veritable honours*. Vol. 3. London: 1836
Burns, Melissa. "Jane Austen's *Mansfield Park*: Determining Authorial
  Intention." *Persuasions On Line*, 2005
Burrows, John William. *Southend-on-Sea*, and district historical notes.
  Southend-on-Sea: J.H. Burrows 1909
Byrne, Paula. *The Real Jane Austen: A Life in Small Things*. New York:
  HarperCollins 2013

Caplan, Clive. "A Bogus Tale: Ellman, Charles Austen and HMS Aurora." *Jane Austen Society Report for 2009*, 11–13

– "The Ships of Charles Austen." *Jane Austen Society Report for 2009*, 143–60

– "The Ships of Frank Austen." *Jane Austen Society Report for 2008*, 74–86

Chelmsford Chronicle, 1812, 1813

Cook, James. "Captain James Cook's Description of the Sea Coast of Nova Scotia, Cape Breton Island and Newfoundland." In *Report of the Trustees of the Public Archives of Nova Scotia for the Year 1958*, 19–37. PANS: Halifax, NS, 1959

Copeland, Edward. "Money." In *Jane Austen in Context*, edited by Janet Todd, 317–26. Cambridge: Cambridge University Press 2005

Cordingly, David. *Seafaring Women: Adventures of Pirate Queens, Female Stowaways, and Sailors' Wives*. New York: Random House 2007

Corley, T.A.B. "Jane Austen and Her Brother Henry's Bank Failure 1815–1816." In *Jane Austen Society Report for 1998*, 12–23

Dresser, Madge, and Andrew Hann, eds. *Slavery and the British Country House*. Swindon: English Heritage 2013

Fingard, Judith, Janet Guildford, and David Sutherland. *Halifax: The First 250 Years*. Halifax: Formac 1990

Fraiman, Susan, "Jane Austen and Edward Said: Gender, Culture, and Imperialism." *Critical Inquiry* 21, no. 4 (1995): 805–21

Fraser, Edward. *Napoleon the Gaoler: Personal Experiences and Adventures of British Soldiers and Sailors during the Great Captivity*. New York: Brentanos 1914

Gentleman's Magazine. Vol. 102, pt 1, 1832

Gibbon, Frank. "The Antiguan Connection: Some New Light on *Mansfield Park*." *Cambridge Quarterly* 11 (1982): 805–21

Gilson, David. *A Bibliography of Jane Austen*. Oxford: Oxford University Press 1982; rev. ed. St Paul's Bibliographies, Winchester (UK) and Delaware (USA), 1997

– "Cassandra Austen's pictures." *Jane Austen Society Report for 1993*, 299–301

Gwyn, Julian. *Ashore and Afloat: The British Navy and the Halifax Naval Yard before 1820*. Ottawa: University of Ottawa Press 2004

– *Frigates and Foremasts: The North American Squadron in Nova Scotia Waters 1745–1815*. Vancouver: University of British Columbia Press 2003

Haliburton, G. Brenton, ed. *A Colonial Portrait: The Halifax Diaries of Lady Sherbrooke, 1811–1816*. Raleigh, NC: Lulu Press 2011

Hallam, W.T. *When You Are in Halifax*. Toronto: Church Book Room 1937

Hallet, A.C. Hollis. *Early Bermuda Records, 1618–1826*. Bermuda: Juniper Hill 1991

Hallet, C.F.E. Hollis. *Bermuda Index, 1784–1914: Index of Births, Marriages, Deaths as Recorded in Bermuda Newspapers*. Vols 1 and 2. Toronto: University of Toronto Press 1989

Hammond, M.C. "The Naval Connection." *Jane Austen Society Report for 1998*, 174–8

Harman, Claire. *Jane's Fame: How Jane Austen Conquered the World*. New York: Henry Holt 2009

Harris, Reginald V. *The Church of St Paul's in Halifax 1749–1949*. Toronto: Ryerson Press 1949

Hasted, Edward. *The History and Topographical Survey of the County of Kent*. Vols 4 and 7. 2nd ed., reprint. Yorkshire: E.P. Publishing 1972

Hickman, Peggy. "The Jane Austen Family in Silhouette." In *Shades from Jane Austen*, written and illustrated by Honoria D. Marsh and Peggy Hickman. London: Perry Jackson 1975

Hill, Richard. *The Prizes of War: The Naval Prize System in the Napoleonic Wars, 1793–1815*. Stroud: Sutton 1998

Hillan, Sophia. *May, Lou & Cass: Jane Austen's Nieces in Ireland*. Belfast: Blackstaff 2011

Honan, Park. *Jane Austen: Her Life*. London: Phoenix 1997

Hopkinson, David. "Frivolities and Affections." *Jane Austen Society Report for 1997*, 89–96

Hubback, J.H., and Edith C. Hubback. *Jane Austen's Sailor Brothers: being the adventures of Sir Francis Austen ... and ... Charles Austen*. First published 1906. Reprint. Lavergne, TN: Biolife 2011

Hume, Robert. "Money in Jane Austen." *Review of English Studies* 64, no. 264 (2012): 291–310

Hussey, Christopher. "Godmersham Park, Kent: II." *Country Life*, 23 February 1945

Ingalls, Sharon, and Wayne Ingalls. *Sweet Suburb: A History of Prince's Lodge, Birch Cove and Rockingham*. Tantallon, NS: Glen Margaret Publishing 2010

James, P.D. Foreword to *800 Years of Women's Letters*. Edited by Olga Kenyon. Godalming: Bramley Books 1992

Jarvis, Michael. *Bermuda's Architectural Heritage: St George's*. Bermuda: Bermuda National Trust 1998

Jensen, Carl L., ed. *The Medical World, A Practical Medical Monthly*. Vol. 4. Philadelphia: C.F. Taylor 1886

Johnson, Claudia. *Jane Austen: Women, Politics and the Novel*. Chicago: University of Chicago Press 1988

Jones, Hazel. *Jane Austen and Marriage*. London: Continuum 2009

– *Jane Austen's Journeys*. London: Robert Hale 2014

Jowitt, Claire. *The Culture of Piracy, 1560–1630: English Literature and Seaborn Crime*. Farnham, Surrey: Ashgate Publishing 2013

Kaplan, Deborah. "Domesticity at Sea: The Example of Charles and Fanny Austen." *Persuasions* 14 (1992): 113–21

– *Jane Austen among Women*. Baltimore: Johns Hopkins Press 1992

Journal of the House of Commons, Sess. vol. 70. London, 1814–15

Kert, Faye. *Prize and Prejudice: Privateering and Naval Prize during the War of 1812*. Research in Maritime History, no. 11. St John's, NL, 1997

Keverne, Richard. *Tales of Old Inns*. 5th ed. London: Collins 1952

Keymer, Thomas. "Rank." In *Jane Austen in Context*, edited by Janet Todd, 387–96. Cambridge: Cambridge University Press 2005

Kindred, Sheila Johnson. "Charles Austen's Capture of the French Privateer *La Jeune Estelle*." *Jane Austen Society Report for 2006*, 50–3

– "Charles Austen: Prize Chaser and Prize Taker on the North American Station 1805–1808." *Persuasions* 26 (2004): 180–94

– "Finding Fortune and Family: Jane Austen's Naval Brother Charles in Bermuda." *Jane Austen Society Report for 2010*, 37–48

– "The Influences of Naval Captain Charles Austen's North American Experiences on *Persuasion* and *Mansfield Park*." *Persuasions* 31 (2009): 115–29

– "Jane Austen's Naval Brother Charles on the North American Station 1805–1811." *Royal Nova Scotia Historical Society Journal* 10 (2007): 25–46

– "Two Brothers, One City: Charles and Francis Austen in Halifax, Canada." In *Jane Austen and the North Atlantic*, edited by Sarah Emsley, 9–21. Chawton: Jane Austen Society 2006

Kirkham, Margaret. *Jane Austen, Feminism and Fiction*. Brighton: Harvester Press 1983

Lambert, Andrew. *The Challenge: Britain against America in the Naval War of 1812*. London: faber and faber 2012

Lane, Maggie. *Growing Older with Jane Austen*. London: Robert Hale 2014

– *Jane Austen's Family through Five Generations*. London: Robert Hale 1992

— "The Real Lady Susan." *Jane Austen's Regency World*, September/October 2016, 47–50

— *Understanding Austen: Key Concepts in Six Novels*. Robert Hale: London 2012

Lavery, Brian. *Life in Nelson's Navy: The Ships, Men and Organization*. London: Conway Maritime 1994

— *Life in Nelson's Navy*. Stroud: Sutton 2007

Laxton, Paul, and Joseph Wisdom. *The A to Z of Regency London*. Publication no. 131. London: London Topographical Society 1985

Lee, Hermione. *Biography: A Very Short Introduction*. Oxford: Oxford University Press 2011

Le Faye, Deirdre. *A Chronology of Jane Austen and Her Family*. Cambridge: Cambridge University Press 2013

— *Fanny Knight's Diary: Jane Austen through Her Niece's Eyes*. Winchester: Jane Austen Society 2000

— *Jane Austen: A Family Record*. Cambridge: Cambridge University Press 2004

— *Jane Austen's Country Life: Uncovering the Rural Backdrop to Her Life, Her Letters and Her Novels*. London: Frances Lincoln 2014

— *Jane Austen's 'Outlandish Cousin': The Life and Letters of Eliza de Feuillide*. London: British Library 2002

— "Journey, Waterparties & Plays." *Jane Austen Society Report for 1989*, 24–30

Lewis, Samuel. *A Topographical Dictionary of Ireland Comprising the Several Counties, Cities, Boroughs, Corporate, Market, and Post Towns, Parishes, and Villages, with Historical and Statistical Descriptions*. Vols 1 and 2. London 1837

Litz, J. Walton. "Chronology of Composition." In *The Jane Austen Handbook*, edited by J. David Grey. London: Athlone Press 1986

London Gazette, 1808, 1810, and 1852

Manning, John. "John Manning to His Brother, 3 August, 1812." *Current Archeology*, no. 275 (February 2013): 4–5

Marshall, John. *Royal naval biography: or, memoirs of the services of all the flag-offices; superannuated rear-admirals, retired captains, post-captains and commanders*. London: Longman 1827

Mercer, Keith. "Sailors and Citizens: Press Gangs and Naval-Civilian Relations in Nova Scotia 1756–1815." *Royal Nova Scotia Historical Society Journal* (2007): 87–113

Morgan, Susan. "Captain Wentworth, British Imperialism and Personal Romance." *Persuasions* 18 (1996): 88–97

Naftel, William D. *Prince Edward's Legacy*. Halifax: Formac 2005

Naval Chronicle, Containing a General and Biographical History of the Royal Navy of the United Kingdom with a Variety of Original Papers on Nautical Subjects. Vol. 3, 1800; vol. 25, 1811

Naval Chronicle: The Contemporary Record of the Royal Navy at War. Vol. 5. Edited by Nicholas Tracy. London: Chatham Publishing 1949

Nicholson, Nigel. *Godmersham Park, Kent, before, during and since Jane Austen's Day*. Chawton: Jane Austen Society 1996

Nokes, David. *Jane Austen: A Life*. London: Fourth Estate 1997

Notman, Suzanne. "The Austen File." *The Bermudian*, vol. 69, no. 8 (August 1999): 17–19, 59–61

– "Fanny Austen's Letters" *The Bermudian*, vol. 70, no. 3 (March 2000)

O'Byrne, William, ed. *A Naval Bibliographical Dictionary: Comprising the Life and Services of Every Living Officer in Her Majesty's Navy, from Rank of Admiral of the Fleet to That of Lieutenant, Inclusive*. London: John Murray 1849

Packwood, Cyril O. *Chained on the Rock*. New York: Eliseo Torres and Sons 1975

Padfield, Peter. *Broke and the Shannon*. London: Hodder and Stoughton 1968

Pavy, Frederick William. *A Treatise on Food and Dietetics Physiologically and Therapeutically Considered*. London: J. & A. Churchill 1875 https://archive.org/stream/treatiseonfooddi01pavy#page/n5/mode/2up

Payne, Jessica K. *Southend-on-Sea: A Pictorial History*. Chichester: Phillimore and Co. 1985

Paysant, Joan. *Halifax: Cornerstone of Canada*. Halifax: Windsor Publications 1985

Piers, Harry. *Robert Field: portrait painter in oils, miniatures and water-colours and engraver*. New York: Frederick Fairchild Sherman 1927

Pollitt, William. *Southend, 1760–1860*. Southend-on-Sea: Public Libraries and Museum Committee 1939

Pope-Hennessey, John. *Anthony Trollope*. Boston: Little, Brown 1971

Rodger, N.A.M. *The Command of the Ocean: A Naval History of Britain, 1649–1815*. London: W.W. Norton 2004

– *The Wooden World: An Anatomy of the Georgian Navy*. London: Collins 1986

Royal military Calendar, or Army service and commission book, Containing the progress of promotion … colonels … 3rd ed. Vol. 3. London, 1816

Royal Nova Scotia Gazette, 1805–1811

Said, Edward W. *Culture and Imperialism*. New York: Knopf 1993

Selwyn, David. *Jane Austen and Children.* London: Continuum 2010

–, ed. *Jane Austen: Collected Poems and Verse of the Austen Family.* Manchester, UK: Carcanet 1996

Slater, Michael. *Douglas Jerrold, 1803–1857.* London: Duckworth 2000

Southam, Brian. *Jane Austen and the Navy.* 2nd ed. Greenwich: National Maritime Museum 2005

– "Jane Austen and North America: Fact and Fiction." In *Jane Austen and the North Atlantic,* edited by Sarah Emsley, 22–37. Chawton: Jane Austen Society 2006

– "Jane Austen's Sailor Brothers: Francis and Charles in Life and Art." *Persuasions* 25 (2003): 33–45

Spence, Jon. *Becoming Jane Austen.* London, New York: Hambledon and London 2003

Stark, Suzanne. *Female Tars: Women aboard Ship in the Age of Sail.* Annapolis, MD: Naval Institute 1996

Sturgess, H.A.C. *Register of Admissions to the Honourable Society of the Middle Temple from the Fifteenth Century to 1944.* Vol. 1. London: Butterfield 1949

Sutherland, Kathryn. *Jane Austen's Textual Lives from Aeschylus to Bollywood.* Oxford: Oxford University Press 2005

Times, The (London), 1808, 1810

Tomalin, Claire. *Jane Austen: A Life.* London: Penguin 1998

Tracy, Nicholas. *Britannia's Palette: The Arts of Naval Victory.* Montreal and Kingston: McGill-Queen's University Press 2007

Trimmer, Sarah. *A Description of a Set of Prints of Ancient History: Contained in a Set of Easy Lessons. In Two Parts.* London, 1786; *A Description of a Set of Prints of Roman History: Contained in a Set of Easy Lessons.* London, 1789; *A Description of a Set of Prints of English History: Contained in a Set of Easy Lessons.* London, 1792

– *A Geographical Companion to Mrs. Trimmer's Scripture, Ancient and English Abridged Histories with Prints.* London: J. Harris 1816

Tucker, George Holbert. *A History of Jane Austen's Family.* Guernsey: Sutton 1998

Uden, Grant, and Richard Cooper. *A Dictionary of British Ships and Seamen.* New York: St Martin's Press 1980

van der Merwe, Pieter, and Richard Took. *The Spectacular Career of Clarkson Stanfield, 1793–1867: Seaman, Scene-Painter, Royal Academician.* Newcastle Upon Tyne: Tyne and Wear Museum 1979

Vickery, Amanda. *The Gentleman's Daughter: Women's Lives in Georgian England.* New Haven: Yale University Press 1999

Vincent, Thomas B., "The Inquisition: Alexander Croke's Satire on Halifax Society during the Wentworth Years." *Dalhousie Review* 53 (1973): 404–30

Ward, Edmund. "Seven Years Residence in Bermuda 1809–1816." *Bermuda Historical Quarterly* 5, no. 4 (1948): 192

Weekly Chronicle (Nova Scotia), 1805–1811

Weir, Hugh. *Houses of Clare: Historical, Genealogical and Architectural Notes on Some Houses of Clare.* Whitegate: Ballinakella Press 1986

White, Gabrielle D.V. *Jane Austen in the Context of Abolition: 'a fling at the slave trade.'* New York: Palgrave Macmillan 2006

Wilkinson, Henry C. *Bermuda from Sail to Steam: The History of the Island from 1784 to 1901.* Vols 1 and 2. Oxford: Oxford University Press 1973

Willoughby, Rupert. *Chawton: Jane Austen's Village.* 2nd ed. Bridport: privately printed 2003

Winfield, Rif. *British Warships in the Age of Sail, 1793–1815.* London: Chatham Publishing 2005

Wynne, Elizabeth. *The Wynne Diaries: The Adventures of Two Sisters in Napoleonic Europe.* Edited by Anne Freemantle. Oxford: Oxford University Press 1982

ARCHIVAL SOURCES

Austen, Charles, to Admiral Sir George Berkeley, 23 October 1807, ADM 1/49, TNA.

Austen, Charles, to Cassandra Austen, 25 December 1808. MA 7820, MLM. Bequest: Gordon N. Ray, 1987, New York, NY.

Austen, Charles. Private journals and pocketbooks. AUS/101 (1815); AUS/102 (1815); AUS/103 (1815); AUS/105 (1816); AUS/109 (1817); AUS /111 (1820); AUS /120 (1826); AUS/125 (1827); AUS 161, AUS/162 (1851), NMM

Austen, Charles. Logbooks: HMS *Indian,* HMS *Swiftsure,* HMS *Cleopatra,* HMS *Namur,* TNA

Austen, Frances (Fanny) FitzWilliams, to Esther Esten, James Christie Esten, and Harriet Palmer, 1810 and 1812–1814. MA 4500, MLM. Bequest: Gordon N. Ray, 1987, New York, NY

Belcher, Andrew, to the Halifax Vice Admiralty Court, 31 August 1808, Vice
     Admiralty Court of Nova Scotia fonds, RG8/IV/52, 23488, LAC

Berkeley, Admiral Sir George Cranfield, to William Pole, Secretary to the
     Admiralty, 23 October 1807, ADM 1/497, TNA

Bermuda Book of Deeds, BA

Bermuda Prize Book, 1795–1813, BA, PA 421

Broke Philip, RN, to his wife Louisa, Sir James Saumarez Collection, 3 October
     1811, HA 93/9/78; 11 December 1811, HA 93/9/85; and 1 January 1812, LAC

Broke, Philip, RN, to Charles Austen, 11 December 1824. MA 4500, MLM.
     Bequest: Gordon N. Ray. 1987

Burial records for Old St Pancras Church, P90/PAN1/180, 167, no. 1335. London,
     England

Chapman, R.W. Miscellaneous papers, MSS Eng. lett. c. 759–61, Bodleian
     Library, Oxford, England

Esten, Esther, to Charles Austen, 26 July 1808. MA 4500, MLM. Bequest: Gordon,
     N. Ray. 1987

George, Samuel Hood, to Lady George, 18 October 1809, George Family Papers.
     MG1, vol. 2160, no. 244, NSARM

George, Samuel Hood, to Lady George, 24 May 1810. George Family Papers.
     MG1, vol. 2160, no. 302, NSARM

George, Samuel Hood, to Sir Rupert George. George Family Papers. MG1,
     vol. 2160, NSARM

Hulbert, George. Cash Book 1808–1812. HUL/ 23, NMM

Knatchbull, Lady (Fanny Knight). Pocketbooks, 1805–1813. Kentish History and
     Library Centre, Maidstone, Kent, England, as quoted in Le Faye, *Chronology*

Norwood, Winckworth. Journal. MG13, vol. 4, 1805, NSARM

Palmer, John. Will, 17. PROB 11/1358/10, TNA

Pocket Magnet, or elegant Picturesque Diary, for 1814, belonging to Fanny Austen,
     in the collection of King's College, Cambridge, England

Stanfield, Clarkson (alias Roderick Bland), to Mary Stanfield, 29 August 1813.
     Ms 79/159, Box 1, Stn 1/3, NMM

Register of Baptisms: The Parish of St Paul's, Halifax, Nova Scotia. Robert Stanser,
     Rector. St Paul's Church Archives, Halifax, NS

Strangways, L., to John Grove Palmer, August 1820, within a letter from John
     Grove Palmer to Charles Austen, 18 August 1820. MA 4500, MLM. Bequest:
     Gordon N. Ray 1987, New York, NY

Vice Admiralty Court of Bermuda fonds, BA

Vice Admiralty Court of Nova Scotia fonds. RG8/IV/142/file 1 and RG8/IV/52, 23448, LAC

Webster's New International Dictionary. Springfield, MA: G & C Merriam, revised 1913

Williams, Sir Thomas, to the Admiralty. ADM 1/748, 7, no. 1272, September 1812, TNA

Index